The Chinese Economy Facing Unprecedented Turbulence

David Daokui Li

Translated by
Hui Cooper

ACA Publishing Ltd

Published by ACA Publishing Ltd
London - Beijing
info@alaincharlesasia.com ☎ +44 20 3289 3885
www.alaincharlesasia.com

Published by ACA Publishing Ltd, in arrangement with
People's Publishing House

Author: David Daokui Li **Translator:** Hui Cooper **Editor:** Martin Savery

Original Chinese Text © 百年变局下的中国经济
(bai nian bian ju xia de zhong guo jing li)
2020, People's Publishing House, Beijing China

ALL RIGHTS RESERVED. NO PART OF THIS PUBLICATION MAY BE REPRODUCED IN MATERIAL FORM, BY ANY MEANS, WHETHER GRAPHIC, ELECTRONIC, MECHANICAL OR OTHER, INCLUDING PHOTOCOPYING OR INFORMATION STORAGE, IN WHOLE OR IN PART, AND MAY NOT BE USED TO PREPARE OTHER PUBLICATIONS WITHOUT WRITTEN PERMISSION FROM THE PUBLISHER.

English Translation text © 2023 ACA Publishing Ltd, London, UK. A catalogue record for *The Chinese Economy Facing Unprecedented Turbulence* is available from the National Bibliographic Service of the British Library.

The greatest care has been taken to ensure accuracy but the publisher can accept no responsibility for errors or omissions, or for any liability occasioned by relying on its content.

Paperback ISBN: 978-1-83890-016-8
eBook ISBN: 978-1-83890-017-5

Contents

A Great Change in the World vii

Understanding the World

1. TO PROGRESS, CHINA MUST LEARN OPEN-MINDEDLY FROM THE US, JAPAN AND GERMANY ... 3
2. LOOKING AT THE NEW NORMAL OF CHINA AND THE WORLD FROM DAVOS ... 12
3. RESURGENCE OF NATIONALISM IN THE WEST ... 18
4. UNDERSTANDING 'BREXIT' ... 22
5. REAPPRAISING OUR UNDERSTANDING OF THE US ... 27
6. KEEP LEARNING HOW TO DEAL WITH THE US ... 33
7. ACTIVELY AND EFFECTIVELY DEAL WITH THE NEW ERA OF SINO-US RELATIONS ... 41
8. THREE LOW-LEVEL MISCONCEPTIONS TO BE AVOIDED IN REASONABLY DEALING WITH SINO-US TRADE FRICTION ... 48
9. CHINA'S NEW ROLE ... 55
10. UNDERSTANDING THAT CAPITAL IN THE 21ST CENTURY CANNOT DO WITHOUT CHINA ... 60
11. THE AIIB GIVES IMPETUS TO REFORM OF THE INTERNATIONAL GOVERNANCE SYSTEM ... 69

Understanding the Chinese Economy

1. MACRO CONTROL ... 79
   What is a modern market economy? ... 79
   Why are Private Entrepreneurs Worried? ... 88
   What to do about 'flight from the real to the virtual' economy? ... 93
   How is China's Economy to Run a High-Quality Development Marathon? ... 99

How Does 'China's Economic System' Upgrade
from Version 1.0 to Version 2.0? 104
Can China Break Through the Middle Income
Trap? 109
Will China Miss the Fourth Industrial Revolution? 118
Is There Still Room for China's Economy to Catch
Up and Surpass? 132
Chinese Economy: Looking Forward to 2035
and 2050 139

2. FINANCE AND REAL ESTATE 146
General Context of China's Financial Development 146
Financial System Modernisation Is the Key to
Crossing the High-Income Countries Threshold 153
The "Crux" of Stabilising the Economy is Major
Financial Structure Adjustment 162
How to Reform the Financial Supply Side? 170
Local Government Financing Must Be Cut Out of
the Banking System 176
Need for Targeted Therapy with Loose Mobility on
Structural Deleveraging 182
Probing the Causes of China's Real Estate Bubble 188

3. THE INTERNET AND THE NEW ECONOMY 197
Cnsumption Integrated With Production: China's
Internet Economic Model is Just Getting Started 197
The Biggest Starting Point of "Internet+" Should Be
to Promote Reform 204
It is Not "Autonomous Driving" But "Smart
Driving" That Will Disrupt the Automobile
Industry 207
Traditional System Should Embrace Internet
Finance 213
Three Questions About Facebook's Libra Currency: 218

4. REFORM PRACTICE AND CHINESE ECONOMIC
THOUGHT 223
Economic Summary of 40 Years of Reform and
Opening Up 223
The Song Dynasty Led the World, the Qing
Dynasty Fell Behind Western Europe 235

Establish a People-Centred Official Assessment System	241
Institutional Innovation Key To Xiong'an New Area Development	246
Learn from the World Bank's Experience To Reform the Infrastructure Investment System	251
China's SOE Reform Viewed from German Car Maker VW's "Diesel Emissions Scandal"	260
Tackle Urbanisation Today on Behalf of Future Generations	269
Notes	275

A Great Change in the World
How to Understand the World and the Chinese Economy?

To understand the world, we look at the essence of the great change that has not been seen in a century

The essence of the great change is that the emerging countries represented by China are rising, while the relative influence of the Western countries, with the US as the 'bellwether', is declining. They are unable to continue to dominate the world alone as they have done over the past century.

The direct consequence of the decline of the relative influence of the Western countries is that their politics have become more and more localised, populist and grassroots orientated. Why? Because the Western elite have long been the leaders of the international order, the decline of the West's international influence has led to people at the grassroots level venting their anger at the elite. Taking the US as an example, the basic demands of the grassroots political support represented by President Trump, who came to power in 2017, is to revitalise the American economy and society, particularly the American manufacturing industry. A typical example of this can be seen in Detroit, a once brilliant city now in decline. This is where Trump's votes come from. However, the American elite are more focused on the overall international situation and ideology, which is incompatible with the president today. At home, Trump's grassroots support takes aim at the elite and the bone of contention is China. They keep on saying that the elite are too soft on China and that they have betrayed the interests of the US. However, the elite are also dissatisfied with China. They are mainly worried that China's strength will disrupt the international order carefully built by the US. On international issues, the common ground of these two groups is China and this is the direct impact on China of a great change that has not been seen in a century.

Specifically, we should see that the American working class, represented by this president, are essentially indifferent to ideology, or China's international role, and they know nothing at all about China's external publicity such as "how marvellous our country is". What they care about is employment and increasing the wages of blue-collar workers in the US! What they want to restore is the economic prosperity and social stability of the US seen in their past glorious period of isolation and the main scapegoats are new immigrants who do not agree with the traditional American values, especially those who believe in Islam. In their political system, China is only an external contradiction, not an irreconcilable one!

With this judgement, we can then accurately grasp the demands of the American working class represented by Trump and do everything possible to make them realise that China's economic rise should help solve their economic pain. This can be done by actively expanding the scale of China's automobile imports from the US or reviving the economy of areas in long-term decline such as Detroit in exchange for their acceptance of the historical trend of China's rise. It should be said that the Chinese government and Western populists are not so far apart that there is no room for cooperation.

To understand China, we must see that China under the great change is different from the Japan, Soviet Union and Germany of the past

We must realise very clearly that China today is totally different from the Japan, Soviet Union and Germany of the past.

Let us look at China and Japan. In terms of per capita GDP at purchasing power parity (PPP), the Japanese economic development level in the past reached about 80% of that of the US, while China's economic development today is only 29% of that of the US. Yet, as a large economy capable of catching up with and surpassing the rest, China's development potential is much greater than was Japan's in the past. Furthermore, in the past, the proportion of Japan's export dependence on the US was much greater than that of today's China (in 1990 Japan's exports to the US comprised about 30% of its total exports while in 2018, China's exports to the US only accounted for 19.29%). More importantly, Japan is completely dependent on the US in terms of its military, politics and even its whole system. Japan's security depends on the security agreement between Japan and the US, and the US military is stationed in Japan; Japan's post-war constitution was drafted by military lawyers when the US army occupied Japan. The Japanese who are held by the Americans cannot argue but can only make adjustments rigidly according to the route pointed out by the Americans, thereby stepping into the 'lost 20 years'. Although the real lives of the Japanese people don't seem to be as bad as many people would have thought in more than 20 years of low growth, it is undeniable that Japan did not continue the trend of fully catching up with and surpassing the US, and today Japan is no longer a worthy competitor of the US in the field of international politics and the economy.

China today is completely different from the Soviet Union in the period when the US and the Soviet Union were contending for hegemony. China's domestic society and economy have undergone diversified development, the market economy ideology has been deeply engrained in the minds of the Chinese people and the scale of the privately-run economy has far outstripped that of the state-owned economy while in the past, the socio-economic system of the Soviet Union was narrow and rigid, and there was little room for the development of a free market economy. Today, China's economic and social vitality and creativity are far from comparable to those of the Soviet Union. China's current ideology is largely consistent with international mainstream ideology which includes promoting the construction of ecological civilisation, energy conservation and emissions reduction, combating climate change, bravely shouldering international responsibilities such as maritime escort duty and UN stability maintenance, supporting globalisation, actively participating in the operation of international organisations, respect for the existing regimes of all countries and refraining from staging coups and installing puppet regimes. On the contrary, when the Soviet Union and the US were competing, the strategic goal of the Soviet Union was to export revolution and overthrow foreign regimes that were not to its liking. The ideology of the US and the Soviet Union were almost completely mutually opposed, as incompatible as fire and water.

China today is also totally different from Germany when it competed with the US. In those days, Germany was in full swing under the control of the old imperial thinking and its basic idea was to expand its territory so as to expand its long-term interests through one or two wars. Generally speaking, this era is over. Israeli writer and historian Yuval Noah Harari has said clearly in his *21 Lessons for the 21st Century* that the world today, including the US government, has abandoned the development strategy of gaining national interests and development through wars. For example, although militarily Israel is fully capable of destroying or annexing neighbouring countries, such action does Israel no good, instead it leads to trouble. Russia is no exception on the Crimea issue. Russia is not simply reverting to force to forcibly seize Crimea, and there is no tit for tat between the US, Europe and Russia, or to counter force with force.

What we need to see particularly is that the economic, social and cultural links between China and the US today far exceed those between the US and Japan or between the US and the Soviet Union in the past, when few large American companies invested in the Japanese economy, and foreign direct investment (FDI) accounted for less than 1% of Japan's average annual investment. Today, China is the largest market for almost all major companies in the US, or the largest country for investment. Chinese students studying in the US far outnumber Japanese students studying there. The degree of integration of interests and mutual understanding between China and the US is much higher than that between the US and Japan. It is particularly noteworthy that in the contemporary Chinese government, a considerable number of decision-makers have worked or studied in the US. However, such a scenario was extremely rare with regard to Japanese government decision-makers in the past and today. After a long term observation of mine, I found that the number of staff in the Japanese Ministry of Finance and the Central Bank who have studied in the US is very small. Hence, we must not simply copy the pattern and results of the competitions between the US and Japan, the Soviet Union and Germany to analyse today's world.

China is by no means the same as the Japan, Soviet Union and Germany of the past, and China will never repeat their mistakes!

To cope with great change, we must do a good job of handling our own major issues

Most importantly, we must be soberly aware that for such a huge country with an ancient civilisation, China's development over the past 40 years is by no means a gift from the US, although sincere cooperation between the two countries has provided a boost. Being yourself is fundamental!

Sino-US trade friction clearly tells us that for China's economic development, the old ideas are no longer feasible. They are to rely on exports to make up for an insufficient domestic market, to attract foreign capital and to let foreign capital introduce new technology, but in the current pattern of Sino-US relations, they are already at a 'dead end', therefore, there must be new ideas.

But how to obtain them? We must return to the most basic experience of reform and opening up, do our homework well and get three major issues right.

First, we must regain the incentive for economic development. The current problem is that the incentive mechanism for economic development is not smooth, particularly when it comes to local officials that are subject to many constraints. On economic issues, authorisation is far from enough, while inspection, supervision and accountability are more than enough, and positive motivation is far from enough, binding people hand and foot. We cannot learn reform by studying documents, while practice and innovation are true reform. We should restore the trend witnessed during more than 40 years of reform and opening up of local governments whereby the key objective was economic development, they had the courage to explore, boldly innovate and reform, and help enterprises to seek development. At the same time, we should also give private entrepreneurs clear property rights protection, giving them clear and equal treatment with SOEs and foreign enterprises. SOEs must diversify their property rights, and there should be a clear authorisation for managers. A modern enterprise system should be established to let SOEs really be market-oriented enterprises rather than government departments facing higher authorities. The basic principle that the state "manages capital but doesn't manage operations" should be implemented.

Second, major social issues, including education, healthcare and care for the elderly, cannot be completely pushed onto the market, and government responsibility cannot be absent. At present in China many contradictions are not simply economic but social, like education, healthcare and care for the elderly. They must be accurately solved by combining public management policies with the market. For example, the population issue requires complete liberalisation of family planning policy from now on. Childbearing should be properly encouraged, while a very precise and flexible public policy is needed. For another example, regarding education issues, we must emphasise the government leading in the stage of compulsory education and that private capital must not be blindly introduced. Because private capital is bound to be profit-oriented, and profit-oriented elementary education inevitably takes care of short-term effects, it distorts the goal of compulsory education. The fundamental purpose of compulsory education is fair development, affording the same educational opportunities to all recipients. Also, higher education must emphasise long-term quality development rather than short-term attainment of degrees. On the issue of care for the elderly, the current system must be thoroughly reformed and flexibility should be increased while, at the same time, supplementing it with various care plans for the elderly.

Third, against the backdrop of Sino-US trade friction, we should place more emphasis on opening up and learning with an open mind. The essence of opening up to the outside world is to learn rather than simply to obtain markets, capital or technology. The government, enterprises and people should learn all the beneficial practices of foreign countries. This is the foundation of economic progress and social development.

We should, first of all, seriously and modestly learn the spirit of the rule of law, the most valuable feature of the US. In the US, after any major event occurs, it eventually seeks resolution at the legal level, and the decision of the US Supreme Court is considered final. This time, for the dispute between the working class and the American elite, both sides are seeking legal solutions. So China must learn from this and build the rule of law into a basic cohesive force. From house demolition to national policy, the dispute ends in a court judgement and this is where we have the most to learn from the US.

In addition, we should learn the spirit of Japan's delicate management. Although Japan's enterprises and government often make mistakes at the strategic level, delicate management is their trademark, and globally their level is second to none. Our enterprises and all citizens must seriously study this point.

We should also learn Germany's methods of accurately regulating the market economy. Germany has a very successful precise regulation system in the real estate and financial fields. Why does Germany precisely regulate the market economy? This is because it suffered from the *laissez-faire* market economy during the Weimar Republic between the first and second world wars. After the second world war, the Germans carefully summarised their experience during that period and put forward the concept of a market economy. Until today, there has been no major crisis in Germany's real estate and financial markets, on the contrary, Germany's real economy, including manufacturing industry, is booming.

At the same time, we should also seriously learn from Britain's strategic thinking. Over the past 500 years, Britain has basically made no mistakes on major strategic issues, winning every time in its strategic competitions with France, the Netherlands, Portugal, Spain, Germany, Japan and other countries. Britain is good at following the trend of history. Now, it is optimistic about China, and it is the first Western country to propose joining the Asian Infrastructure Investment Bank (AIIB) and to actively participate in promoting the internationalisation of the Rmb. From the perspective of Britain, we should see China's continued upward confidence. Over the past 500 years, Britain has never misjudged the general trend of history and today they have chosen China with practical actions so shouldn't we have confidence in the future of our nation?

For a long time, as a scholar I have had the honour to travel at home and abroad, and to participate in various conferences and forums, to visit and investigate various universities, enterprises, government agencies and international organisations, and to communicate closely with my domestic and foreign counterparts in economics, and with business and government leaders. In recent years, I have directly felt the great change the world is experiencing, and from time to time I expressed what I felt I had to get off my chest.

The main body of this book is an analytical report based on these research activities, and there is also a condensed version of other research reports. The main theme of these articles is the great change in the world and China's economic and social response. The articles are often limited to current events that are taking place and may not stand the test of future changes, so I would like my readers to keep this in mind when reviewing my work.

Looking back on the text of this book, I must make it clear that any book or article is the result of collective work, and behind the scenes there are large numbers of devotees who have made silent contributions. They are the people I particularly want to give my thanks to. First of all, I would like to give my thanks to Ms Liu Lingyun, the excellent editor of the *New Wealth* magazine in Shenzhen. For a decade, she regularly messaged me via WeChat or email to discuss some hot topics related to the magazine and invited me to respond. With her magic pen, those quick drafts of mine took on a new look. With clear-cut conception, they inadvertently become hot articles on the internet. Much of the text in this book originated like this. Over the past decade, I met her in person no more than three times, however, such monthly cooperation between us was neverending, which can be regarded as a small miracle of content creation in the era of electronic communication. Over the years, I have taught a group of postgraduate students as well as doctoral candidates that have developed into the most diligent and capable researchers in the world. They were the first commentators and processors, and what's more, the collectors and verifiers of the basic research material of the articles in this book. They include Hu Sijia, Chen Dapeng, Zhang Chi, Li Yusha, Wang Xushuo, Zhang He and Lang Kun. Also, special thanks go to editor Cao Chun of the People's Publishing House. She made me profoundly realise a very simple but neglected truth: in today's world, everyone thinks they can write a book; however, they forget that a diligent and extremely responsible and insightful editor is the magical element that turns a manuscript into a high-quality published product.

Understanding the World

Chapter 1

To progress, China must learn open-mindedly from the US, Japan and Germany

What else must China do to progress?

Without a doubt, we must comprehensively and open-mindedly absorb the essence of development of other developed countries. This is the key to whether China can truly become a large, powerful and influential country. If we are unable to keep learning, we will struggle to make the leap from moderately developed to developed, from a large country to a powerful country.

In the early days of reform and opening up, the target of learning for the Chinese, in the field of economics at least, was Japan. At that time, the Sino-Japanese relationship was at its peak. China sent out delegation after delegation to learn from Japan. Hua Guofeng, Hu Yaobang and other Chinese leaders all visited Japan, Chinese economists and management experts carefully studied the 'Japanese Model'. All of this has left a legacy which can be seen today. For example, the establishment of the state Council Development Research Centre is, to some extent, the result of learning from Japan.

Ma Hong and other economists of the older generation particularly emphasised learning from Japan.

Many years later, China's target of learning gradually turned to the US. Large numbers of students and visiting scholars travelled far to the US to visit, study and exchange. Because the US is the world's first power, very naturally this trend has continued to the present day. This is particularly distinctive in universities and research institutes. Whenever the university elite speak, they speak of Harvard, Stanford and MIT. This makes sense, to some extent, because American science and higher education lead the world. However, it must be noted that the US is not without its own problems. The global financial crisis that broke out in the US in 2008 is clear proof of this. Since 2012, although the American economy recovered faster than other developed countries, it failed to bring tangible benefits to all sectors of society, so rounds of protests broke out. Social problems in the US are becoming more and more serious, and the gap between rich and poor has a marked tendency to expand.

In recent years, China has also studied and examined the European model more carefully. One important reason for this is that at the international strategic level, the US is gradually coming to regard China as a potential competitor; however, Europe, especially Germany, has had increasingly close relations with China. Even Britain, the US's longstanding ally, has also adopted various strategic friendly gestures towards China.

Facing the major powers who have their own unique advantages, what should we learn from them? Obviously, we should learn from the most essential success factors of all countries and integrate them into the comprehensive advantages of China's traditional politics, economics and national governance. In this way, China can truly become a large and powerful country with great influence in the world.

Learn the essence of American advantages: openness and inclusiveness based on the rule of law

As a superpower in today's world, the foundation of US power is undoubtedly innovation. From science and technology to enterprise systems and business models, the US has long been the envy of other countries and the gold standard to be aspired to, including for other developed countries. So, what is the foundation for the US's innovative vitality? It is its open, inclusive and pluralistic spirit. Only by embracing inclusiveness can we make those seemingly disparate ideas eventually develop into sparks of innovation. An important aspect of US inclusiveness is its racial and cultural diversity, and this comes from the openness of its system.

The concept of an 'open society' has long been praised highly by George Soros and his mentor at the London School of Economics, Karl Popper, whom Soros respects. Openness can ensure that people with different ideas are able to integrate into mainstream society. In the US, those very creative geniuses, from Elon Musk, Bill Gates and Steve Jobs to Mark Zuckerberg, as well as Thomas Edison and Nikola Tesla in the early years, are both geniuses and eccentric talents. They all have their own eccentricities in their behaviour and thinking, but they were all embraced by American society, eventually becoming the giants who changed society.

The foundation of America's inclusiveness, openness and freedom is the rule of law. Any major public scandal, from the trial of O J Simpson to the presidential race between Al Gore and George W Bush, Jr, as long as it rises to the legal level and is settled by the legal system, the vast majority of the American public are willing to accept the results. Even today, many Americans scold Bush, but few people cry for Gore, while most Americans believe O J Simpson was guilty but no one publicly challenged the judge's ruling at that time. To draw a parallel with the sporting world, no one said that basketball player Michael Jordan's last winning shot should be disallowed for a foul. Respecting the decisions of the judicial system is like respecting the rules of the game officiated by sports referees, daring to fight and admitting defeat, this reflects the lovely American spirit of the rule of law!

I remember when I studied in the US for my doctorate degree, one of my tutors was Oliver Hart. He was a professor at MIT and later went to Harvard. His academic contribution was to collect court cases and make an intensive study into the concept of 'property rights'. I always believe that this is a work that deserves the Nobel Prize in economics. When I was writing my graduation thesis, a much publicised case happened in Boston. An international student from Ireland was accused of abusing a baby to death. At the first instance trial, a sentence of life imprisonment was delivered, which aroused public dissatisfaction, and the judge later commuted the sentence to a misdemeanour. I have repeatedly asked Professor Hart about this case as an example, saying that judges are also human, hence they must be susceptible to human error, or even bribes, so why not introduce the fairness and efficiency of the court into the study of property rights, and even the whole law and economy. He always smiled without answering my question. Once, he told me gently: "In the US no one will believe this kind of research. Americans believe that the court is the court, and the impartiality of the court is beyond doubt." I still remember this conversation. We foreigners are deeply impressed by the respect for the judicial system across all social classes in the US. For many years, I have been thinking that American academia also has a restricted area.

China is a multinational country with a vast territory and a long history, which is completely different to other Asian countries, such as South Korea and Japan. Therefore, it is entirely possible and necessary for China to learn from the US in terms of openness, inclusiveness and diversity. The starting point of this learning process should be the education system.

The American higher education system is highly respected all over the world, however, it should be noted that the US has a large number of distinctive primary and secondary schools. Although the quality of many of these schools, especially in poor communities, is extremely low, don't forget that there are also a large number of elite primary and secondary schools in the US. For example, Phillips Exeter Academy, Mark Zuckerberg's high school, has trained many of the American elite. Its reputation in the US should be higher than Harvard University, as it is more difficult to enter this secondary school than to enter Harvard. Many high-quality primary and secondary schools, even if they are not elite schools, have their own characteristics. In recent years, I have come into contact with some of these schools. What impressed me deeply is that on the first day of admission, the schools repeatedly emphasise that the students must embrace values of tolerance and equality. The students are not allowed to discriminate against their classmates because of their looks, skin colour, intelligence level or family background, but are taught to respect everyone. This inclusive atmosphere enables every student to learn and grow freely.

In recent years, China's higher education has made rapid progress. From the number of scientific research papers published to the number of prizes won by undergraduate students going abroad to participate in various competitions, and even the quantity and quality of absorbing top scientific research talents, China is rapidly catching up with and surpassing many countries. If there is no major incident, it can be predicted that in the next 20 years, China can indeed have a number of colleges and universities emerging that rank among the world's first-class universities. But what is worrying is that our primary and secondary education does not embrace the kind of tolerance, openness and diversifity seen in the US that allows all kinds of talent to flourish. This is something we must learn from the US.

Learn the spirit of delicate management from Japan

Any Chinese friends who have been to Japan are impressed by its delicacy management. In Japan, from street vending machines, fast-food restaurants, underground rail system, enterprises, and even government departments, all aspects of operation reflect the essence of delicate management. The enduring competitiveness of Japan's automobile industry is the concentrated embodiment of its delicate management: the close cooperation between an auto parts production and assembly plant can ensure the quality of Japanese auto parts and make them economical and durable, beating competitors in other countries at the same price. Japan's delicate management is often directly transformed into its scientific, technological, military and other advantages.

Of course, it cannot be said that delicate management is the sole factor for the success of social development. Objectively speaking, Japan's strength lies in its emphasis on technology and detail, and its weakness lies in poor strategic thinking. In fact, the mistake Japan has made for a long time lies in the lack of strategic management and insufficient direction for research but expending a lot of energy on the management of specific details. Over the past 20 years, Japan's economy was in a downturn and the fundamental reason was that under pressure from the US, the Japanese government made repeated policy and strategy mistakes in its economic system. From the rapid appreciation of the Yen to overly loose monetary policy and extreme fiscal expansion, every step was passive. However, this does not present an obstacle for Chinese enterprises, governments, schools and other sectors of society to meticulously study the essence of Japan's delicate management. This spirit of delicate management ought to be more important than any specific practice or institutional arrangement.

China has a vast territory and abundant resources, but due to the low level of long-term economic development, the Chinese people are habitually satisfied with basic living conditions, so the requirement for delicate management is far less than in Japan. At the same time, the degree of delicate management also varies in China, being relatively higher in the southern coastal metropolis than in the big cities in the north.

Learning delicacy management from Japan should be a complementary lesson for China to continue to rise and grow into a powerful country economically and militarily. In this regard, Japan is a teacher to China.

Learn from Germany to accurately regulate the market economy

Germany's market economy system has evolved over years since the Second World War to contain outstanding characteristics. Then, what is the core factor?

In 2015, I co-wrote with Roland Berger, a noted German economist and management consultant, *The Future of China's Economy: The German Model for the Chinese Economy*. Generally speaking, the most noted characteristics of the German market economy are that it is fully aware that an unconstrained market economy brings all kinds of market failures and social fairness problems. Therefore, accurate regulation must be carried out on the market economy.

Germany's market economy system was refined after serious reflection on its painful experience in the Weimar Republic during the Second World War. The basic lessons learned by the Germans are that an unconstrained market economy, like a great scourge, leads to huge macroeconomic fluctuations. Just as a democracy without any constraints brings political disaster – in those years, it was in a democratic system that lacked the constraints of the rule of law in a real sense. Hitler made full use of nationalism to mislead Germany onto the fascist road.

Germany's market economy system has a series of very precise regulatory systems. For example, in the real estate sector, special emphasis is placed on management of the rental market to not only protect developers who invest in building and renting out houses and to encourage such activity, but also to protect tenants who rent houses. Landlords generally cannot easily increase rent, nor can they easily evict tenants. As for loans for ptoperty purchases, the German government has a set of very prudent measures to discourage families from hastily purchasing a house with a loan. As another example, in terms of estate tax, the German tax system is open-minded toward entrepreneurs who inherit from their predecessors and continue to operate – if the next generation can continue to operate a productive enterprise handed down from the previous generation for over ten years, the estate tax is almost completely exempted. That is to say, estate tax is carefully designed to ensure the longevity of German family businesses.

The German system also accurately protects vulnerable groups in the market economy. It is undeniable that the market economy is indeed very unfair on some participants, including not only people who have bad luck and accidents leading to disability and disease, but also people who are born with a weak sense of market competition and limited competitiveness. To these people, the German system gives considerable tolerance and adequate subsidies. In the late 20th and early 21st century, under the leadership of Chancellor Gerhard Schroder, Germany carried out drastic reforms of social welfare policies, all social welfare subsidies were carefully operated under one platform to ensure that every family in need of assistance could get a package of government assistance, meanwhile the public were encouraged to supervise each other to prevent welfare abuse. This not only ensures fairness but also improves efficiency.

In Germany, such institutional designs for accurately regulating the defects of the market economy can be found everywhere. Learning the essence of the German market economy is to break either the superstition of the 'omnipotence of the market economy' or the dogma that 'government can do anything', and accurately, realistically and practically regulates problems that emerge in the market economy.

In China, after years of reform and opening up, whether it is the advantages and disadvantages of the market economy, or the capacity and limitations of government, we have all seen them clearly, therefore, we particularly need to learn from the experience of Germany.

Generally speaking, China still has huge room to rise. In the process of continuous progress, we particularly need to seriously study the essence of the models of the world's excellent large economies. The openness, diversity and inclusiveness of the US, the delicate management of Japan, and Germany's various measures and systems to accurately regulate the market economy should be three required courses for China's continued upward economic development. If we can conscientiously study them and make constant practice, China will certainly be able to incorporate things of a diverse nature and eventually develop into an exceptional and important major power with its own unique advantages and great influence in the world.

Chapter 2

Looking at the New Normal of China and the World from Davos

Under the new normal of China and the world, the annual meeting of the World Economic Forum (WEF) in 2015 also presented some rather distinguished new characteristics, and the implications of these are worth analysing.

Geopolitics and the Conflict Between Civilisations Changes the World Pattern

The theme of this annual meeting was 'new world pattern', and the impact of geopolitics on the world pattern was the focus of the agenda. Before the meeting, the terrorist attack that happened in Paris made this agenda particularly important.

At the meeting, President Poroshenko of Ukraine, Iraqi Prime Minister Abadi and US Secretary of State John Kerry gave speeches one after another or participated in dialogues. The talks centred around geopolitics as well as how to deal with terrorist attacks. In his speech Abadi clearly pointed out that the current situation in the Middle East was extremely complicated, which could not be described as a simple clash of civilisations but had developed into a conflict between extremists, such as the so-called Islamic State and mainstream Islamic society. Therefore, stabilising the Middle East while mobilising the mainstream political forces of Islamic countries outside the Middle East, like Indonesia and Malaysia, to jointly respond Islamic extremism is an important global response to extremist terrorists.

In other words, the terrorist attack that happened on the streets of Paris could not be simply explained and responded to as a clash between the West and Islam. In my view, the so-called Patriotic Europeans Against Islamisation of the Occident (PEGIDA) movement that emerged in Germany went completely in the wrong direction. Differences within Islamic countries may be greater than differences between Islamic and Western countries. If we fail to grasp this focus, contradictions will intensify, not only will terrorist events spiral out of control but they will also spread. In January 2015, the Japanese hostage incident in the Middle East also reflected these characteristics because, in terms of religion, conflict between Japan and Islamic countries is not the most direct.

The Ukraine crisis was a frequent topic of conversation at the WEF. One breakfast meeting was about how Russia should deal with the Ukraine crisis economically. Several hundred people attended, and the scale as well as the enthusiasm of the participants was a rare scene among the breakfast meetings held behind closed doors. Those who attended included people from various circles of Israel, South Africa, the US, Russia and other countries. The Russian organisers wanted to gain some beneficial experiences from real-life examples of how Israel and South Africa deal with international sanctions. However, the basic viewpoint of participants from other countries was that Russia was 'doomed' in this round of crisis, that its economy would decline further in the future, but that the Russian authorities were seriously underestimating the gravity of the situation. At the meeting I was the only one from China. In my speech in the final stage, I strongly suggested that the Russian authorities must strengthen economic cooperation with Eastern countries to partially alleviate their economic difficulties.

China's influence can be seen everywhere

By and large, meeting participants were relatively optimistic about China's economic development. Especially since there were new ideas in Premier Li Keqiang's speech at the most important golden moment of this round of the annual meeting. He used European analogies familiar to participants to effectively communicate to his audience the transformative experience of Davos and "speed, balance and courage", the basic essentials of skiing, to describe China's firm determination to promote economic restructuring.

Of particular interest was that in this round of the Forum, the participants' attention to China's economic development was gradually replaced by China's impact on the world economy. Therefore, at some meetings on China's economy itself, such as the lunch I attended to discuss China's economic prospects, the discussion among participants was not as enthusiastic as in previous years, maybe people thought that the risks of China's economy were basically controllable. However, in other seminars, everyone unconsciously discussed China's economy. For example, at the seminar on India's economic development prospects, almost every speaker talked about China. China had become the most important benchmark and driving force for India's development and reform.

By witnessing various discussions on India and dialogues with Indian participants, my basic conclusion was that this round of reform in India was quite likely to succeed. Judging from the various reactions of the participants, Indian Prime Minister Modi is indeed a reformer with more drive and executive force. Moreover, unlike the local traditional political elite, he is comparatively close to real life. It is said that he is more used to giving speeches in Hindu. From this point of view, China must pay more attention to India and Chinese entrepreneurs should also pay more attention to the development of the Indian market.

Compartmentalisation of the world economic structure

During the WEF, the European Central Bank (ECB) officially launched a quantitative easing policy. In terms of strength, it also slightly exceeded previous expectations, an important turning point to emerge from the European economy. The basic viewpoint of the participants was that while quantitative easing was conducive for recovery of the European economy, it would also bring some political divisions within Europe. German Chancellor Angela Merkel was quite dissatisfied with the ECB's policy, thinking that excessive easing would hinder the process of reform in some Euro-zone countries. As the leader of Europe, Germany did not seem to play its due leading role in the implementation of the easing policy, only complaining about it.

In addition, many participants believed that the central banks of Europe and Japan were implementing an easing policy, the monetary policy of Britain and the US was gradually shrinking, while Switzerland had abandoned its foreign exchange (forex) controls, all of which would exacerbate volatility in international forex rates. Perhaps a feature of the new normal of world finance is substantial exchange rate volatility, to the point where - as the most important international currency - the trend of the US dollar would be to deviate from other major international currencies. During this process, in fact, there should be a good opportunity for the internationalisation of the Rmb because, as a relatively stable currency and with its influence gradually rising, the Rmb could provide a new choice for investors from all over the world.

In 2015, the International Monetary Fund (IMF) discussed whether to include the Rmb in the basket of special drawing rights. Analysed from various actual situations, the Rmb should be part of the IMF's basket of currencies, moreover, the IMF itself was also very supportive of this reform. However, the problem lay mainly with the US. When the time comes, we will see whether the US Finance Ministry is broad-minded enough to allow the Rmb to join the basket of currencies. If it clearly voices its objection, it will show the world that US unilateralism and hegemonic thinking are continuing. Even if the US wins on this issue, it will lose its prestige as a world economic and financial leader.

The new sector of the world economy is composed of economies with a rapid recovery in the short term, such as Britain and the US, or Russia and other slow-growing economies deeply affected by the decline in resource prices and geopolitics, or Europe, a recovering economy, as well as China, which is still in a steady upward trend; this is the latest pattern of compartmentalisation and diversification of the world economy.

Science and technology are changing society

This round of the WEF paid particular attention to the impact of science and technology on society. In a dialogue, Bill Gates and his wife particularly emphasised the use of science and technology to help backward areas escape poverty. Thanks to the availability of good crop seeds, such as drought-resistant corn seeds, and the promotion of low-cost vaccines, infant mortality and the rate of children dying young have dropped dramatically. In particular, they stressed that China was the biggest contributor to poverty alleviation and expressed optimism about China's prospects for sustainable development. Bill Gates said that over the past 30 years, developed countries had always said that China couldn't do this or that but the facts always proved them wrong. China is developing. He believed that as long as China could maintain 5% economic growth in the future, China's contribution to the world economy, including poverty alleviation, would still be huge.

This Forum also invited the heads of Facebook, Microsoft, Google and Vodafone to talk about the world pattern. One of their basic views was that the development of science and technology is changing the behaviour of the general public's participation in politics. In the future, politics will give more consideration to the feelings of ordinary people.

In another dialogue, what surprised me was when several experts at the Forum carried out a conversation via video link with young people from four locations around the world, and the result was very good. Several young people from Madrid, the Philippines and Tunisia posed a sharp contrast to the senior experts at the scene; from age to viewpoints, they were quite different. With this in mind, I think that the format of the WEF may change in a few years, namely, that many discussion sessions will be attended by young people outside the venue from all over the world. The WEF will no longer be a gathering place for the elite but may become more inclusive for young people and a more representative discussion of major world economic and political issues.

Chapter 3

Resurgence of nationalism in the West

A political and economic change is taking place in Western developed countries. From the result of "Brexit" – Britain's decision to leave the European Union (EU) following a referendum on its membership on 23 June 2016, and Trump winning the US general election on 8 November, to the loss of Italy's referendum on constitutional amendment on 4 December, they all reflected this change.

Resurgence of Nationalism in the West

How should we view the theme of this change in the West? On this issue, in early November 2016 I consulted former British Prime Minister Gordon Brown in an open forum and his reply was that the Western public are generally dissatisfied with their reality, so they project this dissatisfaction onto the political elite.

In our dialogue, I raised the question that a new wave of nationalism is emerging in the West. Gordon Brown agreed with me. He expressed the view that the core of the wave is the rise of nationalism in the West and that it is the revival of the 1648 Westphalian System whereby each nation state does things in its own way, with mutual non-interference. Spain, Great Britain, the US, the era of promoting globalisation through imperial hegemony, seems to be going away.

Then where will the direct spearhead of the resurgence of Western nationalism be directed? As Western scholars say, all politics is local politics, the spearhead of the wave of Western nationalism is mainly directed at domestic political elites, such as Hillary Clinton. However, the fundamental reason behind the attack on domestic political elites is dissatisfaction with the tide of globalisation over the past years.

Eight years ago, in the campaign for presidential candidate Barack Obama, the former US Finance Minister, former president of Harvard University and noted economist, Larry Summers, clearly pointed out that globalisation does not seem to have brought as many benefits to Americans as they thought, the reason being that the US has no ability to compensate the low-skilled segment of the population frustrated by globalisation. Unfortunately, although elites like Summers are eloquent in analysing the defects of globalisation, at that time he did not expect Donald Trump's victory at all. On 1 November 2016, one week before the US general election, in an open lecture held in the Schwarzman Academy of Tsinghua University, with all sincerity and seriousness he said that although the FBI had restarted the investigation into Hilary Clinton, there was still an 85% chance of Hilary winning the election.

What are the direct consequences of this wave of Western nationalist politics? In the field of international politics, the Western developed countries are likely to withdraw on a large scale from international affairs, including international governance. The US is unlikely to lead the wave of globalisation as it has in the past, on the contrary, it will try its best to find a way out of the wave of globalisation.

Actively promote a new type of globalisation with Chinese characteristics

So, in the short term, what negative impact will the wave of Western nationalism have on China? In the long run, how should China respond?

From the perspective of history, the Smoot-Hawley Tariff Act the US introduced between the first and second world wars triggered protectionist retaliation in Europe, thereby directly causing a global recession and indirectly led to Hitler's coming to power. This terrible lesson is still fresh in our minds and many sectors of American society should not allow the same mistakes to happen again.

More importantly, compared to 90 years ago, international trade today has become extremely complicated and global economies are intertwined and affect each other. Therefore, the US may aim at some fields that have a great impact on public opinion, comparatively little on the real economy and take some protection measures, such as the case of tyre warranties. Generally speaking, China's exports as a proportion of GDP dropped to 20% from 35% before the financial crisis, and the proportion of its GDP current account surplus also decreased to an expected 2.2% in 2016 from 8.8% in 2007. Therefore, China's economic dependence on foreign countries has greatly decreased and the recent emergence of Western nationalism and anti-globalisation on China's economy will not have much impact.

In the long run, China should tightly grasp the new wave of nationalism ignited by Western conservative leaders to seize the momentum, raise the banner of new globalisation with Chinese characteristics and become the leader of a new round of globalisation.

Speaking specifically, the new globalisation with Chinese characteristics should have three features.

First, the large numbers of emerging markets must be the main body of the new globalisation with Chinese characteristics. China should tightly grasp them and try to achieve a closer trading relationship with them. They are the biggest beneficiaries of the new globalisation, China must try every means to reach a round of multilateral or bilateral free trade agreements (FTAs), such as the Regional Comprehensive Economic Partnership (RCEP) and a Free Trade Area of the Asia Pacific (FTAAP). China must actively hold consultations with them to form a wave of global integration led by emerging market countries, coping with the tide of anti-globalisation of developed countries by the method of "encircling the cities from the rural areas".

Second, the beneficiaries of the new globalisation with Chinese characteristics must be ordinary people. This point is extremely important. Unlike the US-led traditional globalisation, the new globalisation must emphasise that its beneficiaries are ordinary people. The key is to strengthen infrastructure construction in low and middle-income countries, strengthen investment in labour-intensive industries, and relocate part of China's labour intensive-industries to these countries. At the same time, the emphasis should be on the integration of trade and physical investment, not on the Wall Street-led liberalisation of financial investment and integration.

Third, take the 'Belt and Road Initiative' (BRI) as a breakthrough. To the BRI-related regions or emerging-market countries with mature conditions, we should consciously and gradually sign bilateral or multilateral trade investment integration agreements. Taking BRI as a link, conduct research and establish a 'Belt and Road' development bank. Make good use of international finance resources and speed up the construction of the 'Belt and Road'.

China has become the world's second-largest overseas investor and the world's largest saver. Its own market economy system has highly competitive and adaptable; as such, it is fully qualified to actively participate in and promote the process of economic globalisation amid the resurgence of Western nationalism. Relying on emerging markets, we can gradually build closer economic and trade cooperation with them, so as to gradually enhance China's image as a responsible large country. This is precisely the strategic opportunity for major international development that the resurgence of Western nationalism in today's world has brought to China.

Chapter 4

Understanding 'Brexit'

Britain's decision to leave the European Union (EU), commonly referred to as Brexit, following a referendum on the nation's membership of the trading bloc on 23 June 2016, undoubtedly had a sudden and violent impact on the world economy, which was gradually recovering from the international financial crisis. Some compared it to the series of financial jolts caused by the bankruptcy of Bear Stearns; some equated the power of the referendum to the bankruptcy of Lehman Brothers in its capacity to trigger another global recession; some American financiers even predicted that the British referendum would precipitate an American economic recession with estimated GDP losses of 20% to 30%, and that its force would exceed that of the 2008 international financial crisis.

Then, what is the essence of Brexit? From the EU referendum to the American presidential election, is there any common pattern worth our reflection? Let me use a very simple metaphor to explain its profound mystery more directly.

Imagine that in a tranquil village several hundred families are living a self-sufficient idyllic life. Gradually, the village blends into the outside world. As a result, some villagers suddenly find that their products are very popular outside the village, so they make a fortune; other villagers find that the products of other villages are better than theirs, so they can't sell theirs and their economic income drops sharply; while some other villagers who originally planted crops find that the grain outside their village is cheaper than their own but they don't know how to shift from planting crops to planting agricultural products that are welcomed outside. This is the impact brought to the village by globalisation.

If we look at the village as a whole, integration into the outside world is undoubtedly a good thing. Because villagers can concentrate on the production of products needed by the big market, those products that are not competitive will not be produced by themselves but it's OK to buy them more cheaply than before, and the total income of the whole village has increased significantly. However, the problem is the uneven balance of joy and hardship; many residents who have to give up their original way of life become very upset and confused.

At the same time, another group of people are also very upset, and they are the leaders of the village committee. In the past, when the village encountered a major problem, the director and the village committee would hold a meeting and give their final say, but now the situation is different. The village has been integrated into the outside world, so the final say on many domestic matters depends on greater leaders outside. For instance, the village's standards of hygiene and product quality must be decided by outsiders. In addition, when other villages encounter difficulties, our village needs to help, just as other villages help us when our village is in difficulty. Therefore, many matters are decided by greater leaders outside the community and the words of the village leaders do not work as well as before.

This produces two groups of people dissatisfied with the competition in the big market and economic cycle. One group is the veteran governmeny officials who are accustomed to making decisions and having the final say, or young leaders who think like veteran officials;

the other group is the villagers who can't sell their products and don't know how to change careers. The two groups come up with the same solution, hence, the village director, who is accustomed to the old way of thinking and who wants to go back to the days when he had the final say, suggests that we simply hold a show of hands to decide whether to go back to the happy life of the few people in the small village. The key detail is that the voting rules are not based on the amount of money in their pockets, one dollar for one vote, but one person, one vote, absolutely 'great democracy'. The selfish calculation of the village director is that through the poll he can see how many people oppose the village's integration into the external economic cycle. If voters vote "no", why not close the door and allow the director and the village committee to make their own decisions and have the final say as was the case before.

The timing of the vote is very important. Recently, many residents have been depressed which, to a great extent, is because for a period of time the whole big market outside has been experiencing a cyclical decline but many villagers can't tell whether it's a decline of the whole market economy, or a major cyclical economic adjustment that has impacted their livelihood. In short, all the complaints are attributed to the village's decision to join the big market. Therefore, the voting result comes out: the village announces that it will not join the big market outside, and the village leaders continue to close the door, and make their own decisions and have the final say as before.

The village leaders who are, in a petty, calculated way, taking advantage of the fierce resentment of the villagers, through simple democratic violence, regain the rights they were deprived of, and this is the essence of Brexit.

Speaking more academically, in the era of global competition, a country's government should actively redistribute income, benefiting the majority of people, at the same time, strengthening civic education and training, and letting local villagers whose interests have been damaged improve their competitiveness so as to better participate in the global economic cycle. But the village director feels that it is difficult to do these things, so it is better to make a decision and let democracy rule, allowing the people who do not have inside information to get back the illusion of past glory.

The essence of Brexit is democratic tyranny through populism and an overt plot by some individual elites to be masters of their own destiny regardless of the fundamental long-term interests of their own people. This is not a conspiracy but an overt plot visible to all.

This kind of story is also on show in the US. The Republican candidate Donald Trump is from the far-right elitist class. They think that the US is a fundamentally great nation that possesses excellent systems and institutions. The US's current problems, in Trump's view, stem from the fact that it employs an open door immigration and is a key player and participates in the international relations. Therefore, these far-right American elites think that if we close our doors, have no migrants and do not allow free trade, things will turn out better for us; the US president does not have to take into account external opinions, and such a leader is doing better than before. This is a political alliance reached between Trump's grassroots support base whose interests have been damaged and the right-wing elements today's recessionary global environment, also enlightened by Brexit.

In this situation, the world needs a rational voice as well as politicians with long-term vision.

Currently, the economic chaos brought about by Brexit is, of course, very unfortunate and painful to related enterprises, but the pain is also the best education, especially for the working people who support Brexit without really understanding what it means, but thinking of returning to a closed, non-globalised era, making the other like-minded 'villagers' and 'village officials' think twice.

The prospects for Britain after the referendum are unclear. It cannot either rule out the possibility that the political impact of the referendum will be entirely eliminated after the British political system undergoes a complex operation, or the result that the referendum develops into Britain's complete secession from the EU. Facing this complicated international situation, as a major developing country, China must carefully prepare a plan, keeping close communication with a British government which has left the EU as well as maintaining close relations with the EU itself.

Any world wave provides development opportunities for those countries that are prepared and have a plan, and brings great challenges to those who are not prepared and respond hastily. As a developing country, China should belong to the first category, should be able to turn complexity into simplicity and challenges into opportunities.

Chapter 5

Reappraising our understanding of the US

The world today is witnessing structural change no seen in a century, and this is the basic judgement of China's leaders regarding the current situation. The key element of this structural change is that the behaviour of the US has suddenly changed. Not only was Trump's election a surprise but a series of policies after his election were even more confusing. What is wrong with the US? Is the US we used to know the real US? This can't help but remind people of a past event from 70 years ago.

Chinese Academics are in urgent need of 'The Chrysanthemum and the Sword of the New Era'

In 1941 the Pacific war broke out. The US declared war on Japan and officially entered the second world war. With an urgent need to understand the national character of Japan, the American intelligence authorities authorised the distinguished American anthropologist Ruth Benedict to write a research report. This report gave a comprehensive analysis of some Japanese personality traits that looked very contradictory: on the one hand, the Japanese people are gentle and docile; on the other hand, they display a radical, wild warrior spirit.

In 1946, according to her report to the American intelligence authorities, the author published *The Chrysanthemum and the Sword*, a book that is famous today, which played a key role in Americans' understanding of Japan and in enabling them to deal with Japan's post-war problems. Nowadays, Chinese academics are in urgent need of 'The Chrysanthemum and the Sword of the new era' in order to understand what the real US is.

Frankly speaking, although many Chinese scholars and members of the elite have studied and worked in the US, and they think from the bottom of their hearts that they know the country best, in fact, their understanding of the US is probably extremely one-sided. Because most of them, including myself, studied in the US, and they all studied in elite universities, their tutors and classmates are all members of the upper echelons of American society. Taking myself as an example, when I studied at Harvard University for my doctorate degree, nearly all my tutors were Jews and all self-identified as 'Reformed Jewish' (meaning Jews without unconditional belief in the Jewish faith). After I graduated, I worked at and visited Michigan University and Stanford University, and later often dealt with various institutions of the World Bank and Wall Street. Those I was in contact with were mostly the cream of the elite of American society. I'm afraid they don't fully represent real Americans.

Today, US President Trump was elected mainly because he doesn't represent the elite but more the working class in the US. So, after all, what is an American? And what is the national character of the US?

Dual national identity of the US

It must be admitted that American society is not just made up of the American elite, the origin of their national identity is more far-reaching than that. Prior to his death, Harvard political scientist

Samuel P Huntington (himself a Jew) wrote in *Who Are We? America's Great Debate*: The national identity of the US was not shaped in 1775 but when the initial settlers came to North America in the early 17th century. These Anglo Protestants who came to North America were not colonists but settlers. They didn't come on behalf of Great Britain to explore and expand but fled religious persecution in their homeland in search of a new life in a new land, and it was from that time that the national identity of the US was shaped.

Then, what on earth is the national identity of the US? From this perspective, it can be summarised in two statements.

First, Americans are pious Protestants with a firm belief in god. Some people say that 300 years have passed, has this national identity of the US changed? No, today, the US has the highest proportion of believers in all Western countries, much higher than Europe! The proportion of weekend church-goers is also the highest. In this sense, the US is a country which has truly inherited the Protestant tradition. Donald Trump himself is also a Christian with strong self-discipline and never drinks alcohol. We generally believe that Americans advocate individual freedom and ideological emancipation but this is not the true American tradition which dates back to the settlers of the early 17th century.

Second, isolationism. The US's geological position is different from any European countries (including Britain), having a vast territory and being a continental country with few neighbours (only Mexico and Canada), the Americans have been advocates of isolationism since the founding of the country. In fact, open the economic history of the US since the settlers came in the early 17th century and most of the time, the US was in a closed state, had not opened up its territory and had no desire to colonise overseas. The 25th president of the US William McKinley finally decided to send troops to the Philippines after an extremely bitter internal mental struggle. He once said: "I asked for help... pacing up and down the floor of the White House late into the night... I knelt on the ground more than once to pray to Almighty God. Finally, one night I received the voice of god…, that is, we have no choice but to occupy the Philippines." This is essentially different from Britain's expansion of territory around the world in those days.

Early in the 19th century, the essence of the famous 'Monroe Doctrine' behind US foreign policy was that the US government could not bear to see Britain and the other European powers establish colonies all over the world and seek spheres of influence everywhere. Anyone who is a little familiar with American history knows that during the first world war, the US tried to avoid controversy. After the outbreak of the second world war, the US adopted the same strategy until the Japanese made a surprise attack on Pearl Harbour. Some people say that the Japanese surprise attack on Pearl Harbour was an overt plot of President Roosevelt's, meant to arouse ordinary Americans' fighting spirit to justify participation in the world war, and this is the US. Of course, what Samuel Huntington described in his book is the traditional US, and what he worried about was that the culture of the settlers would be destroyed by later immigrants, particularly the immigrants from Mexico. Once that happens, the US will no longer be the US of the past, it will change its political colour.

In contrast, the major historical exchanges between China and the US, from the Republic of China era and the period of the War of Resistance Against Japanese Aggression to the Cold War period, they all took place after the US had completed its transition to internationalism, defeating the isolation of the Puritans. The various manifestations of the US with which we are familiar are only fleeting moments, they don't represent normality in the long history of the US. The US we are familiar with is the elitist US, the internationalist US, the US manipulated by the 'Reformed Jewish' (including Dr Henry Kissinger and Dr Zbigniew Brzezinski). The Trump we see today and what he represents is the more traditional US, the one where the Pilgrim Fathers went to settle, and the spirit Trump represents is the US that Samuel Huntington believed should stay true to its original aspiration and firmly stick to it.

Reapprasing our understanding of the US and exploring the essence of Trump's ideas

According to the above logic, we should reappraise our understanding of the US. The US has its duality: it is a Puritanical US, which lives a poor life, is self-contained, and claims its own continent as its spiritual and material home; it is also an elitist US of expansionism, heroism and hegemonism, which tries to expand its influence around the world and disseminates its beliefs. These two identities have interacted in American history and it should be said that the US we see today may have returned to its traditional side.

It is in accordance with the above analysis that we should understand the essence of Trump's ideas.

Firstly, Trump does not necessarily want to bring China down. On this issue, he, his adviser Steve Bannon and some other senior officers of the US Defence Department have different views. From an international relations standpoint, his idea is to return the US to the era of the 'Great Isolation' before the beginning of the 21st century, not a US that seeks to influence elections and expand around the world. On this issue, there is no fundamental conflict between China's peaceful development and Trump's basic ideas. If handled properly, Trump may be regarded as an important opportunity for China's peaceful development.

Secondly, Trump's US, that is, the traditional US, does not understand many things about China. Because this iteration of the US is characterised by strong religious faith, they do not understand the Confucian culture that has evolved in China since the Western Zhou Dynast, let alone the Chinese culture described by Chen Yinke as having "reached its peak in the Song Dynasty". They think that the Chinese have no faith and are dissolute. In this respect, we must make a great effort to communicate to the traditional US, telling them that this is a pluralistic world and that there is no contradiction between Chinese Confucianism and Christian tradition, and that, to a large extent, the two can be bridged and learn from each other.

Thirdly, this traditional US represented by Trump is more concerned about the economic situation and social stability of the US itself and doesn't necessarily seek to block China's economic development. They are concerned about trade deficits and surpluses, about trade issues such as exchange rates and tariffs. In essence, they do not necessarily care about China's domestic economic policy and economic system as long as these policies and systems do not pose a threat to US enterprises and trade.

Therefore, regarding the Trump administration and Trump himself, we should firmly grasp the key to trade balance. On this issue, the Chinese government should break with routine and take some concrete measures to seek a win-win situation in exchange for the trust of the Trump administration. This request of the Trump administration is fully understood by traditional American society, as this is also where the interests of traditional society lies.

Reappraising our understanding of the US is of great significance for us to understand the Trump administration and the changes in the world structure not seen in a century. Today, the intellectuals in China who in frequent contact with the American elite must start learning again.

Chapter 6

Keep learning how to deal with the US

In his memoir *Dealing with China*, the American investment banker and former Finance Minister Henry Merritt Paulson, Jr summarised eight basic principles from the standpoint of Americans in dealing with China. Item three is "Speak with one voice without confusing China", item six is "Find more ways to say 'Yes' instead of saying 'No'", and item eight is "Act according to the reality of China"... All of these principles reflected the top-level wisdom of the American side.

But now, the US has changed!

The Trump administration has long forgotten these basic principles while the American elites who are familiar with China distance themselves from Trump, consequently, the high-level advisers around Trump are not in the US main stream.

The US has changed. This is a basic point of the great changes not seen in a century that are now taking place in today's world, among which the change in the Sino-US relationship is at its core. In this context, we Chinese are in fact more in need of a 'practical manual' for *Dealing with America* and should go back to basics and be smarter and wiser in our dealings with the US.

Then, how to deal with the US? My opinion is that first of all, we should start from understanding the US's domestic political operational mechanism and the mentality of the American people. Here is a penny for your thoughts, I will present three obvious observations and analyses.

First, the domestic affairs of the US always take precedence over international affairs. When you open the *New York Times* or the *Washington Post,* the most international newspapers in the US, generally you can find that for the daily top five news items there are at most two news about international affairs and even less news about China. The popular daily paper *USA Today* is even more domestic-oriented. What particularly stands out is how much news that Chinese pay a lot of attention to doesn't attract any attention from Americans at all. For instance, the US Congress passed the 'Taiwan Assurance Act of 2020' but this kind of news almost never appears in mainstream American news media.

What does this mean? It means that the American public and the majority of the policy makers prioritise domestic matters. Even if they care about trade relations between China and the US, their starting point is always concern for US interests. Judging from this, Trump, who always puts "America First" when considering problems, offers nothing new in this regard, only that his policies are extremely short-sighted while other politicians may have a longer-term vision.

Related to this, the vast majority of American politicians and people in the media lack even a basic understanding of China, even today when China is so important interrnationally. Here are two examples. One is that in 2005, two American congressmen proposed a bill on Rmb exchange rate manipulation. At the time, they proposed imposing an additional tariff of 27.5% on China's exports. The initiators were Senator Chuck Schumer from New York State and Senator Lindsey Graham from South Carolina who had never been to China before. That year, some meddlesome people invited the two to China and their first stop was a lecture room at Tsinghua University. I was a commentator on the scene. In the lecture, Schumer said publicly that it was the first time he had left North America and indeed the first time he had held a passport. Considering that he is an important congressman from such an internationally-oriented area as New York, it is amazing that he had never left North America before. Another example is that in 2004 I invited five Western figures (including one from Singapore) with great influence on international public opinion to have a dialogue, including Carl Bernstein who could be called the godfather of the American press and who commented on television every day. He and Bob Woodward investigated the 'Watergate scandal' and eventually brought down President Nixon. He was far more influential than Thomas L Friedman who the Chinese are familiar with and who often comments on China issues, and he also came to China for the first time. During the conversation, we talked about China's Taiwan Issue. He said, not without exaggeration: "Taiwan, where is Taiwan? I forgot about Taiwan a long time ago. What does Taiwan have to do with us?" This is the typical American mentality.

The conclusion is that we must consider China-US relations from the perspective of ordinary Americans and only by doing so can we truly understand what the Americans want and want to do. We cannot only consider what the Harvard, Yale and Washington elite are thinking and saying. In the Trump era, the influence of the American elite was greatly reduced. Ordinary Americans' concerns about China stem mainly from employment and job security concerns. They worry that China's development will take Americans' jobs away and affect their employment. For them, the low price and high quality of Chinese consumer goods, compared to jobs, is far less important! In fact, they couldn't care less about what China's economic aggregate is in the world, and such political partiality of ordinary people is eventually reflected in the decisions of American politicians. Although politicians in the US capital often regard China as 'public enemy number one', to ordinary Americans this is not the case. The house of representatives, elected every two years by ordinary Americans, has more reflected this mentality of the US. So historically the American congress has twice overthrown the interests fought for skilfully by the American president on the international stage. One was the International Trade Organisation (ITO) agreement at the Bretton Woods Conference in 1944, the other one was the proposal to establish the League of Nations and led to its establishment by President Wilson in 1920 after the first world war ended.

In *Who are We? America's Great Debate*, Samuel Huntington's last best-seller before his death, he clearly pointed out that the national character of the US was forged in the early 17th century when the Puritans emigrated to the New World. The US is a country surrounded by sea on three sides with only two neighbours and its people can live happily all their lives without going abroad. Compared with other large countries the American people are more introverted and pay more attention to domestic affairs. This tells us that we must firmly bear in mind what the American general public care about and want when we deal with the US. We must explain clearly to the American people that China's development has also helped the US create jobs. For instance, China is the biggest market for General Motors (GM) and for many years its largest source of profit outside North America. Operating in China has generated large profits for GM, ensuring that GM doesn't have to lay off workers inside the US and helps the company shoulder the heavy burden of pensions for retired workers, helped it through the financial crisis, and return to the stock market.

Second, American society is always pluralistic, more often than not the president represents a minority viewpoint and his decisions are often attacked, so the president's views do not represent all Americans. We are accustomed to taking the American presidents' decision as that of their people, thinking that it represents the will of the country, leading us to mobilise all our energy, including the capacity of public opinion, to bombard decisions of the US administration. But this is often not the case. In reality, pressure on the US president comes more from home, the president's biggest opposition is domestic political enemies, not the Chinese government. Because the US has a presidential system, not a parliamentary system, the president and congress are often split, and the relationship between the senate, house of representatives and the president is often incompatible. Therefore, we must not regard the US as a monolithic bloc; on the contrary, we must actively identify and strive for potential groups friendly to China in the US.

From the perspective of various stakeholders in China-US relations, American multinational corporations (MNCs) and intellectuals used to be the greatest supporters of the development of China-US relations. Now they are wavering in some major respects, but this doesn't mean it is hard to recover the situation. On the contrary, we should make great efforts to win support from MNCs, Wall Street, as well as high-tech industries on the east and west coasts, and university elites for China-US relations. Taking the 'Huawei case' as an example, in fact, the US high-tech industry, including the semiconductor industry, does not support the US government's decision to sanction Huawei because they know that in the short term this will lead to a decline in corporate profits and even operational difficulties, because the policy will affect at least one-third of their business volume; in the long run, they will lose the strategic opportunity to benefit from China's development, because the policy will break the strategic pattern that ties these high-tech companies China interests. Breaking this pattern is likely to encourage China to create its own high-tech ecosystem.

For another example, some US politicians and public opinion leaders, such as Steve Bannon and Mark Cuban, owner of the Dallas Lone Rangers Basketball Club, have been clamouring to kick Chinese companies out of Wall Street. But this is an absolutely terrible idea. In fact, it is extremely important for Chinese enterprises to go to be listed on Wall Street. It is precisely because Chinese high-tech enterprises, such as Alibaba and Jingdong, are listed in the US that allows American investors to share the dividends and added value brought by China's development. More importantly, this is the foundation for the American financial industry to continue to dominate the world, and the key to the continuous development and growth of financial assets denominated in US dollars, and to safeguarding the status of the US dollar as the largest international currency. Therefore, the clamour of Bannon and Cuban is at best equivalent to the fans' barroom chat about a sports match.

Again, for another example, American universities, especially research universities, need excellent Chinese students to continuously enter their university system, to participate in their scientific research and to bring in large amounts of tuition fees. Therefore, in fact, American universities firmly oppose the US government's alarmist and McCarthyist investigation of Chinese students and scholars.

In brief, the investment institutions on Wall Street, the current high-tech industries on the east and west coasts, and the universities can actually become a stable apparatus for China-US relations. China must unswervingly strengthen ties with these social groups and take their concerns into account. It is much more effective to deal with Trump through them than for us to launch a public-opinion offensive! For example, for American MNCs, it must be made clear that they are the key target of China's next phase of opening up, but the premise is that the US must abandon its trade protection policy. In short, we must understand that the US is never a monolithic bloc and that the extreme measures of the White House represent only emotional and narrow nationalism, not the whole US.

Third, American politics is essentially a legal game. Take Trump's request to build a security wall on the border between the US and Mexico, as an example. He found a loophole in the law that the president could declare a national emergency to bypass budget restrictions. Members of congress knew that the president had taken advantage of a loophole in the law but were embarrassing to dwell on the matter because if they vetoed this budget of Trump and challenged the national emergency law, Trump had the right to veto Congress, while Congress was unable to mobilise more than two thirds of its members to veto the president. What could congress do?

Trump's Democratic opponents took up the arms of the law to fight him. A federal judge in North California directly ruled that Trump's national emergency law violated the US Constitution and had no legal effect. Trump was incensed, saying that the judge was originally appointed by Obama and was deliberately restraining him. But no matter how much Trump complained, he had to act according to the rules of the game. The next focus of struggle was whether the US Supreme Court agreed with the judgement of this federal judge.

In this sense, it is no doubt contradictory when Trump listed Huawei as a national security threat and a monitored object, while also claiming that Huawei was a bargaining chip in US-China trade deals. Chinese enterprises must make full use of related US laws and regulations to contend with Trump. For example, they must precisely target federal judges who especially dislike Trump and get to know more about technology companies and the technology industry to initiate a lawsuit against Trump's Huawei policy in their jurisdiction. Of course, we need to do our homework carefully and find a top team of lawyers in the US.

Of particular importance, negotiations with the US, including negotiations with the US government, are essentially negotiations with American lawyers. We must know ourselves and the American lawyers and beat them at their own game. The law-based American political operation mechanism means lawyers play a decisive role, and the lawyer culture runs deep in every political operation in the US, including external negotiations. In negotiations, lawyers are often more destructive than constructive, because lawyers focus most of their energy on issues like "What should I do if you don't follow the contract", but not on "Let's rack our brains and find a third solution". In fact, Robert Lighthizer, the US chief representative in charge of Sino-US trade talks, is a lawyer. To negotiate with American lawyers, we must follow their ideas and *modus operandi* in dealing with them. Firstly, right at the beginning we must 'draw a red line', clearly stating what is not negotiable and what is negotiable; secondly, "consolidate at every step", advancing step by step; thirdly, explain repeatedly what harm it will do to the other party and your own party if the negotiation fails. It is better to have no results than to make concessions in principle. Once the principle is determined, we must hold to it firmly. The premise of knowing yourself and the enemy is to hire top American lawyers as consultants on the periphery. The professional ethics of the American lawyers is first class because professional reputation is above all else and transcends national boundaries; information that should not be disclosed is never disclosed.

In short, the US has changed, and today's Sino-US relations are undergoing fundamental changes. In this situation, we need to go back to basics again and again to gain a deeper understanding of the US. We should learn to consider Sino-US relations from the standpoint of the US and we should also be familiar with the rules of the game of American political operation. The ancients said: "Know the enemy and know yourself, and you can fight a hundred battles with no danger of defeat." This is an importan point to bear in mind regarding the "great changes not seen in a century" of today's world.

Chapter 7

Actively and effectively deal with the new era of Sino-US relations

Since 2018, there have been some extremely complex changes in Sino-US relations. These changes, objectively speaking, were all provoked unilaterally by the US side. So, how to view these changes? Will Sino-US relations fall into the 'Thucydides' trap' of full-scale confrontation, as many people, such as Professor Graham Allison of Harvard University, have said? What is the most likely form of this round of trade disputes between China and the US? How will it evolve? What will be the final outcome? How will China's related industries, such as high-tech and manufacturing industries, be affected?

The basic reason why Sino-US relations can't fall into the Thucydides' trap

On Sino-US relations, we should have a very objective and sober judgment. The most fundamental and important point is that the demands of China and the US are different: China's development goal in the future is not what the US imagines it to be, they think that China wants to become the US of today. Chinese leaders repeatedly stressed in the report of the 19th National Congress of the Communist Party of China (CPC) and on various international occasions, including the WEF, the Bo'ao Asian Forum as well as in all speeches in the UN, that China will resolutely maintain the existing international order but will never start all over again, that China will advance by firmly following the logic of the development of world history, and that the trend of development of world history is peace and development, openness and accommodation, or more specifically, that China does not seek military domination and influence like the West does.

Although China's strategic aim is completely different to Europe in years gone by and the US today, people always ask whether China will change when it becomes strong in the future? Will it be like the US today and deploy military forces around the world to project diplomatic influence and seek political agents? It can be said that this is by no means the prospect of China's future development. It is difficult to simply replicate China's unique cultural tradition and the current governance system in other regions.

In terms of cultural tradition, what the Chinese pursue deep in their hearts is harmony in diversity. While based on Christianity and Judaism, what the Western cultural tradition talks about is 'faith', faith or belief in one god, demanding that people in other regions also pursue the same belief. Therefore, what the Latin American countries practiced in former times was that among the common people, believers could be exempt from taxation while non-believers' property and even lives could not be guaranteed. This mighty force of faith is completely different from the norm in China.

Going hand in hand with this is that the Chinese people have a deep-rooted concept of 'home'. Historically, overseas Chinese living all over the world were often forced to go by the circumstances of their lives only to return to their hometowns after their successful overseas development, achieving wealth and power. Contrary to this, the Western countries are more about pursuing 'harmony and uniformity'. Cecil John Rhodes dominated Rhodesia (today's Zimbabwe) in the south of Africa and was engaged in diamond mining. He never married and before his death he donated all his property to Oxford University, setting up the 'Rhode Scholarship'. His ideal was to gather young students in former British colonies to study at Oxford University so that their own countries would be influenced by Western ideas and values. This is the typical mentality of a Westerner. The Chinese culture and traditions are not so obvious. China, even in its most glorious historical periods, did not try to expand its territory or religious beliefs overseas.

Currently, the 'Two Centenary Goals' put forward by Chinese leaders, in the final analysis, comprise territorial integrity and socioeconomic prosperity, as well as the improvement of people's living conditions that it has brought about. Economic prosperity itself is not a zero sum game and China's economic development can bring a win-win situation to the world. Moreover, China's claim for territorial integrity is very clear, the boundaries are also very clear, mainly to solve the issues of Taiwan, the South China Sea and the Diaoyu Islands (known as the Senkaku Islands in Japan). These requests do not constitute the most essential conflict with the core interests of the US, after all, the Pacific Ocean puts China thousands of miles away from the US. In geopolitics China and the US are probably the two world powers that are furthest away from each other. .

How will this round of the trade dispute between China and the US Evolve?

The immediate cause of this round of the trade dispute was undoubtedly Trump's election as the president of the US. As a nationalist and businessman, it is not strange that Trump provoked the Sino-US dispute on trade. As early as at the end of 2017, Chinese leaders had made very clear ideological preparations for this.

In essence, the most direct aim for Trump to provoke this round of the trade dispute was election and his campaign slogan – 'Make America Great Again'. Let's analyse it carefully, at present, the core interest and the biggest pain point of the US is not that its high-tech enterprises no longer have an advantage, nor is it the decline of its macroeconomy. In fact, in high-tech areas the US today still has an all-round overwhelming advantage over China, and the macroeconomy of the US is also going through a very good period in its history. At the end of 2018, the US jobless rate fell to 3.7%, and the fall continues.

At present, the biggest pain point in the US is that there are a large number of urban areas that used to be economically developed but are now extremely depressed, the most typical one being Detroit. I used to teach at Michigan University, a suburb of Detroit, and recently I took my family and drove back to Detroit. The scene we saw could be basically described as a post-apocalyptic wasteland, extremely sad. How to revitalise the economy in areas like Detroit is, in fact, the most pressing problem facing President Trump and the American people. Of course, Silicon Valley wants to maintain its absolute lead in high-tech forever but this is not Trump's core political demand. After all, the people in Silicon Valley are Trump's sworn political enemies.

On revitalising the traditional American manufacturing industry and solving the Detroit problem, China can actually provide support because China has a huge and rapidly developing consumer market, and the US still has superiority in the production of many manufactured products. For instance, there is still great growth potential for American auto exports to China, so investment in multiple production lines could be considered to increase production capacity by one to two million vehicles, which would create 100,000 new jobs. China's market can digest all these products. China's annual car sales are about 30 million, so adding another two million is no problem at all. Calculated according to the export price of US$25,000 per vehicle (converted to medium and high-end models with a retail price of about Rmb150,000 in China), that could reduce the US's US$50 billion trade deficit with China each year. This is a very large number and exceeds the total US soybean exports to China.

We must note that as a businessman Trump is also a good negotiator. The first principle of his negotiations is to make extremely rude and seemingly absurd demands while, at the same time, using extreme threats. At this critical moment in Sino-US trade negotiations, it is no coincidence that ZTE was heavily fined by the US Department of Commerce. That must be seen as a major, carefully planned threat carried out by the Trump administration, and this is also a negotiating tactic. In China, although we have no advantage in the field of tech, we must see that this round of provocation by the US is a provocation to the global production and supply chain. Although China does not fully grasp the core technology in many fields, as an important part of the world production chain, we can put forward effective responses and threats against the US in other areas. For example, we can, according to China's current laws and regulations, penalise Apple mobile phones, Apple computers and other products that are almost exclusively produced in China, so as to counterattack the unreasonable sanctions imposed by the US on ZTE.

In general, at present China's economic recovery has exceeded social expectations, and exceeds the growth requirement to achieve the goals of building "a moderately prosperous society in all respects" by 2020 and realising "socialist modernisation" by 2035. Hence, China can fully afford trade friction in the economic field. However, we must clearly see that the US faces short-term elections, and its goals are short term while China's goal is long term. So, on the whole, if by engaging in trade friction, China's political system can resist; in the US the short-term nature would make this approach unviable.

According to this series of analyses, it should be said that it is entirely possible for China and the US to reach a mutually satisfactory and win-win agreement. The final result of trade friction should be to maintain the current pattern of globalisation and the smooth operation of the global market supply chain. At the same time, China and the US also take care of each other's interests: China supports the US industrial revitalisation in key areas, while China's major issues of concern in the economic and non-economic fields also receive support from the US.

The effect of this round of trade friction to China's emerging industries of strategic importance

It must be noted that at present, China's economy is in the process of rapidly catching up with and surpassing the US. In terms of structure, China's industrial layout has been basically completed. China is rich in human resources, including young engineers, and the government's support for scientific and technological innovation is also more proactive than the US, so the big picture of China's industrial upgrading will not change. But after this round of trade friction, China's strategy of supporting the development of the science and technology industry is likely to change, for example, project support for scientific and technological innovation may be more open. It may also support some foreign-funded enterprises to develop new technologies in China, as long as they are in China and they cooperate closely on R&D with Chinese enterprises, they can obtain support from the Chinese government.

At present, in some sectors with high profits, there has been a comprehensive trend for Chinese enterprises to catch up. For instance, in the field of sport utility vehicles (SUVs) and medium and low-end family cars, China's independent brands have not only experienced a rapid rise in sales but also have a strongly growing market share. We have reason to believe that in the field of electronic chips and chip processing, China will also make great progress soon. Because these industries are very profitable, the initial investment is relatively large, however, on the whole China does not lack the funds required for early investment.

What is most uncertain and needs the joint efforts of all sectors of society is the construction of some technology platforms that seemingly have no profit points, for example, the design of operating systems and the proposal of Chinese standards in network protocols.

With this kind of work, in the short term, a single company has no obvious profit point, but plays the most basic supporting role in the development of the whole IT industry. This is the biggest difficulty in the process of China's industrial upgrading. Because, after all, we are latecomers in the field of operating systems (OSs). The Apple, Microsoft and Android OSs have formed a pattern of tripartite confrontation and there is great uncertainty about whether China can produce a new OS. Others say that WeChat will be an OS in the future, that every time we turn on the phone, the first interface is WeChat, all programmes should have WeChat as the entrance, for example, for the use of shared bikes and to order meals. This might be one direction, however, it still seems unclear, and all parties need to work together. On this issue, China's internet giants, especially the 'BAT system' (Baidu, Alibaba, Tencent), have an unshirkable social responsibility. The development of these enterprises must be combined with solving the pain points of society and national problems.

I believe that due to China's huge market, talent accumulation and sufficient funds, in the near future China's high-tech industry will certainly be able to form a situation of mutual cooperation and competition with the US. This is also a huge benefit for the world. The world cannot only depend on the US engaging in hig technology. More competition and more choices are good for the people of the world, including the American people. If Microsoft had a monolopy on computers and Apple didn't exist, I believe that the user experience would be greatly diminished.

In short, we have entered a new era of all-round competition between China and the US. How to deal with the new challenge is a major test for the leaders as well as the people of the two countries.

Chapter 8

Three low-level misconceptions to be avoided in reasonably dealing with Sino-US trade friction

At present, Sino-US trade friction is at a stalemate, there is strong uncertainty with all kinds of information changing rapidly, unsettlingh investors and ordinary people, and causing widespread anxiety. The Trump administration is used to releasing all kinds of contradictory information and complex signals, sometimes aggressive, exerting extreme pressure and acting wilfully, sometimes taking a more relaxed attitude and actively preparing for negotiation. In this regard, the Chinese people should remain rational and pay special attention to preventing three low-level misconceptions.

Misconception one: the Trump administration = America

The first misconception is to simply think that the Trump administration is the whole US, lumping together the Trump administration and the American people, making no distinction between all levels of the American people, escalating opposition to specific policies of the Trump administration into opposition to the US as a whole. This is undoubtedly a low-level mistake. We must remain sober-minded and never make mistakes on this point.

We must see that on many issues, especially on policies toward China, Trump is unable to represent the interests of the American people at all levels. In general, most American people are friendly to China. They have gained actual benefits from Sino-US trade and are willing to continue to push forward trade development and even Sino-US relations. Here at least three interest groups are included.

The first type of interest group is one we are familiar with, the conventional 'international elites'. They take a clear stand for internationalism, emphasising that globalisation is good for the world, yet insisting that the US should create and lead the rules and process of globalisation. The representative figures are Henry Kissinger, Ben Bernanke, Larry Summers and Henry Paulson, among others. They want China and the US to deepen cooperation under the globalisation system created and maintained by the US but the focus is mainly on the interests of the US itself. Generally speaking, they believe that China and the US should cooperate and hope that the two countries will reach agreement through negotiations.

The second type of interest group is the general public, the largest interest group in the US. They lack understanding of China affairs, or even of the whole world, caring only about their jobs, income and consumption. The majority of this group have benefited from Sino-US economic and trade relations, and cooperation. For instance, the companies they are working for profited from Sino-US trade and these profits are partially converted into their income, thereby raising their living standard. A typical example is General Motors (GM). For a long time, GM's main profits came from its cooperation with SAIC Motor in Shanghai. After the 2008 global financial crisis, GM was in serious trouble, delisting and going bankrupt. But after corporate restructuring, it relisted on Wall Street in 2010, a key factor being investors' acknowledgement of GM's profit-making capacity and global development prospects, particularly in the China market. In this context, Sino-US trade cooperation saved GM, as well as safeguarding the normal income and lives of its staff. In addition, this group of people have also benefited from high-quality, low-cost consumer goods exported from China with Sino-US trade enabling them to buy daily necessities, such as refrigerators, electric fans, clothing, toys and other items at a lower price.

The third type of interest group is the hardline representatives of the US military-industrial complex. Out of partial and local interests, they hold that strategically China is the enemy of the US, therefore the US must expand military spending and strengthen military construction, and that more military forces need to be deployed around China to contain it. Speaking frankly, the interests of this group of people are inconsistent with the interests of the US as a whole, they can never represent the fundamental interests of the American people.

In short, we need to see that the Trump administration's policies are the result of the game being played by the above-mentioned three interest groups. Sometimes, the interests represented by the first and second groups are dominant and Sino-US cooperation continues to advance. Recently, it seems that the interests of the third group have become dominant, thereby intensifying the conflict between China and the US. However, in any case, we cannot generalise our criticism of the Trump administration, expand criticism of specific Trump administration policies to the whole of American society, and even into opposition to the US as a whole. If we do, it will undermine the pertinence of our countermeasures, affect the accuracy of our political analysis and decision-making, and will hinder our ability to reasonably deal with the Trump administration's China trade policy.

Misconception two: the oversimplification that everything the US demands is contrary to our interests

The second low-level misconception is that we should oppose whatever the US demands and support whatever the US opposes. This simplistic thinking, if you lose, I win, is harmful. In fact, on many issues, particularly on economic and trade issues, we should ignore what the Americans want, but first clarify what the Chinese economy itself needs. We must clearly realise that for the Chinese economy to develop qualitatively, to be innovative and to be upgraded, reform and opening up must continue to progress.

We must realise that the intellectual property (IP) rights must be further strengthened, which is vital to raise our economic vitality as a whole through innovation; the rule of law must also be strengthened, which is vital to all market operations, including the stock market; the reform of SOEs must also advance. As of end-2017, the value of state-owned assets was as high as Rmb183.5 trillion, twice as much as GDP, so it's necessary to improve operating efficiency and for the internal mechanism of SOEs to be reformed in accordance with economic laws.

US demands can be summarised into two levels. The first level is that the Americans are eager to intervene, eager for success, bossy and aggressive; this attitude and style is absolutely unacceptable to China. At this level, we should resolutely respond to and reject unreasonable US demands and its gross interference in our internal affairs.

The second level regards US demands some concrete changes to be made by the Chinese side which, to a certain extent, are consistent with the direction of reform established by China itself. We must be clearly aware that many aspects are in line with China's long-term development interests and must not be blindly opposed because they have been requested by the Americans. This means that we must distinguish between US negotiating tactics and specific negotiating demands, and distinguish between legalistic thinking, interference in other countries' internal affairs, and the attitude of imposing domestic legal provisions and implementation methods on foreign countries from the actual demands of the US. We cannot mechanically think that we cannot negotiate or talk things over with the US.

Misconception three: opposing everything American and failing to study what might be to our advantage

The third misconception is that because of the Trump administration's tough China policy, we oppose everything American and no longer open-mindedly study the many aspects of the US that can be beneficial to us. As we move forward along the road of national rejuvenation, we must learn from the strengths of all countries in the world. At present, the US is the number-one power in the world. The reason why it has become a powerful country must be something unique that we should learn from. We must never blindly negate everything American just because some people over there regard China as a strategic opponent and try to contain us, or are arrogant and bossy, treating us as students.

Specifically speaking, the following characteristics of the US and the American people are worth learning from.

Firstly, the positive and optimistic attitude of the American people is particularly worth learning from. For instance, many American sports fans firmly support their favourite teams but there are few fights between the die-hard fans of different teams. If one's team doesn't perform well in a game, or even for a season, the fans still don't give up but acknowledge the match result, never finding excuses but encouraging their team to look for problems and move on. The most typical example is the Boston Red Sox in the MLB American Professional Baseball League. They didn't win the title for 90 years but their fans are well known countrywide for their good humour and loyalty, and many of the fans are professors from Harvard and MIT.

Secondly, the cultural characteristics of American people's tolerance and respect for diversity are also worth learning from. The US is a multiethnic and multicultural country, known as a 'melting pot'. Generally speaking, since the founding of the US, the tolerance of American society towards multiculturalism has been increasing, Americans mostly respect others' innate traits and life choices, and are able to work in harmony with those different from themselves. It is because of this that people of different colour, ethnicity, character and sexual orientation can enjoy a relatively stable and comfortable life and give full play to their intelligence at work. Tolerance and respect for diversity are the most basic and important soil for innovation and progress.

Thirdly, generally Americans respect the law and rules. Taking the current situation as an example, although many people scoff at Trump's actions, he was after all the freely elected president, the product of the American political system. So Americans obey his governance and will not illegally impact the White House and the immigration office. Americans prefer to settle disputes with Trump through legal channels, they support lawyers to sue Trump's executive orders in the circuit courts and the Supreme Court, so as to correct the president's misconduct. Americans' awareness of rules and laws is often not understood by the outside world. Many people think that the US is an extremely free society and people can do whatever they want. But this is not the case at all.

Similarly, China can also learn open-mindedly from Japan, Germany, Britain and other countries. We can learn from the Japanese for their delicate management spirit, tirelessly doing a good job of the 'details' for decades. We can learn from the Germans for their precision, discipline, rational thinking and long-term vision. We can learn from the British for their attitude of seeking truth from facts and their alertness and powers of observation. Generally speaking, in the past 500 years, Britain has not made any major mistakes in international strategy, and this international political operation capability is worth learning from. At the same time, we should also learn from the British people's ability to debate and analyse facts, and to refine theory in the field of social science, especially in economics. Britain is the origin of modern economics and, to date, is still one of the best practitioners of economics, or even the whole field of flexibly applying social scientific thinking.

In the current international environment where Sino-US trade fiction is increasingly complex and there are even signs of escalation, we should learn from all countries in the world with an open mind. Only by doing so can China overcome the current difficulties and move on to realise the dream of the great rejuvenation of the Chinese nation.

Chapter 9

China's new role

The view from Davos

The annual WEF meeting held in Davos, Switzerland, is an important window through which to see changes in the global structure, particularly the one held in January 2017 which is likely to become a milestone meeting reflecting future changes in the world economy.

At this meeting, Chinese President Xi Jinping expressed China's views on a series of major issues in the world today, most notably, that: "In today's world, there are problems that must be solved in terms of economic growth, governance and development model"; that "We should not only have the wisdom to analyse problems, but also the courage to take action"[1]; and that we must realistically promote globalisation, not reverse it. This was the clarion call for a new type of Chinese-style globalisation and clearly established China's position as a new leader in global governance and globalisation.

In sharp contrast, the participants' analysis of Trump's future administration and of changes in the political and economic structure of all the Western countries in the future was pessimistic. It can be concluded that the West is gradually withdrawing from its leadership in globalisation and global governance, and that each country will fight its own battles and move into a relatively chaotic period of development. This means new leadership opportunities for China.

Trump's coming to power marks the end of the era of American dominance

At the Davos Forum, Ian Bremmer, president of the Eurasian Group and an international politics scholar, pointed out vividly that Trump's coming to power was not so much a reflection of American people's dissatisfaction with reality, rather, it was a more profound reflection that the US has bade farewell to its position as the world's absolute leader.

He pointed out that Trump had repeatedly criticised Clinton, George W Bush Jr and Obama for a series of administrative mistakes but, in fact, he wanted to criticise their policies for leading to the decline of America's relative status, and for the fact that the US is no longer a great power whose every word carries weight. The decline of America's relative status has brought all kinds of impacts on people, including the elite. For instance, it is impossible for the US to dominate the political structure of the Middle East on its own, and the US cannot mean what it says about international trade. This has led to a loss for all Americans. Hence, in essence, the US must accept its new historical status as a member of a diversified global system.

Trump cannot represent the will of the people and the foundation of his administration is extremely unstable

Many WEF participants pointed out that Trump was not a president who truly represented the will of the majority of the American people; on the contrary, he came to power in a strange combination of circumstances and with ingenuity. In fact, he did not receive the support of most of the voters in the election, he lost the popular vote to Hillary Clinton and, to some extent, he made use of the dissatisfaction of some white-collar workers in two midwestern states and the eastern state of Pennsylvania, and came to power by taking advantage of the electoral system. Therefore, Trump's coming to power was completely different to the background of Ronald Reagan and Margaret Thatcher when they came to power, and has actually led to division in American politics rather than unity.

As expected, after the Davos Forum, when Trump was sworn in, millions of people protested in the US and around the world. The Trump era was probably an era of division rather than one of consensus.

At the political operation level, it may have meant that many senators were unwilling to cooperate with the White House because they worried that people in their constituency were disgusted with Trump, thereby affecting their re-election chances.

Trump administration's governance ability questioned

In various group meetings at Davos, WEF participants cast doubt on the Trump administration's ability to govern. Many economists pointed out that the Trump administration was not backed by economists with rich economic policy experience, which was completely different from the Reagan era. In those years, the 'supplyside school' was supported by scholars such as Harvard professor Martin Feldstein whereas there was not a single well trained economist in the Trump administration.

In sharp contrast to serious scholars, there was a 'big shot' member of Trump's team in Davos, wearing sunglasses, with an entourage and reporters crowding back and forth from each sub forum. He was Anthony Scaramucci. He and I were on the same stage in an open forum to discuss the future of global monetary policy. He had no special point of view. After the meeting I found that he had graduated from law school and was a former senior executive of Goldman Sachs investment bank. He later founded his own asset management company. He very much fits the stereotype of someone who works on Wall Street.

In addition, the Trump administration lacks former government officials with administrative experience. Its members are mainly former senior executives of large enterprises, Goldman Sachs and retired generals. They may not be proficient in how government and Congress operate, which may cause the Trump administration to encounter many difficulties in its early days in office, having trouble making progress.

Based on the above analysis, not only is the Trump administration's base of popularity among the people very unstable, but its policymaking and implementation process may also be extremely difficult. However, Trump himself is an extremely high-profile politician who is not afraid of controversy, therefore the Trump administration is likely to be defeated repeatedly on the battlefield of traditional policy making, but under circumstances where he continuously keeps hitting a brick wall on all sides, Trump is very likely not to play his cards according to common sense. China must be mentally prepared to deal with that.

China should confidently and calmly hold high the new banner of globalisation to pragmatically deal with the new changes

Facing the policy impact of various Trump administration provocations, China must adhere to the overall situation and respond positively. China must not deal too much with Trump in low-level public opinion wars, instead we should deal with calm, distinguishing between the Trump administration's false moves and real moves, but not over-responding, at the same time, seizing on the Trump administration's weakness in the core link, such as its close relationship with large American enterprises including Goldman Sachs, so China can keep a close watch on several large American enterprises with international influence, strengthening communication with them and making them understand that reversing globalisation has an adverse impact on the American economy, particularly for large American companies.

The world has entered a new era of relative contraction of Western countries represented by the US, while China has made great strides in international governance and globalisation. The 2017 Davos Forum distinctly underscored this scenario in no uncertain terms. This is a new era which provides new opportunities for China's development.

Chapter 10

Understanding that capital in the 21st century cannot do without China

After the global financial crisis broke out in 2008, the West entered a painful recovery period. Although the GDP of the major developed countries has increased, almost all the developed countries suddenly found that the world is not as beautiful as it was before the crisis and that economic recovery seems to mean recovery of the rich and the reopening of Wall Street. Where is the market economy of the developed countries destined to go? What reforms should be pushed forward? Although the developed countries today have the confusion of the late 1970s and early 1980s, there is no unified ideology with clear symbols and direction, neither is there a supply-side school of thought as advocated by Mrs Thatcher and President Reagan, nor any Keynesian economics pursued so energetically by President Roosevelt.

Against this background, as soon as *Capital in the 21st Century*, the new work of French economist Thomas Piketty, was published, it comfortably topped the list of Western best sellers, triggering a heated debate in the process.

How should Chinese readers understand this book? Are his viewpoints reliable? Will his predictions come to pass? Is his prescription for the contemporary market economy accurate? Is it possible to implement it? This is crucial for China which has integrated into the global market. Therefore, it is necessary for us to make a very careful analysis.

Piketty's two findings

In his book, Piketty quotes large numbers of his own and other economists' statistical data to expound his two findings.

Firstly, over the past 300 years, in the operation of market economies in developed countries (here I intentionally avoid the use of 'capitalist economy' because capitalism has an obvious ideological connotation, in the popular view it is often used to describe the institutional arrangement of market economies in developed countries in the late 19th century and early 20th century, while today the basic economic system of the developed countries is completely different to the system 100 years ago), there have been obvious regular changes in the ratio of capital to national income[1]. From 1700 to 1910, this ratio was as high as 600% to 700%; from 1914 to 1945, it dropped and stayed at 200% to 300%; but in the 1980s, after Britain, the US and other countries began to implement neo-liberal policies, the ratio gradually went up to 500% to 600%, and it is still rising. At the same time, wealth income as a proportion of overall GDP is increasing, from about 20% in 1975 to 25% to 30% in 2010.

Secondly, the book's other finding is that the concentration, or inequity of capital ownership is rising. For example, capital held by the richest 1% of the population in the US has increased to more than 20% today from less than 10% 20 or 30 years ago.

Based on the two findings, the author came to the conclusion that there are serious problems in the modern market economy, the stock of wealth is increasing and the share of wealth in GDP is also increasing, but the distribution of wealth is increasingly uneven. In today's developed countries, the share of wealth of the rentier class has returned to the level before the first world war, the rentier class is recovering and the market economy aligned with the concept of democracy and fairness is diminishing. Therefore, extreme measures must be taken to solve the problem. A policy suggestion put forward by the author is to tax people with high net assets and capital at a high level worldwide so as to solve the problem of the widening wealth gap.

It should be said that Piketty and his research team have studied for nearly ten years and there is conclusive evidence for the two historical findings they made. Although a reporter from Britain's *Financial Times* raised some questions, the whole economic circle accepted Piketty's statistical research work. This is an important contribution to his research and must be fully affirmed.

How to explain and understand Piketty's findings

The question is how to explain these two important findings and, on this basis, predict whether these two major trends will continue?

In his book, Piketty claimed that the two trends are an inexorable law of the development of the contemporary market economy and only once systematic measures are taken can their development be restrained. But his explanations for the two trends caused great dispute in economic circles, and a majority of mainstream economists challenged him based on their research on related literature.

Firstly, what is the reason for the increase in the ratio of capital to income? Will the increase continue? To this question, Piketty put forward a simple theory: ratio of capital/ income is decided by net savings of an economy (expressed by s, namely, gross national income (GNI) minus national consumption including government spending, then excluding depreciation, with the result divided by GDP) and the actual GDP growth rate (g). The higher the s/g, the higher the ratio of capital/income. He thought that because technological progress in developed countries slows down, g is falling, but s is unchanged, therefore, the ratio of capital to income is increasing.

In fact, this simple statement holds only under stable conditions, namely, where s remains unchanged. But Piketty's first finding is that capital and income are increasing, which means that s is declining. Because depreciation is directly proportional to capital stock, when capital is high to a certain extent, depreciation eventually devours the whole gross savings, even leading to zero net savings. More importantly, when investment keeps rising, capital stock inevitably rises; however, marginal output eventually continues to decline and this is the basic conclusion of hundreds of years of economic research. Here, in particular, we should take into account that it becomes increasingly difficult to replace manpower with capital, in economic jargon, the marginal elasticity of capital-labour substitution decreases, which means capital-output efficiency becomes lower and lower, the capacity for return on capital decreases and even the overall return on capital declines as a proportion of national income. That is to say, Piketty's findings may not be a simple way of predicting the future.

Secondly, regarding an increase in the concentration of wealth or capital distribution, Piketty also posits a simple theory. He held that as long as r (about 4.5% in developed countries) is larger than g (about 1.5% in developed countries), the distribution of capital/wealth in such a society will be more and more uneven, and those with a large amount of capital get richer and richer.

This theory is not necessarily consistent with reality. The reason is that even if the returns on capital rises, capital owners may squander it and their unproductive capital may be constantly transformed into consumption in the economic process. At the same time, their productive capital may be depreciated continuously, therefore, the wealth of the rentiers themselves does not necessarily continue to rise.

In reality, in many countries the inheritance of wealth and capital is discontinuous. In China there is a saying: "Being poor does not exceed three generations, nor does being rich." For nearly 20 years I and my team have carried out analysis of the ancient Chinese economic structure, and we found that the per capita GDP from the Northern Song Dynasty (960-1279) to the middle and late Qing

Dynasty (1644-1911) was declining, and the rate of economic growth was also very low, generally under 0.3%. Against this background, the return on capital and land far exceeded GDP growth. However, because the savings from a large amount of capital did not enter the field of production but turned into unproductive wealth, and at the same time, because there was no eldest son inheritance system in Chinese history, wealth was evenly distributed among the rich man's numerous descendants, resulting in the relative concentration of wealth across generations being not very high. The decline of the family was very common in Chinese history.

Considering the limitations of Piketty's findings from the perspective of China's economic rise

In addition to the above discussion on research methods, from what perspective can we consider Piketty's two findings?

I think we must study the development of the global market economy, including the rise of China's economy as a whole, to achieve a comprehensive and profound understanding. That is to say, our vision must not be restricted to the 20 developed countries, which is the biggest limitation of Piketty's research.

We know that after the end of the second world war, a wave of national independence against colonisation was set off all over the world, many non-developed countries, especially former colonial countries, had moved towards an independent development path and their economic development was relatively closed.

Therefore, it can be said that in nearly 30 years after the end of the second world war, the market economy of the developed countries, including Britain and the US, was developed in a relatively closed self-perpetuating cycle. In this context, the scarcity of labour relative to capital was on the increase and labour became relatively expensive. Moreover, the implementation of various social welfare and security systems made labour income as a proportion of GDP relatively stable at a high level, while the proportion of capital income relative to GDP was fairly low. This led to a pattern of relatively slow capital accumulation in developed countries in the nearly 30 years after the second world war.

However, after the 1980s, due to the acceleration of globalisation, and especially the rise of a group of emerging market countries led by China, the return on capital and technology of developed countries became higher and higher all over the world. At the same time, the abundant cheap labour force in emerging market countries forced great changes in the labour markets of these countries, including the weakening of trade unions and the relative deceleration in wage growth. This revolutionary change led to a rise in the rate of return on capital in developed countries. For example, German workers' wages have grown slowly over the past 20 years but corporate profits have risen rapidly, which precisely explains why the proportion of capital stock in developed countries has been rising during this period.

Following this thinking, we can see that currently, important structural changes have taken place in China's economy: there ia a relative shortage of labour force, the proportion of labour income as a proportion of GDP has begun to increase and the wages of blue-collar workers have began to rise. Because China's economy plays an important role in the global economy, this will cause a chain reaction globally, leading to new structural changes on a global scale. This will lead to a relative improvement in the negotiating ability of labour and capital, the proportion of labour income will likely increase progressively and the rate of capital accumulation in developed countries will slow down. Because China's savings rate is still high, the ratio of China's capital stock and GDP will continue to rise.

China's impact must be taken into account when considering changes in the world economic sructure. If China is ignored in the process of analysis, it distorts the economic facts. In fact, if the income and wealth distribution of people all over the world are calculated together then, over the past 30 years, the proportion of the top 10% of global income relative to total global income, and the proportion of the top 10% of the world's wealth relative to the total wealth must be reduced; in other words, the overall global income gap is narrowing. Why? Because income levels in economies such as China, which was extremely poor 30 years ago, have increased significantly today, and the level of wealth has also increased significantly. Therefore, if we look at this globally, I'm afraid Piketty's two findings will be reversed.

Policy recommendations are particularly worthy of scrutiny

So, are Piketty's policy recommendations tenable? Or should we impose high taxes on high earners and wealthy people as he has said?

In this regard, his analysis particularly lacks depth. Because there are many factors that affect the institutional arrangement of a society's market economy and many key details need special study. For instance, in Germany, also a market economy, representatives of stakeholders, such as trade unions or employees, are introduced into the corporate governance structure, not only restricting the power of capital but also promoting labour-capital cooperation. The proportion of workers' strikes is much lower than in Britain and the US, and there is no such phenomenon as a widening gap between rich and poor as there is in the US. As another example, Germany does not have financial industry development that is divorced from the real economy like the US does, and the development of its financial industry is also strictly regulated. While the development of real corporate enterprises has been continuously supported by the government, family-run enterprises are completely exempted from paying estate tax to enable them to sustain operation from one generation to the next. This long-term support for the management of productive capital and encouraging family businesses to participate in management through capital ownership seems to be an important long-term institutional arrangement which is conducive to economic development, resulting in a win-win situation for capital and society. In short, there are too many institutional arrangements in the operation of local market economies, enabling them to promote harmony between capital and labour, therefore, there is no need to take extreme measures aimed at wealth or capital, as these measures often lead to division of the whole society and decline in the speed of economic development.

The essential difference between wealth and capital

Finally, it must be stressed that Piketty's research failed to clarify the difference between wealth and capital. Wealth should be in a broad sense, namely, it includes either productive capital, such as stocks, or consumer wealth capital, such as housing; while capital generally refers to the factors of production that directly participate in the process of production and distribution, it can expand the scale of production and bring returns. It is very important to clarify the two concepts, because in a modern society the gap in wealth distribution is mainly reflected in the gap of productive capital. Take Bill Gates, for example; his main wealth is not his houses, cars and collections, but his stake in Microsoft whose value makes him one of the wealthiest people in the world.

Moreover, the essence of productive capital is completely different to consumer wealth, and the two are not proportional either. People with more productive capital do not necessarily consume more. Therefore, the expansion of a wealth gap mainly comes from the gap in productive capital, it does not mean the widening of the social welfare gap, on the contrary, people with more productive capital do not necessarily enjoy a higher proportion of social welfare.

If the whole society really agrees with the philosophy behind Piketty's high wealth tax, it would be better to impose a progressive tax on ultra-high consumption, including ultra-high consumer wealth.

Only by clarifying these two concepts can we understand the key in the process of system reform – reduce the excessive intervention of high-wealth groups, especially high productive-capital groups, in social decision making. Once high-wealth groups, especially high productive-capital groups, have a particularly big say in social decision-making, they will change the development direction of the whole society. However, they may not represent this direction, and this must be the key for discussion. Simply focusing the discussion on the overall distribution of wealth itself can be quite misleading.

To sum up, Piketty's book is good at topic selection, detailed in data, but careless in theory and rough in policy recommendation.

But here I particularly want to stress that the influence of a best seller often goes far beyond the academic field. Although Piketty's *Capital in the 21st Century* may not be fully recognised by his peers academically, it is very likely that it will trigger a great debate and revolution in the political and economic ideas of Western countries. The ideological heritage of Margaret Thatcher and Ronald Reagan may be shaken and reversed because of a French economist's best seller.

Chapter 11

The AIIB gives impetus to reform of the international governance system

After the Asian Infrastructure Investment Bank (AIIB) was proposed by General Secretary Xi Jinping in October 2013, it attracted global attention. A large number of the US's staunch allies, including Britain and Canada, have defected, expressing their willingness to join or consider joining, thereby becoming founding members of the AIIB.

This is a golden opportunity. China should seize the rare opportunity, sound the horn of the international economic governance reform and bring a long-lost new wind to the world economy!

Background: the Bretton Woods system is facing reform

In July 1944, the international conference held in Bretton Woods, New Hampshire, USA, established the basic framework for the 70-year-long international economic governance after the second world war. At the time, the Chinese nationalist government sent a massive delegation led by K'ung Hsiang-hsi, second only to the host USA in terms of number of delegates. Mr K'ung, who understood foreign affairs very well, carefully prepared the Chinese plan. But unfortunately, China's national strength was weak at the time, so nobody cared to ask about his plan. The all-powerful, daring and energetic British representative, the renowned economist John Maynard Keynes, was even more proud of his success, and he proposed a package plan. Also, unfortunately, the international order depended on strength, and the final agreement was basically made by the US, therefore Keynes arrived in high spirits but returned in low spirits.

The international system established at this conference consisted of a 'troika': the ITO (that is, the International Trade Organisation, which could not ultimately be established due to US Congress opposition, was downgraded to the GATT (General Agreement on Tariffs &P Trade) but upgraded to the WTO (World Trade Organisation) in 1995) for maintaining free trade, the IMF (International Monetary Fund) for stabilising international finance, and the World Bank for helping the development of poor countries. Over the past 70 years, this system has made certain contributions to solving major global problems and dealing with various crises.

However, at present, this chariot, that has sustained world economic growth for 70 years, is showing a nagging sense of languor and is in urgent need of reform. However, as the maintainer and beneficiary of this system, the US has shown obvious inertia in recent years. Not only was the US unable to put forward any plans for reform but it obstructed and destroyed the existing plans. The most obvious example is that the US Congress has been slow in approving the reform of IMF voting rights, leading to strong dissatisfaction among many member states, including European countries.

The European countries, including Britain, are the real victims of the short-term interests of this round of IMF reforms. Although they are the ones whose voting rights have been cut the most, they still agreed with the reform plan, while the US has made few concessions, yet always expressed opposition, which aroused public anger. This explains why Britain took the lead, and Canada and other developed countries united to rebel, they changed sides and joined China. As a matter of fact, this is an important signal.

Actually, before this, Britain, Canada and other US allies had actively promoted cooperation with China on the internationalisation of the Rmb, in sharp contrast to the attitude of the US. This cooperation didn't go down well with US. This fully shows that the US dollar hegemony which the US is trying to safeguard has become unpopular internationally. The American allies have parted ways with the US on the core issue of the US dollar, and the AIIB issue only displays this new pattern more clearly to the people.

American arrogance: basic problems with the current international governance system

The current international economic governance system led by the US has three fundamental problems.

First, it does not respond to the new demands of emerging market countries represented by China, but still maintains the dominant position of the developed countries in the international governance system. Taking the 1997-1998 Asia-Russia financial crisis as an example, even the IMF itself today has admitted that its policy guidance at the time was wrong. When the financial crisis broke out in Asian countries, the developed countries, including the US, looked on unconcerned, or even hit the Asian countries when they were down. The policy prescription issued by the IMF was: cut, cut and cut even more. Under the circumstances where the financial market was in chaos, instead, it required countries in crisis to tighten monetary and fiscal policy. It was like a house was on fire, and closing the financial tap was supposed to put out the fire. These recommendations were completely wrong, the economic movement was in the opposite direction, which the IMF fully admitted in its self-appraisal. The fundamental cause of the problem is that the IMF doesn't really consider the problem based on the interests of the emerging-market countries. However, what we saw in the 2008 global financial crisis is that the US Federal Reserve and the Bank of England adopted measures completely opposite to the policy promoted by the IMF in 1997, in essence to "relax, relax, and relax even more", which resulted in a relatively effective rescue and promoted the rapid economic recovery of the US and Britain.

It is questionable whether the above-mentioned IMF policies are due to the limited awareness or level of its staff. In fact, according to my experience in dealing with the IMF for many years, the quality of the IMF staff is very high and its management is exceptionally focused, with policy reports (such as the Rmb exchange rate) and contributions subject to centralised examination and approval. The core organ responsible for approvals is the IMF's committee of executive directors, on which the US has an extremely great influence both internally and externally. Because of this, it is impossible for the IMF to seriously supervise and guide US monetary and fiscal policy in accordance with IMF regulations, and public criticism is even more impossible. In other words, the US is the monitor while the IMF is a course representative appointed by the monitor. The monitor does not hand in his course work, so the course representative can do nothing about it.

Second, in the IMF and the World Bank the US is unwilling to give up its veto status, which has aroused public anger. The abovementioned reform of IMF voting rights has made the intention of the US clearly visible to the world, and the previous challenge for the president of the World Bank also showed the dominating conduct of the US, namely, never allowing non-American citizens to be elected. Currently, IMF voting rights reform has become bankrupt while no Plan B has been proposed. On top of this, the internal management of the World Bank is also in chaos currently and morale is low. Facts have proven that the current president of the World Bank is not a strong leader and he may come to be regarded as the weakest president in the World Bank's history. As a professor in the field of health, he is inexperienced and unable to cope with economic development, poverty reduction and even the internal management of a large institution. According to the logic of business organisations, such CEOs should be laid off early. However, the US is unwilling to let its appointed CEO step down because that would be so embarrassing for the White House.

Third, as the largest international currency issuer, the US fails to shoulder its due responsibilities. The recovery of the US economy benefited from its own quantitative easing (QE) monetary policy, however, it accused foreign currencies of appreciating against the US dollar when QE was implemented. Today, once its economy had recovered, the US began to tighten its monetary policy, completely ignoring the impact of this move on other countries, including emerging-market countries. As an international currency issuer, the US's approach of concentrating entirely on its own economic interests with no consideration for other countries is inappropriate in the eyes of the world. According to the above analysis, it is impossible for the IMF to bring up any binding opinions.

Even the US's own strategic allies can no longer bear to see these problems. Therefore, Britain and other countries took their stand and chose to join the AIIB, which shows that the trouble has been brewing for quite some time.

Focus: how should the AIIB innovate its system?

Strictly speaking, the AIIB initiated by the Chinese government is not contradictory to the current international economic and financial institutions because it operates mainly in Asia and its investment direction is mainly toward infrastructure construction. But why has it attracted widespread international attention? What goal can China achieve through the establishment of the AIIB?

I think the most important thing is to bring a new wind to the world. By system innovation, let the world see that as a responsible emerging country, as well as a large country with an ancient tradition of civilisation, China can bring new ideas to the world.

Firstly, the mission must be clear, and the bank's niche should reflect the realm of selflessness and the height of morality. Starting from this perspective, the mission of the AIIB should to seek long-term economic development and prosperity for the broad masses of Asia. In other words, the AIIB does not serve the narrow interests of China, its goal is to bring long-term economic development to the surrounding countries. Such a clear and noble mission will strike a chord all over the world.

Secondly, the governance mechanism must be innovative and it must never engage in American-style hegemonistic clauses. Specifically speaking, it should reflect the interests and listen to the voices of many parties. It can't emulate the system of the IMF and World Bank council of executive directors whereby there is 'one share, one vote', the US is the major shareholder with more than 15%, a majority of more than 85% is needed for votes to be passed, and the US has veto power by design.

I think the AIIB can set up three councils. The first one being the board of directors, with countries allocated seats and voting rights in accordance with the amount they have invested; the second being the representative council, similar to the US Senate (two seats for each American state regardless of size), that is, regardless of the size of the country and the amount of investment, each country has a seat; the third being the consultative council, to include representatives from: labour organisations from relevant regions; entrepreneurs; capital markets; social opinion leaders; and even representatives from the cultural and environmental protection sectors. The three councils work together and make joint consultations. The board of directors has decision-making power, however, major issues should be fully discussed and deliberated before decisions are made, striving to reach a basic consensus before making any specific decisions. This consultative democratic approach is a basic feature of Chinese politics and is also consistent with the current trend of emphasising social responsibility and trying to hear different voices in the era of globalisation. It is different to the IMF and World Bank practice of 'one share, one vote', requiring a majority of 85% to pass, long dominated by the

Americans with their veto power. Such a governance structure of the AIIB will have more global appeal.

Another important AIIB governance issue is the appointment of senior staff such as the president. Learning lessons from the World Bank and IMF, selection and appointment should be on merit, a break from the unwritten rules of the IMF, World Bank and Asian Development Bank (ADB), whereby the president of the World Bank should be American, the president of the IMF should be European, and the president of the ADB should be Japanese. If the AIIB adopts the method of selection on merit, it will comply with the historical wave of globalisation.

Thirdly, cultural construction should be emphasised. Any international organisation is like an enterprise, its culture is the gene that keeps its foundation forever green. The AIIB should emphasis a culture of openness, efficiency and tolerance. Such a culture can attract the elite from all over the world to work for it. This culture can also ensure that the AIIB's decision-making can be reasonable, effective and in the interests of the majority of people in relevant regions.

Fourthly, the AIIB's decision-making should take economic development as the main goal, rather than considering political and ideological factors. For example, if there is a real need for economic development for the target of sanction of the US and other major countries, then the AIIB should consider the actual situation of the region and make decisions independently. After all, the biggest beneficiaries of economic development are the general public, not the ruling class of a country.

The AIIB is a great initiative of China's new generation of leaders. In its establishment, we should firmly take the bull by the horns with regard to system innovation and sound the clarion call for China to promote reform of the international economic governance system. This is China's due contribution to the world as a youthful yet ancient civilisation.

Understanding the Chinese Economy

Chapter 1

Macro Control

What is a modern market economy?

What is a modern market economy? This seems to be a very fundamental academic question in terms of economics so one would deduce that economists should have studied this issue very clearly, however, this is not the case. Today, what is the modern market economy is another topic of great and timely significance because some developed countries have questioned the status of China's market economy while China itself needs to spell out the connotations of a modern market economy to further clarify the direction of reform. China's economic circles today are duty-bound to shoulder this academic responsibility.

The definition of a market economy by foreign economics circles is extremely unsystematic

Until now, the academic discussions of foreign economists have not focused on the fundamental question of "what is a market economy?". From Adam Smith to Paul A Samuelson, and to the author of today's mainstream economics textbook N Gregory Mankiw, what has been discussed is "what is a market?". As to "what is a market economy?" and particularly to the question of "what is a modern market economy?" there have been no systematic expositions, or at most, only a broad definition is given.

Ludwig Von Mises of the Austrian school of economist thought that the "market economy is a social system of division of labour under the private ownership of the means of production". This definition excludes an economy under social ownership or state ownership of the means of production from the definition of "a market". Paul A Samuelson believes that a market economy is "an economic system in which production and consumption are mainly determined by individuals and private enterprises". Mankiw, author of the best-selling economics textbook abroad today described a market economy in his book as "an economy that allocates resources through decentralised decisions where many businesses and families trade with each other in a market for goods and services". Mankiw's description lightly bypasses some fundamental questions of the market economy, including the role of government. The definition of "a market" in the encyclopaedia of economics *The New Palgrave Dictionary of Economics and the Law* is: "a system with a large number of buyers and sellers, and circular trading of specific types of goods". Obviously, it also avoids a series of major issues.

It is noteworthy that Marxist political economics does not give a direct and clear answer to this question either, although there are discussions about market issues almost everywhere in Marx's *Das Kapital*. In Marx's era, the modern market economic system had not been conceived and a series of institutional arrangements for a modern market economy, including a basic welfare system, had not yet been discussed, so it is impossible to find direct answers for today's problems from the giant of thought of that time. Afterwards, with the rise of the Soviet central planned economy, a large number of comparative economists focused their discussions on the antagonismbetween a planned economy and a market economy without a clear definition of what a market economy itself is.

Three goals pursued by a modern market economy

Then, what is a modern market economy, or more precisely, what is a modern market economy system?

Let's firstly discuss the current world and some of the common understandings reached by mainstream groups in society toward the goals of a modern market economy system. There are fundamental differences between a modern market economy and a planned economy as well as early capitalist systems, and they mainly reflect orderly pursuit of the three goals of freedom, equality and fairness.

Firstly, freedom, that is, that in a modern market economy the participants in economic activities should be able to freely participate in economic activities without prejudice to public interest. Here, the participants in economic activities include both consumers and producers and both individuals and private or state-owned enterprises. Without prejudice to public interest, the independent decision-making of market economy participants is not interfered with, and this is the first goal pursued by a modern market economy.

Secondly, equality, that is, that in a modern market economy, transactions between economic entities are not forced but shared equally and voluntarily without prejudicing overall economic order. On the contrary, in ancient slave societies, labour transactions were unequal because slaves were forced to work. A planned economy directly violates the principle of equality and voluntariness because the superior government requires enterprises to conduct transactions under conditions determined by the government.

Thirdly, fairness and order, that is, that in a modern market economy, economic activities should be fair and orderly. For instance, the principle of fairness requires that participants in economic activities with poor luck or relatively low economic talent deserve and get help. The principle of fairness also requires that there is a potential equal relationship between people of different generations, such as contemporary and future people, namely, that contemporary people should not sacrifice the happiness of future people, for example, by destroying the environment to develop the economy. Order requires that there are no huge fluctuations or crises and panic in the macroeconomic financial market.

In short, orderly freedom, equality and fairness are the goals pursued by a modern market economy, as well as the inner essence of a modern market economy. These three embody the basic values generally recognised in the world today, while the early market economy and central planned economy system had some defects in these three respects.

Four elements of a modern market economy system

What kind of institutional arrangements should a modern market economy adopt to achieve the above three goals? Specifically speaking, a modern market economy should have four institutional arrangements, and the most critical of them is that, unlike a traditional market economy, in a modern market economy governments are, in fact, extremely important participants in economic activities, and the practice of a modern market economy in all countries is organised in this way.

Firstly, there should be a series of systems to protect the freedom of economic individuals. There should be both a property right protection system and a consumer protection system. This requires a series of legal mechanisms, such as: *Company Law*; *General Provisions of the Civil Law*; *Property Law*; and *Law for the Protection of Consumers' Rights and Interests*; and relevant institutions, such as courts and consumer protection bureaus, to collectively play a role in achieving the above goals.

Secondly, there should be systems and institutions to maintain market order and economic stability. For instance, through the implementation of *Anti-monopoly Law* to prevent large enterprises with great market power from bullying small enterprises so as to harm the interests of future consumers. For another example, there should be an efficient macro regulatory mechanism because spontaneous market economy transactions often bring huge fluctuations at the macro level, as evidenced by a large number of market economy practices, therefore, various macro control mechanisms must be designed and put in place, including a financial supervision system and central bank system. It also includes external regulation mechanisms because international trade often has large transaction costs and information asymmetry, therefore international transactions tend to be more volatile than domestic ones and this is manifested in the fluctuation of exchange rates and the imbalance of trade between countries. In this respect, a modern market economy system must have a series of market arrangements, such as adjustment of the foreign exchange market and a foreign trade regulation system.

Thirdly, there should be a system to ensure basic social welfare, human resources development, and environmental protection and innovation. The need for social welfare security is to ensure that most groups are motivated and interested in participating in market economy activities. If there is no social welfare security, due to short term bad luck or lack of competence to compete in the market, some people will find it difficult to participate normally in a market economy, and a market economy also finds it very difficult to get the support of people like this, making such a market economy unsustainable due to the gradual erosion of a social foundation.

Human resource development is also very important to a modern market economy system because it can train future market economy participants with certain skills, so governments must help to establish such a system. Taking the educational system as an example, if we rely entirely on private-sector participation, this often engenders short-term behaviour which cannot meet the long-term needs of a market economy.

As to environmental protection, special institutional arrangements are needed for environmental protection because the fundamental difficulty of environmental protection is that contemporary people cannot fully consider the welfare of future people. As a whole rather than as individuals, contemporary people often ignore the welfare of the next generation and future generations, thereby causing excessive damage to the environment. Once the environment has been damaged, the cost of future repair is out of proportion to the benefits of today's destruction. Therefore, outside forces are needed to restrict the behaviour of existing enterprises and contemporary economic activities to achieve long-term environmental protection requirements.

In terms of scientific and technological innovation, there must also be a corresponding mechanism to provide guarantees. Scientific and technological innovation often has strong externalities, the elevation of social welfare brought about by a scientific and technological invention is often greater than the greatest benefit the inventor can get. Therefore, there must be a corresponding non-market mechanism to protect it, such as strengthening intellectual property (IP) rights and supporting investment in scientific and technological research.

Fourthly, there should be mechanisms to maintain, encourage and restrict government behaviour, including the public finance system. Because government is an extremely important participant in a contemporary market economy, we must pay attention to the government's own behaviour and incentives. At the same time, we should also strengthen the constraints on government behaviour, yet this point is often ignored in today's mainstream economic discussions. For example, the impact of the public finance system is not only on the source of government funds and income, more importantly, it has a direct impact on every aspect of government behaviour. For instance, if the government taxes the enterprise sector directly, it often pays special attention to the operation and development of enterprises; if the government taxes the household sector directly, then it often pays attention to increases in household income; if the government derives taxes directly from transactions or appreciation of real estate or other financial assets, then it is naturally more interested in the market operation of the finance and real estate sectors. Therefore, the public finance system and government behaviour are inseparable.

Has China embarked on the path of a modern market economy?

After years of reform and opening up, China's economic development has made remarkable achievements. It should be said that China has now established a modern market economy system that is basically adapted to current development and has embarked on the path of a modern market economy.

To be precise, at present China has established a preliminary market economy with respect to property right protection, consumer protection, macroeconomic management, anti- monopoly, monetary policy, finance policy, basic social welfare, ecological protection and public finance, which are playing an important role in supporting current economic development, otherwise, it would have been impossible for China to have become a remarkable, flourishing, rapidly developing economy. We have confidence in this point and must clearly explain it to the West.

However, we must also admit that China's current market economy system and the long-term development goal of China's economy are not yet in synch, so we must persist in reform, especially in terms of social welfare and the government's own operation mechanism, they should be greatly perfected, and this is also the direction of the next reform proposed by the state.

Based on Chinese practice, confront the skepticism of developed economies

We must clarify the basis of what a market economiy system is. On this issue, the existing research abroad is not sufficient, so we must clarify three points.

Firstly, the existence of SOEs should not be regarded as the basic symbol of whether the system is a market economy system. In fact, SOEs are also common in Western developed countries, for example, EDF (Electricité de France) and the national airlines of many countries are all state owned, let alone many oil companies. SOEs are a way to realise a state-owned economy, and a state-owned economy often has the important attributes of a modern market economy. For example, according to my initial calculations, the assets of Singapore's state-owned economy are roughly several times that of Singapore's GDP, and this has greatly assured the long-term stability of Singapore's economy. Therefore, the existence of SOEs is not the key to a market economy, the key is that the state-owned economy must operate under the principles and framework of a modern market economy.

Secondly, government intervention is not a reason to deny the existence of a modern market economy. In fact, nowadays, government intervention in enterprises and other sectors is also common in many developed countries. For example, the US Department of Agriculture has nearly 100,000 staff to provide all kinds of help to domestic farmers for every aspect of farming. Not to mention in finance, banking, monetary and other areas where the regulation and control of market operations by governments all over the world exists from time to time.

Thirdly, the market economy system is not a static, perfect system, it needs to be continuously upgraded and improved through reform, and each country's market economy system has its own problems that need to be solved through further reform and development. We must make it clear to the West that China is not satisfied with the current market economy system and a series of reform requirements have been put forward. On this issue we welcome Western critics to provide constructive opinions but they must not deny the fact that China is already a modern market economy country just because we want to make improvements.

In short, what is a modern market economy? Has China already embarked on the road of a modern market economy? And in which areas should China further reform and improve our market economy system? These are the basic and important academic issues that we must sort out ourselves and clarify to the outside world in our own time.

Why are Private Entrepreneurs Worried?

If we use one word to describe China's economy in 2018, it is "worry". It refers to the fact that the participants in economic activities generally felt worried, the most worried of whom were private entrepreneurs. This worry also extended to 2019, whether small and medium-sized private enterprises or those at the helm of listed companies, most of them thought that it was a challenging year. Although they are in different sectors and competitive positions, and have different worries, there are still some commonalities.

In this case, what are the private entrepreneurs worried about?

Some people say it is foreign trade. This worry is mainly caused by Sino-US trade friction, which they think will affect the medium and long-term development of China's economy. However, in foreign trade, although Sino-US trade friction was once jittery in 2018, the import and export performance of that year was still extraordinary: according to statistics, China's exports in 2018, denominated in Rmb, increased by 7.1% year on year (YOY), imports increased by 12.9%, and total imports and exports increased by 9.7%; among which the imports and exports of privately-run enterprises increased by 12.9%.

Some people say the future is unclear, and investment will slow down. Indeed, due to the slowdown of economic growth, low investment efficiency and, in addition, because supervision is becoming stricter, causing some areas to continue closing down due to bad management, entrepreneurs feel uncertain about business prospects, consequently there is a decline in investment intention. But, from the macro level, the investment index of the private economy in 2018 was very healthy. From the beginning of the year, private investment maintained growth of more than 8%, growth from January to November reached 8.7% YOY, in 2017 it was 5.7%, in 2016 it was only 3.1% in the same period. If only looking at the manufacturing industry, private investment in that sector from January to November increased by 10.3%, 0.8% higher than the national average. This shows that some private enterprises are still investing. There may not be many, and they may be a silent group, but the amount of single investment is large.

So clearly foreign trade and investment alone cannot explain the deep worries of private entrepreneurs.

Some say another major worry for private entrepreneurs comes from difficult and expensive financing. Comparisons must be analysed carefully. Financing has always been a big pain point for private enterprises, is not a problem that suddenly arose in 2018. Besides, after carefully combing through the relevant data, we found that the problem of difficult and expensive financing in 2018 still mostly affected small and medium-sized enterprises (SMEs), and mainly those with bad credibility, while those with good credibility, no matter whether state-owned or privately run, received a fairly high loan rate.

The third worry of private enterprises is, of course, that taxes are relatively high, which leads to high operating costs and diluted profits. In recent years, the profitability of enterprises has been gradually squeezed, and this pressure is particularly prominent. This is indeed an issue of concern but we must not forget that high taxes have always been a pain in China's economy, this is not just unique to 2018-2019. From 2018 to today, following the initial implementation of a series of tax and fee reduction measures, it should be said that the pressure in this regard is expected to gradually ease, therefore it cannot be said that high taxes and fees are a new problem for private entrepreneurs.

We think that the biggest worry among private enterprises is that the private economy is facing major adjustment, and this major adjustment is related to their industrial development process. Except for a few industries, this has little correlation with the nature of private enterprises and SOEs, therefore, if we talk about difficulties in the development of the private economy, we cannot go to their rescue to blindly rescue production capacity that should be eliminate and interfere with normal market clearing, this runs counter to the requirements of China's economic transformation and upgrading.

In 2018, I took the lead in completing a project entitled: *An Economic Summary of China's Reform and Opening Up in the Past 40 Years*. In order to obtain first-hand material, we visited many places and investigated a large number of physical enterprises, and found several prominent problems. In a sub-provincial city, I met an entrepreneur who was extremely pessimistic about the future. After a careful investigation and interviews, we discovered that his enterprise was mainly engaged in elevator and glass-curtain wall business. Domestic competition in these two industries was extremely fierce and profits were very low, prompting them to expand into the international market. However, this type of expansion is not easy, and often the final competition in bidding takes place among Chinese enterprises. He said of the elevator and glass curtain wall business: "The Europeans created the industry, the Japanese refined it, and the Chinese have broken it." The reason why? Vicious, malignant competition. Going a step further, I learned that there are now more than a hundred glass-curtain wall enterprises and six hundred elevator enterprises in China. In a mature market economy, such a subdivided industry cannot support the competition of hundreds or even one hundred enterprises. For instance, in the elevator industry, in a mature market economy, there would be about ten big enterprises in total to share the market. Looking globally, OTIS from the US, Schindler from Switzerland, Thyssenkrupp from Germany, KONE from Finland, Mitsubishi and Hitachi from Japan occupy more than 60% of the market.

From this we made an important observation: for the Chinese privately-run economy, particularly those in the middle and lower reaches of the industrial chain, their production concentration ratio is too low, and they engage in low-level vicious competition, they need to be bigger, stronger and better, thereby facing the challenges of mergers, reorganisation and structural adjustment. In fact, all developed market economies have gone through this painful process. For example, the three major automobile manufacturers in the US were formed after continuous mergers and reorganisations. From the current overcrowded state of enterprises competing to develop into the state of equilibrium of a mature economy with a high industrial concentration, the process will be extremely painful for any private entrepreneurs, as well as for the banks. However, this transformation process is inevitable for China's economic transformation and upgrading.

During the process of survival of the fittest following the 20%/80% principle, the best way out is usually to quit in an orderly manner. For the 'survivors' who have the 'last laugh', they can, of course, choose to stay on and enjoy higher business profits. For the 80% of the long-tail enterprises which lack competitiveness, it is better for them to cut short the suffering and make a timely exit rather than be dragged to their deaths and crushed by excessive competition and extremely low profits.

At present, we don't know how many bad debts such a merger and reorganisation process will bring. Take the elevator industry, for example. At present, national brands have a market share of about 30%, among which the ten leading enterprises account for about 15%, while the remaining 15% is shared by more than 600 domestic SMEs. Supposing that the result of mergers and reorganisation is that all the several hundred SMEs making elevators go bankrupt, all their assets are devalued, and their bank loans turn into bad loans then, according to the industry average, that would result in asset impairment of more than Rmb200 billion. Considering that there is excessive competition in many industries in China, mergers and acquisitions (M&A) is needed, meaning that many bank loans would also need to be restructured.

Therefore I think that, at present, the most worrying factors for private entrepreneurs are the exit arrangements necessitated by industrial upgrading and the closely related financial arrangements. To this end, we should be ready in the next few years.

For entrepreneurs, they must ask themselves a question: stick it out or quit as soon as possible? If they opt to quit, they should consider trying to diversify into new industries while their business is still good; if they do not quit, they should try every means to expand and acquire other enterprises: this is what they must do.

For banks, industrial restructuring funds must be established from now on, and they must consider how to deal with the asset restructuring of enterprises that exit the market. They should consider how to regain the valuable experience of setting up asset management companies on a grand scale at the beginning of the 21st century.

China's economy is now facing the process of transformation and upgrading, a major aspect of this process is to reflect on how to accelerate the pace of M&A activity in many industries. Some private enterprises are having a hard time, so they must pay attention to and properly deal with the problems they may encounter. If handled well, the problems can be transformed into opportunities for economic growth; if badly handled, they may become a major burden on the financial sector and related industries. We must not blindly protect backward production capacity and sabotage the order of the market economy under the banner of protecting the private economy.

What to do about 'flight from the real to the virtual' economy?

From the second half of 2016, capital 'flight from the real to the virtual' economy (breaking away from the real economy to invest in the virtual economy) again became a hot topic in China's economic field. Indeed, GDP growth slowed in 2016, and an important reason for that was that the growth rate of private investment in fixed asset investment was only 4%, less than half the growth rate of overall fixed asset investment. The growth rate of private investment and closely linked manufacturing investment slowed down and was inseparable from the reluctance of funds to flow into the real economy.

Against this backdrop, the regulatory authorities of China's capital markets issued a series of policies, pointing to the problem of capital 'flight from the real to the virtual' economy. At the end of 2016, the China Securities Regulatory Commission (CSRC) made it clear that it would crack down on the 'demons' making waves in the capital markets; the China Insurance Regulatory Commission (CIRC) stopped 'universal insurance', and also gave exhortations and punishment to individual institutions that used insurance capital to carry out capital operations in the capital market; recently, the CSRC revised several provisions on the refinancing of listed companies.

Will the actions of these regulators help solve the problem of capital 'flight from the real to the virtual' economy? This needs to be analysed to find the root cause of the problem.

The first cause of capital 'flight from the real to the virtual' economy is high cost

Most enterprises in China's manufacturing industry are private enterprises and their operating costs have indeed been rising in recent years: since 2008, the increase of labour costs has been rising faster than both the Consumer Price Index (CPI) and the Producer Price Index (PPI), causing a gradual decline in enterprise profit margins. At the same time, the international market remains depressed. China's imports and exports have shown negative growth for two consecutive years, confronting the private economy and manufacturing industry with various difficulties.

Currently, there is much discussion about private enterprise tax. However, it must be noted that over the past few years, the tax burden of the private economy has not significantly increased in terms of tax system design. High taxes and fees have always been in existence, and the major change after 2016 was to replace business tax with value added tax (VAT).

According to our actual investigation, the policy of "replacing business tax with VAT" increased the tax burden for enterprises in the short term. Business tax is often fictitious and there is no actual collection of tax from many enterprises, while VAT is actually paid. The important reason for this is that business tax is traditionally levied by local tax bureaus. Out of consideration for the local economy, the local tax bureaus often consult with local government. In order to encourage enterprises to invest, they reduce or exempt them from business tax in some way, or at least they do not directly levy business tax at the tax rate specified in the tax system. Since business tax was changed to VAT, the China State Administration of Taxation (SAT) has become the main body of taxation, however, SAT does not have a close relationship with local enterprises, therefore, it often collects taxes according to regulations. My research in Jiangsu and other places also found that the tax burden of enterprises increased significantly after "replacing business tax with VAT".

In addition, at present, labour cost is a hot topic of discussion. The burden on enterprises of some fees such as the 'Five Insurances and One Fund (endowment, medical, unemployment, employment injury, maternity insurances and Housing Provident Fund)' and labour-cost related fees is rather heavy and while, of course, there is room for a decrease, it should be noted that this type of tax has been in place for a long time.

Comparatively, after 2008, there was another important factor directly leading to the rising costs of private enterprises, namely, large-scale infrastructure construction was largely financed by local governments through various investment platforms, and these investment platforms usually had implicit guarantees from governments at all levels. Moreover, investors in such infrastructure do not consider the long-term financial burden and are often more concerned about maintaining fixed-asset investment in the short term, thereby elevating GDP. Therefore, many regions do not hesitate to borrow from banks and trust institutions at high interest rates, and this has the effect of crowding out normal loans from banks and other channels for enterprises, especially for private enterprises. Corporate loans from banks related to infrastructure are small in scale, while quantities are more numerous with higher transaction and approval costs, therefore banks and trust institutions charge higher interest rates on loans to them instead. This is an important reason why high financing costs lead to a downturn in the real economy.

The second cause of capital 'flight from the real to the virtual' economy is that there is structural 'false fire' in the financial system

'False fire' in the financial system is not due to the arrival of a bull market. From the overall market value and rate of return of China's stock market, we cannot say that there is a big bubble. But we must acknowledge that there is a structural bubble in China's capital market, that is, in the context of current promissory notes, some high-risk financial products can still provide extraordinary, unsustainable high returns in the short term, such as local government debt and trust products.

A considerable portion of these local bond and trust products should have been restructured or even defaulted on, and their high interest rate is the risk premium provided in response to its larger possibility of restructuring or default but, at present, the rate of restructuring or default is far below the rate at which it should happen. Neither the financial market nor even regulatory authorities want to see this happen, leading to the trend of investors blindly pursuing financial products with a high rate of return. The rate of return on large blue chips and bank stocks is generally very low. Together with Hong Kong stocks, they constitute the lowest-priced stocks in the world's major economies, with their value being far lower than those in Europe and America. But the prices of high-risk stocks, including Growth Enterprise Market (GEM) stocks, remain high. In essence, there is a problem in the pricing of risk in China's financial market. The risk premium, in investors' minds, is too low. They blindly pursue high-risk products, while projects in the low-risk, traditional, real economy are often ignored.

According to the above analysis, to solve China's economic problem of capital 'flight from the real to the virtual' economy, we must fundamentally take two-pronged measures.

Increase the proportion of tax retention, reignite local government enthusiasm and reduce the burden on the real economy

We suggest that the Ministry of Finance increase the tax return to local governments in the short term and the State Taxation Administration increase the tax by an additional proportion and directly return it to the local governments while, at the same time, encouraging local governments to accelerate support for private investment, letting local governments give targeted tax incentives and subsidies in terms of operating costs to private enterprises that have development prospects. This is partially returning to the magic weapon for economic development since the reform and opening up – mobilising the enthusiasm of local governments and taking the initiative to reduce the tax burden on local private enterprises.

Encourage defaults and restructuring, 'squeeze bubbles' in financial markets

To "squeeze bubbles" is to make conscious efforts to make the original high-risk financial products default or restructure. For some high-risk new enterprises, it is wise to warn them of their risks in various ways. In capital markets, once this kind of risk premium can be elevated to a reasonable level, the attraction of high-risk financial products will be greatly reduced and capital will flow more to traditional manufacturing industries where the risk is relatively low although their rate of return is also low.

In 2016, events such as the 'Wanke-Baoneng dispute' that shocked China's stock market and the shareholding notification to the shareholders of the Gree Electrical Alliance should be reconsidered from this respective. At present, the price/earnings ratio of traditional manufacturing industry is very low, showing that capital markets do not think that the operation of these enterprises is highly efficient and do not agree with their internal governance and direction of investment. Therefore, in principle, the forces of capital markets and investors need to be mobilised to put pressure on the insiders of such enterprises, forcing them to reposition their development direction and to restrict their hot-headed and blind investment behaviour, requiring them to increase the remaining capital flow but not to keep it or invest it into some unrelated or even 'red sea' (highly competitive) areas such as EVs (electric vehicles) and mobile phones. Therefore, generally speaking, China's capital markets need funds to engage in M&A activity. Insurance funds may not be fully responsible to take on this task, however, the healthy development of China's capital markets is inseparable from M&A.

Related to this is the refinancing of the stock market, and this is a very important direct financing function of the stock market. The refinancing difficulty for listed enterprises is smaller than IPOs because the operation of such enterprises follows standardised rules, and enterprises financing through standardised operations is smoother than that of non-listed companies.

Therefore, to solve the problem of capital 'flight from the real to the virtual' economy, the key point should be to reduce costs and squeeze bubbles, rather than cracking down on so-called 'demons' or restricting the refinancing scale of enterprises.

Capital 'flight from the real to the virtual' economy will be a long-term problem for China's future economic development that may take quite a long time to solve. We need to take the pulse, recognise the focus and then diagnose the medicine to the case in order to seek a gradual solution.

How is China's Economy to Run a High-Quality Development Marathon?

Seventy-three consecutive years of growth is an unprecedented economic miracle

The report of the 19th National Congress of the CPC has aroused great repercussions at home and abroad. If the prospects described in the report can be realised smoothly, which we are fully confident they can be, it will create a significant miracle in human economic history because there has never been an economy that has experienced 73 years of smooth, fast development (from 1978 to 2050) in human history. Compared with China's amazing economic development results achieved over the past 40 years, particularly its sustained GDP growth rate of more than 9%, it is a greater miracle.

China's 40 consecutive years of growth cannot be said to be completely unprecedented. Japan's development in the Meiji Reform period was very fast, as was the Germany's development after its unification and before the first world war. Therefore, the greater and absolutely unprecedented miracle in the world would be to be able to add the 33 more years of consecutive growth that we are striving for in future to the 40 consecutive years of growth achieved in the past.

Therefore, if China wants to create miracles, it does not lie in speed but in stability and whether China can grow for another 33 years.

Don't stumble but maintain momentum, the two problems we must face in creating miracles

We must face two issues to achieve the goal of 73 consecutive years of growth.

First, how can we avoid a slip in the next 33 years? To China, nowadays the development speed has not been important, if from now on we are able to maintain an average growth rate of 4% annually, by 2050 we can enter the ranks of the 20 most advanced countries in the world. Therefore, the key to the future is not speed but not to stumble. My understanding is that the top economic priority in 2018 is stability and to avoid mistakes. General Secretary Xi Jinping said that high quality and high speed cannot go side by side, that here, high quality is put before high speed, and the first requirement for high quality is not to allow the work to slip. There are many possibilities for a slip, not only financial crises, but also social contradictions as well as the problems of population, health and international relations. It is worth studying how China can resolve various crises without slipping up in the next 33 years.

Second, how to ensure the continuous driving force of development in the next 33 years, and to ensure that we always have the motivation and energy? Recently, I have paid close attention to Traditional Chinese Medicine (TCM). TCM stresses the primordial *qi* of life, meaning that the rise and fall of vitality lies in the amount of primordial *qi* which is stored in the kidneys. Corresponding to an economy like China, the first thing to consider is how to conserve this primordial *qi* and how to keep a balance between *yin* and *yang*, that is to say, to have no slip in our economic work. Next, how to ensure that primordial *qi* can be continuously cultivated, and whether young people's educational level can be continuously raised, and how to avoid people of our age becoming a burden on society after 20 years? This is a personal issue, a family issue and a social issue, and an issue related to national development.

Only by answering the above two questions can China create a miracle of 73 consecutive years of growth and contribute new development experience to the world.

Three key points in running a high-quality development marathon

To maintain continuous growth for the next 33 years means that China's economy from 2018 to 2050 needs to run a marathon. Then, how can we have a good and beautiful run, and how can we achieve a stable, sustainable and high-quality development of our country's economy? After careful consideration of the historical experiences and the basic rules governing economic development, the following three points provide us with much food for thought.

First, strictly guard against major twists and turns, on no account trip up and fall over, sprain your ankle or get a stitch.

Major twists and turns may come from financial risks. Historically, the 1929-1933 world financial crisis, the series of financial crises prevailing in Latin America throughout the 1980s and 1990s, the 1997-1999 Asian financial crisis, as well as the financial panic after the the Japanese capital bubble burst, every time the impact on the related countries and regions set back their economic development by 10 or even 20 years.

At present, China is facing two economic and financial risks. First, the scale of liabilities in the real economy is rather large, moreover, it implies many bad debts, so we should make good use of the current stable situation when the macroeconomy is doing well to promptly clear the bad debts. Second, the liquidity of our country's financial assets is too strong and the ratio of total cash, bank savings and financial products to GDP is beyond 200%. These assets that can be turned into cash can weaken stability of the overall financial system. Therefore, fundamental reform is needed to adjust the structure of financial products, guiding savers to directly hold bonds or other securities with less liquidity, thereby to raise the stability of the financial system.

Major twists and turns may also come from the fact that the external dependence of China's supply chain is very high. Some important upstream products, including semiconductors, crude oil and natural gas, are highly dependent on external, relatively concentrated sources. We need to guard against risks such as the oil crisis from 1971 to 1973. From now on, we should appropriately reduce dependence, increase diversity and increase reserves.

Second, we need to replenish water in advance while it is running, and continuously resolve some basic problems to pre-empt them developing into restrictions in the future.

One problem is labour force quality. With the constant upgrading of the economy, China's labour force competitors will increasingly be workers from developed countries such as Europe, the US, Japan and South Korea. China's ability to retain industrial activity and employment will depend on whether our domestic labour productivity can compare with that of these developed countries. In addition, with the development of science and technology, our workers have to compete with machines that have gradually implemented artificial intelligence (AI) and do things that the machines of today cannot do. From now on, we should proactively increase investment in education, especially the basic education in junior high school and senior high school, not only to improve hard knowledge of mathematics, physics and chemistry but, more importantly, to improve the comprehensive soft qualities such as the humanities and society which are difficult to replicate with technology.

Another problem is the ageing population. In the short term, fertility should be properly encouraged. More importantly, there should be a complete change in thinking. The accumulation of experience, and maintenance of the skills and physical condition of people in their 60s and 70s today is better than that of middle-aged peple in their 50s 20 years ago. There is untapped potential in the elderly population, so reform should be adopted to encourage them to voluntarily participate in social labour, turning a problem into a positive.

Third, make good use of the uphill and downhill on the marathon route, and make good use of normal economic fluctuations.

The market economy has its own fluctuation rules. In *Das Kapital*, Marx, 150 years ago, profoundly revealed the internal contradictions leading to the instability of a market economy. Today, the practice of the socialist market economy is to fundamentally solve the basic problems expounded by Marx by enhancing the role of government. However, this does not mean that government should completely erase fluctuations in the market economy, on the contrary, it should make good use of these fluctuations.

Making good use of economic fluctuations is similar to TCM that says "winter diseases are treated in summer and summer diseases are treated in winter". A good marathon runner reduces speed and adjusts their breathing when going uphill but speeds up and adjusts their muscles when going downhill. For an economy, when the situation is good, supervision should be strengthened to help the financial system remove negative elements and to raise efficiency; when the economy is bad, we should make more public investment and supplement our weaknesses.

We have full confidence that China, which has accumulated valuable experience in reform and opening up, is able to run a beautiful marathon of economic development from 2018 to 2050, to achieve the economic miracle of 73 consecutive years of growth and to realise the grand blueprint for the great rejuvenation of the Chinese nation described in the report of the 19th National Congress of the CPC.

How Does 'China's Economic System' Upgrade from Version 1.0 to Version 2.0?

China's rapid economic growth in the past did not lie in the implementation of industrial policies. In fact, these policies could be said to have been unsuccessful in fields such as photovoltaics (PV) and VCRs where the government implemented industrial policies. Today's Hai'er and Green Electric Appliances were not supported by the government in the early days, the same thing also happened with Huawei in Shenzhen. Many successful growing enterprises today, no matter whether it is Huawei or Hai'er, often received attention from the government only after they emerged, and only received key support from local government in the middle and latter stages of their growth. Hence, the experience of China's economic growth cannot be credited to the implementation of industrial policies but, rather, the explanation is to be found in Adam Smith's *The Wealth of Nations*.

In the past we had many misunderstandings about Adam Smith's works, thinking that he merely encouraged freedom but, in fact, in Volume V of *The Wealth of Nations* he talks a lot about how governments should help the development of a market economy, including why the British monarch at the time had to interfere with the court, why the British had to control the foreign trade of its colony of America, and stipulate that the merchant ships used in American foreign trade must be purchased from Britain rather than France. China's rapid economic growth over the past 20 to 30 years also proved the viewpoint of Adam Smith. The basic experience of China's economic growth in the past can also be called experience Version 1.0 of 'China's Economic System', whereby the government assists enterprises in opening up territory and helps them to cultivate and expand the market.

However, currently the operation of this economic system has encountered difficulties and China's economic growth is slowing down. It cannot be denied that there are many factors leading to the slowdown of economic growth, including surplus production capacity as well as low international market demand, however, the more important reason is that 'China's Economic System' is in a period of transformation and upgrading. Much like the operating system of a computer needs continuous upgrading, today Version 1.0 of 'China's Economic System' is also in the process of being upgrading from a 'low-energy operation status'. I hold that if we want to walk away from economic distress, we must complete the smooth upgrading of 'China's Economic System' from Version 1.0 to Version 2.0, and during this process two points are crucial, namely, the smooth upgrading of the relationship between government and enterprise, as well as the quality and level of government supervision.

There must be a smooth upgrading of the relationship between government and enterprise

In Version 1.0 of "China's Economic System", there is close cooperation between government and enterprises. The government helps the enterprises open up territory, such as attract investment, provide industrial parks and help enterprises recruit workers. However, the old version of government-enterprise relations pushed forward economic growth while also bringing on the problem of corruption, therefore, it needs a timely upgrade. For this, General Secretary Xi Jinping put forward that "building a new type of cordial and clean relationship between government and business"[1], namely, leaders must be both "cordial" and "clean" to entrepreneurs.

It is not an easy job to change the relationship between government and business. Under the deterrence of the current anti corruption situation, some leading cadres are overcautious and indecisive in their work, so the economic work is naturally affected. Therefore, the first key point for pushing forward the upgrading of "China's Economic System" lies in finding a way to build "a cordial and clean relationship between government and business".

It is obvious that "building a cordial and clean relationship between government and business" needs an institutional guarantee. In essence, we must establish a set of incentive mechanisms with clear rewards and punishments while, at the same time, an effective supervision mechanism is needed. The incentive mechanism used to rely on trans-regional GDP growth competition, that is, for whoever oversees high growth of local GDP, the possibility of promotion is high. Looking at it now, this mechanism is too single and insubstantial. Being too single is because the GDP growth competition has led to some local officials to pay too much attention to short-term GDP growth but ignore long-term consequences, thereby leading to problems such as excessive local debts. Being too insubstantial is because the opportunities for promotion are too few, the higher one goes, the more difficult it gets, therefore some officials often take bribes at the risk of their political future to pursue short-term personal economic interests. Therefore, the direction of reform should be to greatly increase the performance salary of officials, to set up performance indicators for every post and make regular assessments. More importantly, officials at all levels oversee important economic and social decisions, therefore they must have a high sense of professionalism. Consequently, their average salary must not be lower than that of managers in the private economic sector with the same qualifications. According to the successful experience of Singapore and other countries, such a team is quite conscious of resisting the pressure of corruption from the market economy. Only having an incentive is not enough, supervision is also extremely important. The supervision of the Discipline Inspection Commission and the Audit Supervision should be institutionalised and long term.

The Quality and Level of Government Supervision Urgently Needs to Be Upgraded

After many years of rapid development, China's economy is no longer the simple market economy it was in the past. On the contrary, at present, the form of market economy is extremely complex, a simple streamlining of administration and devolution of power cannot make it spontaneously develop healthily, instead, it must be properly regulated. For instance, online shopping platforms adopt a competitive ranking, opening up the possibility of fake information whereby not all the highest-ranked goods are certified products; for another instance, the search engine and the tendering ranking are not only unable to provide users with the most effective and timely information but they may be misleading, leading to tragedies like the "Wei Zexi Incident"; pharmaceutical supervision must not listen to one side of the enterprise, because the falsification of clinical trial information is not without precedent. This creates a huge challenge for supervision.

When facing a more and more complicated market environment, if the government's regulatory capacity is not improved on a timely basis, problems will arise. The American financial crisis broke out because "cats are not as capable as mice", the US government's regulatory capacity failed to catch up with the innovations of the financial market. Therefore, version 2.0 of "China's Economic System" must learn from the past, promptly upgrading the government's capacity for precise regulation and supervision. To which, the key is to train a high-quality, high-level and enterprising market supervision team, giving these market supervisors a wage level that is fully in line with the market, and elevating their social status, thereby encouraging them to achieve accurate supervision of the market.

In the next stage of development, to complete the upgrade of "China's Economic System" from version 1.0 to 2.0, we need to focus on how to build "a cordial and clean relationship between government and business" as well as how to achieve precise regulation and supervision. If solutions can be found to these two key issues relating to China's economic upgrading, while at the same time achieving sustained economic development, China's proposals that contribute China's wisdom will also be globally recognised and accepted by the world.

Can China Break Through the Middle Income Trap?

Against a backdrop of continued decline in economic growth, all circles of society have expressed various worries as to whether China can cross over the middle income trap and enter the rank of developed countries. The so called "middle income trap" is a concept proposed by the World Bank in 2006, meaning that after the per capita GDP reaches US$3,000 for a developing country, it is difficult for it to graduate from being a middle-income country to enter the ranks of developed countries whereby per capita GDP exceeds the threshold of US$12,000.

In 2018, China's per capita GDP was close to US$10,000, so how to transcend the "middle income trap" is undoubtedly a major question for study, as well as the first step to achieving the "Two Centenary Goals" (building a moderately prosperous society in all respects by the centenary of the CPC's founding in 2021 and building a modern socialist country that is prosperous, strong, democratic, civilised, harmonious and beautiful by the centenary of the founding of the PRC in 2049).

Which Countries Have Broken Through the Middle Income Trap?

Throughout the history of the world economy in the 70 years after the second world war, of more than a hundred underdeveloped economies, only 12 have managed to break through the "middle income trap", including five East Asian countries, namely, Japan, South Korea, Chinese Hong Kong, Chinese Taiwan and Singapore;

five European countries, namely, Spain, Portugal, Cyprus, Greece and Malta; plus Israel and Oman in the Middle East.

The other countries, including all Latin American countries, are either always below the level of poor countries, or have entered middle-income level, with per capita GDP of US$8,000 to $11,000, but they are hovering there without a breakthrough.

Three Necessary and Sufficient Conditions for Breaking Through the "Trap"

What factors led these 12 countries and regions to break through the middle income trap, while the remaining countries failed to achieve such a leap forward? Recently, myself and Fu Lin, my former Ph.D student who is now an Associate Professor of the Central Finance University, have tried to sort through this issue systematically.

Our research shows that only when three conditions are satisfied simultaneously can a country break the middle income trap; on the contrary, so long as one of the conditions has not been met, a breakthrough will not be achieved. So, what are the three conditions?

The first condition is a government that is stable and supportive of the development of a market economy. This firstly means that the government must be stable, here, a worthy negative example is Thailand. The reason for the stagnation of economic growth in Thailand is because of political infighting, the Red Shirt Army and the Yellow Shirt Army having long been obsessed with street politics. Obviously, such a government cannot even maintain a basic economic standard of living, let alone improve the level of economic development.

A government must not only be stable but also systematically implement policies that can maintain economic growth, including basic policies to unleash the vitality of the market economy, such as the rule of law and basic supervision, including a series of interventionist policies that can maintain economic growth, such as basic health and housing policies to maintain social stability, as well as basic welfare policies to eliminate poverty. In this regard, India is a negative example. Although India claims to be the largest democracy in the world and its politics are basically stable, for a long time, the Indian government's policies were against a market economy. To date, in India there one third of its population still gets grain subsidies, also the Indian government subsidised energy prices for a long time, therefore, at present, the global crude oil price is low so India is in a good situation. However, once the trend is reversed, India's public finances and even the macroeconomy will encounter difficulties.

The second condition is the continuous improvement of labour quality. To meet this condition, firstly, we should ensure basic public health and, secondly, we should provide a good educational environment. The utility of the public health service is to ensure the health of permanent residents and floating residents, so that they can participate more in the market economy, causing the labour participation rate and labour productivity of the population to be continuously improved (the labour participation rate is a major factor in economic development). In the 30 years before the reform and opening up, China had greatly improved its basic health level and the Chinese people's life expectancy was raised to 57 in 1979 from below 40 in 1949, yielding a demographic dividend for economic growth over the next 30 years. However, if there is no guarantee for basic public health, labour productivity is greatly impacted. India and other countries are slow to construct infrastructure. There are many reasons for it, but an undeniable reason is the productivity of construction workers. This low efficiency is closely related to the health level of their basic labour forces.

The more important prerequisite for a high quality population is to achieve a certain level of education. In China, through 30 years of efforts after 1949, the adult illiteracy rate dropped from 80% in the early years after the new China was founded to 22.81% in 1982[2] and further reduced to 4.88% in 2010. Compulsory education has been made universal for nine years and the gross entrance rate of higher education institutions has reached 25%. By contrast, India still has an illiteracy rate of 30%, and this will directly impact the improvement of its productivity because it is difficult to employ illiterate workers in many basic modern jobs.

The third condition is to open up to developed economies. Japanese economists once discovered the "flying geese paradigm" of economic development whereby, among a group of countries, one country takes off first, which then leads the neighbouring countries to take off. We have studied this phenomenon more carefully but found that this is not entirely true, because there are exceptions. For example, Israel has broken through the middle income trap but there are no developed countries among its neighbours.

We think that the mechanism behind this "flying geese paradigm" is that if an economy wants to develop, it must open up to developed countries but generally economic relations between neighbouring countries are already open. Specifically speaking, to transcend the middle income trap, a country must carry out trade and investment with developed countries. As a result, such a country's technological level, business philosophy and social consciousness will unconsciously move closer to that of the developed countries, and its income level and productivity will continuously rise. Israel's main trading partners are Europe and the US, the main trade partner of Japan used to be the US, and the main trade partners of South Korea are the US and Japan; In Europe, the main trade partners of Ireland and Spain are developed Western European countries, this naturally makes these economies keep learning ideas from developed countries.

China Possesses the Conditions to Bypass the "Trap"

Compared with the above three necessary and sufficient conditions, we found that China has the possibility of bypassing the middle income trap. Of course, in several respects, China must continue to make efforts to meet these three conditions.

Firstly, it has a government that concentrates its efforts on economic development. China is unlikely to have the Thai and Filipino style of street political unrest. More importantly, in general, the basic point of China's system and policies is to push forward economic development. Regarding the main spirit of the Third Plenary Session of the 18th Central Committee of the CPC, the popular interpretation is to let the market do the work of the market and the government govern. Viewed from this angle, in most areas of resource allocation, including labour wages, capital and land prices, the market should play an absolute leading role. At the same time, China must let the government play a better role in realising the governance of a modern society so as to provide a solid foundation for the development of a market economy. The most important thing is to give better play to the role of supervision, letting the market economy develop in an orderly and healthy manner, while also ensuring that the government provides public goods necessary for market development. At present, to a great extent, infrastructure construction is a kind of public goods which must be completed by the government. The Chinese government is trying every means to reinforce infrastructure construction and provide this series of public goods.

Secondly, the quality of China's labour force continues to improve. The adult illiteracy rate has reduced to 4%, education levels continue to improve, the level of population health is also among the best in developing countries and our average life expectancy is on par with that of developed countries. It is true that population ageing is a problem facing China's economy, but whether ageing has an impact on economic development needs to be linked to the health level and education level of the population. When income level has not entered the rank of the developed countries, if the health level is high, it is entirely possible to let those individuals who are fit and well educated, and still willing to work, continue to work by extending the retirement age flexibly and reforming retirement benefits.

With regard to public health, China has made tremendous progress, but there is still room for improvement. Comprehensive medical reform must be launched as soon as possible, the construction of a preventative community medical network has great potential, public hospitals can reduce medical costs through reform, and the government provides more financial support through social insurance while simultaneously strengthening management and improving the medical efficiency of public hospitals. In addition, the multi-directional medical supply of private hospitals can be enhanced. All these measures can further improve the health level of Chinese citizens.

Thirdly, China is presently the largest trading body in the world, as well as a country with the same total amount of trade as the US and attracts the largest amount of foreign direct investment (FDI). China's main trading partners are the US and the EU; China has always been open to developed countries. China is continuously learning the experiences of developed countries, moving closer to them in regard to knowledge and philosophy.

To sum up, China is in possession of the three basic conditions for transcending the middle income trap. Meantime, we discovered that the gap with the developed countries in the world is the most basic factor to explain how a country is breaking through the "trap". Currently, China's per capita GDP is only 20% of that of the US, but from the historical experiences of Japan, South Korea and the Chinese Taiwan region, at the present stage, China has at least the potential to achieve a GDP growth of more than 7% (see Table 1). We expect that if China's economy continues to follow the path of reform and opening up, by 2021, calculated at purchasing power parity (PPP), China's per capita GDP should have the potential to reach 26% of that of the US, with the total economy exceeding that of the US; by 2050, China's per capita GDP, calculated according to PPP, can reach 75% of that of the US, and the total economy will be three times that of the US.

Table 1. The change of the GDP growth rate after the per capita GDP of East Asian economies reaches 19% of that of the US (period average %)

	Japan	South Korea	Chinese Taiwan Region
Within 5 Years	8.6	10.8	8.9
5 - 10 Years	9.4	8.6	10.7
10 - 20 Years	6.9	6.3	8.2
20 - 30 Years	4.3	4.0	6.2

Data source: The GDP growth of Japan and South Korea before 1961 comes from Pen World Table 8.0, the data after 1961 comes from the WDI of the World Bank; the GDP growth rate of the Chinese Taiwan region comes from Pen World Table 8.0 (Japan with 5 years means 1956 – 1960, South Korea means 1983 – 1987, Chinese Taiwan region means 1971 – 1975, the later time range can be deduced from this).

Several Reforms and Policies Still Need to Be Promoted to Achieve a Breakthrough

Although China has the basic conditions to break through the middle income trap, only by accelerating the reform and adjustment in several aspects can we fully tap the potential of economic development.

Firstly, against the backdrop of the current decline in economic growth, we must promote structural adjustment to stabilise the economy. The current situation facing China's economy is like that of 1997 to 2001, that is, after the Asian financial crisis. At that time, China's economy also faced a series of problems such as overcapacity and insufficient demand. Because China's macro debt ratio has reached over 200%, therefore, we must fully recognise the nature of the vicious circle brought about by the decline of economic growth, as well as the self-actualisation of related expectations. It is necessary to take some measures to stabilise economic growth, to reverse the expectations of domestic and foreign markets for the decline of the growth rate and to thereby stabilise the financial system.

So, for the moment, we must cultivate and consolidate many new growth points as soon as possible. There is no doubt that infrastructure construction is the weak point of China's economy and what can be continuously supplemented in the short term. At present, China's per capita infrastructure stock is only about 20% of that of Japan, South Korea and other economies. Moreover, China is not short of savings, if the financing channels of infrastructure can be opened, we can create a new growth point that is conducive to long-term economic development and able to stabilise the economy. The fundamental prerequisite for starting this steady growth engine lies in the financing mechanism.

To this, my suggestion is that governments at all levels provide seed funds, guaranteed by the central or provincial government and that infrastructure bonds are issued to society with lower interest rate than the loan interest rate of commercial banks. This is like building a series of "World Banks" within China's economy. It operates in a more focused manner than the CDB (China Development Bank), besides, it can operate relatively independently of the local government, and independently evaluate the feasibility and efficacy of infrastructure construction.

Secondly, we must adhere to the direction of reform. The basic direction of reform put forward in the Third Plenary Session of the 18th National Congress of the CPC is the most important and fundamental guarantee for breaking through the "middle income trap", which must be resolutely pushed forward, and which allows no room for wavering. In a situation where the economy is declining, we must correspondingly quicken the reform oriented toward the market economy, particularly the reform of the SOEs and the implementation of all measures to break up monopolies. If these reforms are in place, it will greatly stimulate the enthusiasm of relevant market subjects, thereby enhancing economic vitality.

Thirdly, we must persist in opening up to the outside world to cooperate and compete with developed economies and, during the process, enhance the competitiveness of China's economy. At present, globalisation has taken a new turn, the developed countries led by the US have put forward a series of new international economic systems that a protective against China. Facing these challenges, China's response strategy should be to continue to adhere to reform and opening up, and to enhance enterprise competitiveness through free trade zones and the "BRI" and other open constructions. After the competitiveness of China's enterprises and even the whole economy is raised, the impact of some international discriminatory protectionist policies on China's economy will be greatly reduced, and Chinese enterprises can then easily deal with various challenges in international negotiations, thereby enabling them to remain invincible in international competition.

To sum up, China has the basic conditions to transcend the middle income trap and its potential for economic development is still impressive. The main issue currently is to reasonably deal with the challenge of economic decline, to quicken the pace of reform and consequently to lay a solid foundation for a new round of economic growth as soon as possible.

Will China Miss the Fourth Industrial Revolution?

The theme of the annual winter meeting of the WEF in Davos in 2016 was very focused on the fourth industrial revolution. Many attendees I met at the meeting all expressed that the themes of the previous annual meetings were mostly conceptual but that this time it was more focused and specific than any previous ones.

This year, the US sent a large delegation, which is rarely the case – five vice state or ministerial-level officials attended the meeting at the same time, including the Vice President, the Secretary of State, the Secretary of Defence, the Secretary of the Treasury and the Commerce Secretary. US Vice President Joe Biden spoke at length about the many challenges brought to the world by the fourth industrial revolution, among which his greatest concern was whether the general public, especially the middle class, could benefit; and how to avoid the recurrence of an embarrassing situation when the readjustment of interests brought up by the fourth industrial revolution could only benefit a minority while the majority would suffer. However, the majority of the American officials were optimistic about the prospects of the fourth industrial revolution. The US Secretary of State John Kerry even said that the US had never faced so many good things as it does today, and the realisation of these benefits is expected to help solve some major global issues.

Then, what will the fourth industrial revolution bring to China? Will China become the victim of this revolution?

China Failed to Fully Catch up with the Previous Three Industrial Revolutions

What is the fourth industrial revolution? According to the definitions by Professor Schwab, founder of the WEF, the four industrial revolutions can be divided as follows: the first industrial revolution started when Watt modified the steam engine in 1775, the second one was the electrification that started at the end of the 19th century, the third one was the computer revolution that started in the 1950s, and the fourth industrial revolution is a comprehensive revolution, including computer popularisation and informatisation engendered by it, 3D printing and innovations in the manufacturing field brought about by robots and other new types of technologies, as well as human health and changes in life style brought about by life science and technology.

Professor Schwab held that the industrial revolution this time will bring more profound changes than the previous three revolutions. The participants of the WEF and Professor Schwab especially stressed that a considerable number of global passengers were left behind by the trains of the previous industrial revolutions, for instance, 17% of the world population still hasn't benefited from the first industrial revolution; the third industrial revolution marked by the application of computers has still left half the world population behind, those who have had no access to computers or the internet. There is no doubt that new winners and losers will certainly emerge in the fourth industrial revolution, and there is a great possibility that this train may leave more passengers behind than the previous three industrial revolutions.

Then, will China, ambitious to achieve modernisation, miss the fourth industrial revolution? Will we be forgotten by the fourth industrial revolution? Can we get on this train of revolution and thoroughly realise industrial modernisation? This is not a seemingly virtual, self-designed issue; thinking it through carefully, this is a serious question for study.

China failed to fully catch up with the previous three industrial revolutions, or at least was half a beat slower than the world. Among them, the first two industrial revolutions plunged China into an embarrassing situation of falling behind and getting beaten. The third industrial revolution awakened China very early, at the time, DIS-130, the first computer developed by China, was basically at the same level as the computer developed by Japan, but when it was in the early stage of reform and opening up, China fell behind both in computer hardware and software. We just got on the second half of the train of the third industrial revolution, rather than being the first passenger to board.

Three Main Reasons To Be Confident that China Will Participate in the Fourth Industrial Revolution

For the fourth industrial revolution, we must firstly have a certain confidence; there are at least three reasons for this.

Firstly, the rapid development of China's education since the reform and opening up. The gross enrolment ratio of higher education in China was only 2% in the 1980s but reached 40% in 2015 while Jilin Province, which ranks first among all provinces, autonomous regions and cities, has reached 52%. To a country whose per capita GDP is only 1/5th of that of the US, especially considering that the dropout rate of Chinese college students is much lower than the 25% of the US, this is an extremely rare achievement. Of particular concern is that for every 7 million university graduates, at least 1 million come from natural sciences, and engineering graduates comprise at least 30%. Meantime, science and engineering education in China is far more systematic and rigorous than in other countries in the world, particularly the US, Britain and other developed countries, where the undergraduate education is mainly general education and the students' basic training in engineering technology is far less than in China. But Chinese engineering graduates basically have the ability to directly participate in engineering and technical work.

China has a large reserve of engineering and technical talent, and this is the most basic capital for us to catch up with the fourth industrial revolution.

Besides, in the most recent decade China's industrial circles have achieved progress in many areas that has attracted worldwide attention. In high-speed railways, construction engineering equipment, information, drones, UAVs and so forth, China has undoubtedly stepped into the first camp in the world, and even achieved a leading position. We can say confidently that in the next five to 10 years, there is hope for China to achieve breakthroughs in military, civil aircraft engines and large passenger planes. At present, China's rapid development momentum in science, technology and industry is also reflected in China's annual number of patent applications, the number of published and cited papers in engineering and natural science has entered the world's first camp.

Secondly, China still has a huge market. Among which, the scale of automobile, high speed rail, UHV power transmission and transformation, power generation and other markets rank among the top in the world, while civil aviation will soon rank first in the world too. These huge markets have created unprecedented advantages for China to participate in the fourth industrial revolution. Because of the huge market, Chinese standards can be formulated, and standard setters often have important advantages in technological breakthroughs and industrialisation. At the same time, the huge market can also breed large companies, like Huawei and Midea, which are all large companies in the first camp of related industries in the world. Large companies have strong financial support and R&D capabilities, thereby giving them great advantages in participating in the fourth industrial revolution.

Thirdly, on the whole, China's economy is still in good shape and with a rapid growth momentum, in sharp contrast to the general economic decline in other economies. China's economic growth rate still maintains at above 6%. Even if there are some difficulties at present, the growth rate of added value in high tech industries is still higher than the development speed of the overall economy. What is closely related to this is that, at present, China still has the highest savings rate in the world, officially about 45%. Of course, this data is a slight overestimation. According to my research, China's current national savings rate is about 38%, still a very high number globally. In 2013, the US's national savings rate was only 17.6%, Japan's was 21.8% (the data of the US and Japan comes from the WDI). China is a rare economy with huge savings. And funds are the booster for the transformation of science and technology into the driving force of enterprises. With this powerful booster, any technology can be applied rather quickly.

Mend Weaknesses: We Should Appropriately Advance, Lead and Open Up the System Improvement That Restricts Innovation

Although we have the above three important advantages, we must see that facing the fourth industrial revolution, China's current biggest weakness, and also the most worrying point, is whether our institutions will restrict our capacity for creativity. The fourth industrial revolution will certainly have a huge impact on the present systems, so if there is no improvement in the systems, they will certainly shackle progress with the fourth industrial revolution.

For example, the application of internet technology has impacted the traditional taxi business. Modern technology allows everyone to use private cars for business, blurring the boundary between private and business use of cars. In the past, a relationship of mutual trust was formed between taxi providers and taxi users via the process of licencing taxi companies. Business cars are designated for business use, they must be bought by taxi firms and handed to workers for their use. Today, large numbers of private cars are left unused, and they themselves can be used for business. This needs to be redefined by law, providing a relatively relaxed environment for private unused cars and workers to turn these private cars into taxis.

For another example, driverless cars can only be used on the road through institutional innovation if there is no clearly defined system to guarantee who will be responsible if the driverless cars go wrong. What legal responsibility should the manufacturer bear? If a crash takes place between a driverless car and a car driven by a driver, how to define responsibility? What should be the difference in standards of conduct for pilotless vehicles and for someone driving a car?

For another example, with the development of biotechnology, personalised gene sequencing will soon become a large-scale market. Under such circumstances, who owns the personal gene information? And under what circumstances can pharmaceutical companies, insurance companies and hospitals obtain the information? A more sensitive topic is that in future fertility may be completely different from today. Is surrogacy feasible? Who has the right to bear children? Who controls our genes? There must be a breakthrough in laws governing these major issues.

What I am appealing to is that facing the fourth industrial revolution, China should make an appropriate advance in consciousness, otherwise we may lose out to competitors in related fields. Because today, technology is changing with each passing day. Even if we start only a little later than the others, the gap between us and the leaders may widen in the future.

Regarding laws related to the fourth industrial revolution, we should keep an open mind; in partial areas we must open a window for new technology, allowing the leaders to continuously probe and innovate. China should not only become a free rider of the fourth industrial revolution, but become more of a leader, and this requires us to innovate and take the lead in systems; so to be bolder, it would be better to let go a little more and make modifications when there is a problem, rather than have a closed mentality of being slow rather than going wrong.

China has never been so close to the world's leading technology wave as today. The fourth industrial revolution is a new wave and, in the process, China should never fall behind. This requires us to appropriately lead and open up the institutions that restrict technical advancement. If institutional innovation keeps up, China can become the perfect leader of the fourth industrial revolution.

What is the New Normal Between China and the World?

The new normal is a commonly used term internationally in recent years since the outbreak of the financial crisis in 2008, used to describe the economic and financial status of developed countries. This term appeared frequently in the recent two winter World Economic Forums in Davos. "Under the new normal, our country's economic development displays three characteristics: a fast pace of change, structure optimisation and power conversion. The growth rate should shift from high speed to medium speed, the development mode should change from scale and speed to quality and efficiency, and the economic restructuring should shift from incremental capacity expansion to simultaneous stock adjustment and incremental optimisation, while the driving force of development should shift from mainly relying on resources, low cost of labour and other factors to being more innovation driven."[3]

What does the new normal mean to China and the world? The judgment on this question is undoubtedly an important issue affecting China's economic, social and enterprise related decisions. Below, we will analyse new normal developments with respect to three types of economies: developed-country economies, emerging-market economies excluding China, and China's economy. To analyse this more extensively, a more solid research framework is needed, otherwise accuracy decreases. Here the time window is set to the medium term development stage of three to five years.

The New Normal of the Developed Countries

Six years after the outbreak of the international financial crisis in 2008, one after another the developed countries entered the recovery process of the post-crisis era. Not only Britain, but also the US, even Greece and Spain that were in the grip of a crisis, had fully entered the stage of gradually coming out of the crisis, constantly repairing the trauma and making adjustments to the deep-seated problems that caused the crisis.

To Britain and the US, the new normal meant that overall economic growth would be slightly lower than before the crisis, but the most important thing was that the growth of these countries after the crisis mainly came from finance, real estate, high technology and high-end services, therefore the biggest challenge they faced was how to coordinate the social contradictions in the process of economic development and economic recovery. The most prominent problem was that the general pattern of globalisation had led to the loss of competitiveness of a large number of low-skilled people in the developed countries. Taking the US as an example, although unemployment continued to go down, there were still a large number of its population who were long-term unemployed, and they were no longer included in the unemployment statistics. Therefore, someone said that the US recovery was a rich person's recovery, the gap in income was widening. In Britain, although the economic growth rate was not low, the wages of employees were falling, and this was an economic phenomenon even the British were extremely surprised about.

After comprehensive analysis, the main characteristics of the new normal in Western developed countries are: an increased focus on domestic politics in the face of globalisation with the spearhead of change directed at the capital elite, hence more emphasis on the fairness of distribution, the constraints on the market mechanism, especially the financial market, at the same time, taxes for high-income people will also be increased. This point can be proved by the popularity and heated discussion of French economist Thomas Piketty's new works since the recent period.

The New Normal of Emerging Markets Outside China

The impact on emerging markets outside China was relatively limited but since 2009, after the developed countries began to implement large-scale quantitative easing (QE) policies and other monetary-easing policies, large amounts of capital poured into the emerging economies. Besides that, the increase in demand for bulk commodities brought about by the rapid recovery of China's economy allowed a gratifying pattern of prosperity and vigorous development to emerge. Unfortunately, the foundation for this round of development was not solid because many countries' market mechanism was not solid and the macro management was not firm, therefore, from the beginning of 2013, when the US Federal Reserve announced that it would withdraw QE, the emerging markets were hit by a new round of divestment. It can be expected that under the impact of monetary policy adjustment on developed countries, the new normal for these countries would be a downturn in the overall economic growth rate, and the process of the downturn would again stimulate some emerging economies to have to carry out some market-oriented economic system reforms.

Therefore, the basic theme of the new normal in emerging markets is to seek the reform of an economic system in the era of slow growth, trying to create an institutional basis for the new round of growth, in short, to 'turn right'. It can be ascertained that some emerging markets are able to grasp the opportunity and push forward reform while some other countries are likely to avoid reform, thereby pushing their economiesw into a more difficult situation.

Four Types of New Normal for China's Economy

Many analysts believe that the basic point of the new normal of China's economy is the gradual decline of the growth rate, as well as the gradual adjustment of the debt level. In my opinion, these analyses are not necessarily comprehensive, and the reason for it is that these analyses pay too much attention to the performance of the macroeconomy, but we need to further analyse some connotations of China's new economic normal, namely, those hidden, very important socioeconomic phenomena that will determine the new normal performance of China's macroeconomy. On the whole, the new normal of China's economy will comprise the following four important aspects.

1. See-sawing of old and new growth points

This will be the most obvious and prominent feature of China's economic new normal. There were two old growth points in China, exports and real estate. They will gradually and repeatedly decline. Partly due to the direct impact from international economic fluctuations, there will be various fluctuations and repetitions in the growth of exports. Generally, because China's economy continues to grow, world markets find it difficult to support China's continuing export growth, therefore the ratio of favourable balances for exports and trade in China's GDP will decline. But this process is not linear, it fluctuates.

Against the backdrop whereby the basic housing demand of urban residents in China has been met, coupled with the fact that the adjustment of the financial markets has increased people's return on investments, therefore real estate growth will also fluctuate. The fluctuating decline of these old growth points will be intertwined with the continuous fluctuating rise of new growth points, bringing pain to the growth of the whole macroeconomy.

There are three points in the new growth of China's economy. The first one is infrastructure investment with a protracted and public consumption nature. The investment includes high-speed rail, underground railways, urban public facilities construction, and air and water pollution treatment. The second one is the transformation and upgrading of various production capacities, including those with high pollution and high energy consumption, and this can't be linear and rise steadily, so there must be fluctuations. This is closely related to the cost of capital market financing and adjustment of government industrial policy. The third one is household consumption. The proportion of GDP accounted for by China's household consumption has increased by 0.7% each year; currently it has increased to about 47%.

The key to the problem is that the exit of old growth points is volatile, while the force of new growth points is unsteady, therefore, economic growth in the future three to five years will fluctuate. And this fluctuation is different to China's traditional macroeconomic fluctuation which comes more from the fluctuation in overall demand, including the fluctuation of investment demand, therefore the government needs to step on the brakes regularly, dealing with it through various policies and administrative means. However, in China's economic new normal, the essence of the macroeconomic fluctuations is the alternation of new and old growth points. And this alternation will lead to the internal driving force of continuous growth being insufficient. Therefore, the basic theme of a macro policy during this period is steady growth, and to take various measures to give birth to new growth points. Perhaps the most important point is the investment in public consumption infrastructure. To some extent, this investment needs to be led by the government, and this is also the main driving force of the government's steady growth.

Related to this is the fact that, due to the high national savings rate, China's current debt/GDP ratio of about 200% will increase, so the so-called deleveraging process will not come in the short term. It is reasonable that a high savings brings high leverage, the key is that there is a great need to increase the long-term debt guaranteed by the government.

2. Progressive economic adjustment

The second manifestation of China's economic new normal has, as a matter of fact, already appeared, namely, the hidden, progressive structural adjustment that has not been fully recognised by observers. This structural adjustment is specifically reflected in the following aspects.

Firstly, continuous wage rises, particularly the wage rises of blue-collar workers; the reason behind it is the complete reduction of the surplus labour force. In contrast to the double-digit rise in the wages of blue-collar workers, which obviously exceeds the growth in GDP, the overall profit rate of capital is declining. In fact, at present, China is in a high cost of capital stage, and this situation in which the actual rate has exceeded 3% was rare in the years of reform and opening up. I believe that after the next round of reform, the actual rate will decline again. After all, the basic character of China's economy is the high national savings rate. Even if at the present level, the wage rises of blue-collar workers has brought on the trend of capital replacing the labour force, all trades and professions are trying to raise the ratio of capital to labour force. With capital replacing the labour force, the capital accumulation will also speed up.

Secondly, the structural adjustment actually being promoted is the development of a new style of urbanisation, except for ultra-large cities, whereby residence registration has been opened up and China's labour force will be ablew to migrate freely for the first time in 60 years. In future, the regional layout of China's economy will exceed the constraints of administrative planning but present the pattern of cities and regions competing for a high-quality population, therefore China's economic geography will undergo major changes. The impact of this process on China's economic development will be extremely far-reaching.

Thirdly, the proportion of residents' consumption and the proportion of the service industry is rising. Besides, the service industry is not only a productive service industry but also includes logistics, distribution, e-commerce, finance and other consumer services. The main flow of labour and employment is also in the service industry.

3. Reform enters a deep-water area

Reform entering a deep-water area will also be a new normal for China's economy. The determination and goals, as well as coverage of this round of reform can be said to be unprecedented. At the same time, it must also be noted that there will be unprecedented resistance to reform.

The driving force for reform should come from two aspects, one is the energy of the upper level to promote reform. This top-down driving force is very abundant now, and the central authorities specially set up a leading group for comprehensively deepening system reform. But the problem is that during this round of reform, the grassroots governments and the SOEs have looked relatively passive, lacking creativity and vitality across the board. There are many reasons for it. One comparatively important reason is that some officials are insufficiently motivated and timid.

At present, of the three most remarkable reforms in the economic field, the first is the reform of the banking system. This reform is presently being pushed forward from the top down, therefore the progress is relatively smooth. The marketisation of the interest rate is likely to be basically completed in the next two to three years. Banks founded by private capital have started their layout, the capital account opening has also been placed on the agenda. The second is the reform of the fiscal system, which is currently in planning, the focus being to improve the tax system, to divide the financial relationship between the central and local governments. This top-down reform may be pushed forward in the near future. The third reform is the reform of the SOEs that everyone has been paying attention to. The essence of the SOE reform lies in further marketisation, further separation of the SOEs from government, and further capitalisation of SOE operations. However, at present, exploration of these aspects is far from enough. In short, reform entering a deep-water area will be the new normal for China's economy.

4. Promotion of Chinese factors in the field of international economy

Since the reform and opening up, China has been basically in the process of accepting the international economic rules and merging with the international financial system. But at this late hour, tremendous changes have taken place in the international pattern. China has been a giant ship among the world economic fleet, due to its high national savings rate and abundant funds, it will soon become the world's number-one country for investment, its overseas investment will exceed foreign direct investment in China, and the scale of its enterprises is also expanding. Therefore, the interaction between China and the world has become a two-way feedback process, not only does China's economy need to further accept the requirements of international rules to raise its international level but, at the same time, China is also constantly putting forward its own suggestions on revising the operating rules of the world economy and continues to push the international community to accept some of its basic demands through various operations. For example, to participate in the establishment of financial institutions including the New Development Bank (NDB), formerly known as the BRICS Development Bank, so as to improve the international economic order. China is no longer a simple recipient of international rules but is gradually becoming an active and pragmatic actor. By putting forward suggestions on reform of the international economic order, it lets the international community better accept the existence of China's economy. This is also the new normal of China's economy in the future.

In brief, after the outbreak of the global financial crisis, China and the world have entered a new normal. This new normal itself is a process of dynamically and constantly shaping the new pattern of China and the world. Careful analysis and seizing opportunities are compulsory courses that all participants in China's economy need to learn.

Is There Still Room for China's Economy to Catch Up and Surpass?

Since 2013, China's economic growth has been slowing down. Data issued recently by the National Bureau of Statistics shows that in the third quarter of 2019 GDP growth decreased to 6.0%. A more dominant statement in the academic community is that China's economy has ended the era of catching up and surpassing, and the continuous decline of the growth rate in the future will be a long-term trend. They have two main reasons for stating this. Firstly, China's per capita GDP will reach the level of US$11,000 and, according to historical experience, when the per capita GDP of an economy reaches this level, economic growth often declines continuously. Secondly, from the perspective of domestic factors, population ageing has become a general trend, and the total labour force is already saturated; in the near future, labour supply will continue to decline.

These types of analyses failed to grasp the most basic nature and the most basic potential of China's economic growth. In fact, if measures are reasonable, after adjustment and reform for a period of time, China's economy should be able to return to the track of catching up and surpassing.

The Logic of Catching Up and Surpassing

To study whether an economy has potential for further growth, an important indicator is the gap between this economy and the world's leading economies. Because they are driven by technology, business model innovation and other forces, the leading economies will continue to grow, and the development level of their per capita GDP will not stagnate at an absolute value.

Today the world's leading economy is that of the US; in 2018 US per capita GDP had reached US$63,000. Calculated at purchasing power parity (PPP) (one US dollar equals about Rmb4), China's per capita GDP is still less than 30% of that of the US. Historically, economies with a per capita GDP of US$11,000, compared with the per capita GDP of the US in the past, the gap was relatively small because the per capita GDP of the US at that time was far below the US$63,000 in 2018.

Therefore, from this perspective, we cannot observe China's economic growth potential according to the absolute level. With regard to catching up and surpassing aspects

such as business model, production technology, market development, management philosophy and system reform, China's economy still has huge room to grow.

China Has Satisfied the Standard of a "Student of Comprehensive Merit" in Breaking Through the "Middle Income Trap"

In the most recent period, the Centre for China in the World Economy of Tsinghua University has made a special study of the so-called "Middle Income Trap" issue. We discovered that in the 70 years after the second world war, only 13 of 100 countries and regions managed to break out of the "Middle Income Trap", raising per capita GDP to US$12,000 from US$4,000 (the World Bank standard). They are Portugal, Greece, Malta, Israel, South Korea, Cyprus, Chinese Taiwan, Spain, Japan, Oman, Ireland, Chinese Hong Kong and Singapore. We found that three conditions enabled these 13 countries and regions to achieve the breakthrough, therefore, we call their standard that of a "Student of Comprehensive Merit".

Today, China has fully satisfied the standard of a "Student of Comprehensive Merit".

Firstly, if a market economy system has taken root and sprouted in an economy, that is a positive inicator. After many years of reform and opening up, although there is still huge room for the economic system to improve, what cannot be denied is that the market economy has taken root in the hearts of the people, and the direction of market reform is unshakable.

Secondly, whether the population quality and human resources meet the basic standards. China's public health level ranks among that of the world's leading countries, particularly among the emerging economies; the education level of the Chinese population, compared to other emerging markets, is particularly outstanding, the gross enrolment ratio in higher education has risen to 37.5%, the illiteracy rate of the population over the age of 15 has decreased to less than 4%; by comparison, India is 30%, yet China's illiteracy standard is obviously higher than that of ordinary emerging economies. The continuous improvement in the public health level (including life expectancy) and education level of the population provide the basic conditions for China's economic growth.

Thirdly, whether to open up to developed economies. The valuable experience of China's rapid economic development over the years is to open up to the outside world and particularly to open up to developed countries. When a country opens up to developed countries, the level of economic growth will continue to approach that of developed countries, and this is also what the Japanese said of the "flying geese paradigm".

Prediction After Per Capita GDP Reaches 20% of US level

Since China's current per capita GDP is 20% of that of the US, more importantly, China's per capita GDP has reached the level that surpasses the middle income trap. With this in mind, what is the exact growth potential for China's economy in the next 15 years?

Let us see the growth situation of the 13 countries and regions after their per capita GDP achieved 20% of that of the US in history: Japan, South Korea and Chinese Taiwan have always maintained an economic growth level of more than 7% (see Table 1), the other countries and regions also continued to show a good growth momentum in this development stage. That shows that China's economy has great growth potential.

The Logic of Great Power Development

We must face up to an important fact, namely, that compared to the other east Asian countries and regions as well as the countries that have historeically managed to break through the middle income trap, China is a country with a vast territory and a large population. Then, will China's economic growth potential be greatly reduced?

I think the answer is not because, as a large country, China's growth potential is greater than small countries. The reason is that China's internal economy is the equivalent of a small world, there is still a huge internal trade potential, which at present has not been fully exploited. For example, the economic gap between the Chinese provinces is no less than that of other countries in the world. The per capita GDP of Zhejiang Province is four times that of Guizhou Province, and this gap is nearly equal to the income gap between China and the US, and what is more important is that Zhejiang and Guizhou can fully realise the flow of production factors, including capital and labour forces, which is impossible to realise between China and the US. Therefore, Zhejiang's capital will continue to trickle down to the economically deprived regions, equally, part of the labour force in these regions will pour into the developed regions. The great potential of this domestic trade cannot be overemphasised.

More importantly, because it is a major economy, once a large unified market is formed, it can continuously support the development of China's enterprises and industries. Take Taobao and Jingdong as an example. Recently, these e-commerce platforms have developed rapidly, and one of the reasons is that they have learned advanced foreign business ideas and business modes but, more importantly, a unified market has been formed in China. Taobao and Jingdong can uniformly sell products nationwide and uniformly deploy logistics, greatly reducing the cost of per unit transactions.

China's large market is also able to support research and development (R&D), with investment into R&D continuing to rise. This is the principal reason enabling China's high-speed rail technology to be deployed abroad. High-speed rail technology can become the blockbuster product for China to "go abroad", not because Chinese engineers are more capable or of a higher level than Siemens engineers but mainly because China has a large population, many cities are densely populated, the traffic volume between cities is huge, creating a huge demand for high-speed railways, and such demand is rare in countries elsewhere in the developed world.

Following this same logic, China's construction and construction machinery enterprises have also become world leaders. Therefore, compared to South Korea, Japan and Chinese Taiwan in the past, China's economy today should possess greater growth potential.

To do good work on the economy of a large country, the key is to break the fetters of population mobility between provinces and regions. Once the labour force can be further circulated among provinces, in terms of the overall situation, there will be a new round of development in China's economy. The specific mechanism is urbanisation. What needs special attention is that the advancement of urbanisation does not mean that the economy of each region will rise simultaneously. For example, there might be a decline in the northeast region, but the growth in other regions will make up for the relative shrinkage of the economy in that region.

Is Ageing a Fatal Blow?

This viewpoint is very popular, but I do not completely agree with it. Firstly, the factor of population ageing cannot be used for analysis and conclusion alone but must be considered comprehensively with the per capita GDP development level, the health level of the population and the quality of the labour force.

The average age of the Chinese population is indeed rising but the level of health is significantly higher than 20, even 10 years ago. At the same time, large numbers of the low-level labour force still have the willingness and capacity to work continuously. Therefore, if the system can be appropriately flexible, ensuring that the retirement system not only does not penalise those who extend their working life into retirement but encourages such behaviour, then the problem of an ageing population can be solved directly.

For instance, at present, the average health level of male blue-collar workers at the age of 55 is better than that of previous generations at the age of 45 to 50 but the current system forces many of them to retire when they are 55 years old. The same applies to female workers aged 50 whose health level is also higher than that of female workers 30 years ago at the age of 45 but they often retire too early, with the result that large numbers of the labour force now waste time in square dancing and pointless household affairs. Once an extension can be applied properly to working life while, at the same time, benefits are given to those who postpone their retirement, and age discrimination is eliminated, all these measures will maintain the participation rate of China's workers to a great extent.

Another factor must also be taken into consideration, namely, that China is an economy with high rates of savings and investment. With the continuous accumulation of capital, the ratio of China's capital to labour force will continue to rise to the forefront globally. Therefore, the amount of capital corresponding to each worker is rising, there is still huge room for improvement in labour productivity, and labour intensity will continue to drop. This goes back to the basic fact that China's per capita GDP is 20% of that of the US. The quality and quantity of labour capital in China still have room to rise.

In the short term, the ageing population has, in fact, promoted the structural adjustment of China's economy. Because of its ageing population, the relative shortage of labour has led to the rise of workers' wages and, in turn, promoted an increase in disposable income, thereby driving continuous growth in consumption, while the weakness of China's economy is consumption rather than supply. Therefore, whether in the short term or in the long term, ageing will not become a fatal factor in China's sustained economic growth.

How Much Is the Negative Impact of Change in the International Economic System?

Many people say that when China's economy as a large country continues to rise, the US and other major countries will all take measures to restrict China's development.

Indeed, the US has the strategic intention to restrict China's economic development and curb its impact on the new world economic order. But we must see that whether or not this strategic intention can be realised will depend to a great extent on how China responds.

The developed countries are never a monolithic bloc, while the US cannot completely dominate the economic governance system of developed countries. The US and Britain, the US and Germany have already had different economic strategies for China. Generally speaking, the international environment is still advantageous to China's sustainable development, it cannot be said that international factors will restrict China's future development.

In brief, after a period of reform and adjustment, after solving some of the elements obstructing current development, such as lazy governance of local governments, high financing costs, slowness in tackling backward production capacity, and clearing bad accounts and bad debts, China's economy can still be rejuvenated and return to the era of medium or high growth. The Chinese enterprises and people should have firm confidence in future economic development prospects.

Chinese Economy: Looking Forward to 2035 and 2050

After the 19th National Congress of the CPC, what does China's economic future look like? What are the characteristics of China's medium and short term economic development in future years? What level of development will China's economy reach when China has built a moderately prosperous society in all respects in 2020? What does it mean to basically realise socialist modernisation by 2035? By the middle of the 21st century, when the second centenary goal is achieved in 2050, what will the picture of China's economy look like? From now on, what are the problems that China's economy must solve? This series of issues deserve careful analysis and serious consideration by the Chinese people.

China's Economy in 2020 When China Has Built a Moderately Prosperous Society in All Respects

Building a moderately prosperous society in all respects is a comprehensive development goal, containing not only various tasks and objectives of economic development, but also other tasks and objectives of social development. Then, in terms of economic development, what does it mean to build a moderately prosperous society in all respects?

A comprehensive analysis shows that when China has built a moderately prosperous society in all respects in 2020, calculated at the market exchange rate, its per capita GDP will reach about US$10,000, calculated at PPP, 30% of that of the US. This development level will be very close to the threshold of high-income countries defined by the World Bank. By then, China will basically bid farewell to the so-called middle income trap.

Purely from the perspective of economic development indicators, it is not difficult to achieve this goal. As long as the economy maintains a growth rate of 6% from now to 2020, this goal can be realised. Just as General Secretary Xi Jinping repeatedly stressed in a series of important speeches: "To build a moderately prosperous society in all respects and to realise the first centenary goal, a landmark indicator is that all the rural poor are lifted out of poverty." "Building a moderately prosperous society in all respects is our solemn commitment to people of the whole country, it must be achieved, and must be achieved in all respects, and there is no room for haggling."[4] I'm afraid this is also the top priority of the work of the party and the government from now on to 2020.

China's Economy in 2035

The report of the 19th National Congress of the CPC points out that by 2035, China will basically realise socialist modernisation, on which the report gives a rather detailed description: "The vision is that by the end of this stage, the following goals will have been met: China's economic and technological strength will have increased significantly, China will have become a global leader in innovation; people's rights to participate and to develop as equals will have been adequately protected, rule of law for the country, the government, and society will basically have been put in place, institutions in all fields will have been further improved, the modernisation of China's system and capacity for governance will have been basically achieved; social etiquette and civility will have been significantly enhanced, China's cultural soft power will have grown much stronger, and Chinese culture will have greater appeal; people will be leading more comfortable lives, and the size of the middle income group will have grown considerably, disparities in urban-rural development, in development between regions, and in living standards will have been significantly reduced, equitable access to basic public services will basically have been ensured, and solid progress will have been made toward prosperity for everyone; a modern social governance system will basically have taken shape, and society will be full of vitality, harmony and order; there will have been a fundamental improvement in the environment, and the goal of building a beautiful China will have been basically attained."[5] Then, from the perspective of economic development, what are the prospects for China's economy in 2035?

From the perspective of economics, we can describe it in two ways. The first way, also a more commonly used way, is to measure by absolute per capita income. By this standard, by 2035, China should be able to reach the development level of the current top 20 most developed countries with a population of more than 5 million, that is, per capita GDP can reach between US$25,000 to US$30,000 at constant prices in 2011.

But we must see that this development picture may not be the goal in the minds of the Chinese people and the decision makers, because the world is changing, all countries are developing, the benchmark for realising socialist modernisation should also be a moving benchmark. The target of what to achieve is relative, namely, that by 2035, what will be regarded as the standard of the most developed country in the world, and this is the second way.

After careful analysis, we think it is entirely feasible for China to enter the ranks of the most developed large and medium-sized countries with a population of more than 5 million by 2035. In other words, according to the level of economic development and affluence of people's lives, China can fully reach the top 30 large and medium-sized countries with a population of more than 5 million. According to today's image, it can reach the level of Israel and Portugal. Based on the current PPP standard, China's per capita GDP will reach 60% of that of the US, and the total economy will be about twice that of the US. This is a significant milestone because historical experience tells us that once a country's economic development level reaches more than 50% of that of the US, generally its economic development will be relatively stable, and the impact of financial and economic crises, external shocks, social unrest and other socioeconomic factors can be easily resolved.

China's Economy in 2050

According to our comprehensive calculation, by 2050, in terms of economic development, the goal of building China into a great modern country that is prosperous, strong, democratic, culturally advanced, harmonious and beautiful should be able to be achieved. In terms of economic development level, by then, it is entirely possible for China to step into the forefront of the world's most developed large and medium-sized countries, the per capita wealth level can enter the top 20 of large and medium-sized countries at that time, the per capita standard of living according to PPP should be able to reach about 70% of that of the US, and the total economy will reach more than 2.5 times, or even 3 times, that of the US. In overall national strength, China will remain at the forefront of the world, and there is hope that China will be at the forefront of the world in science and technology, innovation, ecological civilisation construction, human resource development, life expectancy and other aspects.

We think that this growth target is not beyond reach: as long as China's GDP growth maintains a level of 5.5% in the next 10 years, 4% over the next 10 years, and 3% in the 13 following years, the development goals described above will be achieved.

Our assumption is that the average GDP growth rate of developed countries will be 2%, which is also the average GDP growth rate of developed countries over the past 20 years. At present, internationally, most economists think that in the future, the growth of developed countries will slow down due to ageing population and the slowdown of progress in science and technology, with the latter being regarded as the basic reason: they think that the development of life science technology in the past 50 years has brought tremendous change to people's lives, cars from nonexistence to existence, housing from small to large... all these changes are substantial, while changes in future decades will be partial and local, an upgrade on the existing foundation. In short, the growth rate of developed countries in the next 20 to 30 years is generally considered not to be greater than the growth rate of the past 20 years.

To Achieve the Grand Goal of China's Development, We Must Work Hard

If we want to achieve all the development goals, we must work extremely hard.

Firstly, we must give full play to the advantages of large country development, turning solving the imbalance of development into exploring the driving force of growth. At present, unbalanced development is a prominent problem in China's economy. This imbalance is manifested in many ways, in particular, the development between regions, and between urban and rural areas is unbalanced. This imbalance can be transformed into the driving force of growth through policy and institutional reform. For example, Jiangsu and Anhui are neighbouring provinces, but the per capita income level of Jiangsu is in the forefront of all provinces in China, twice as much as Anhui, which is catching up at full speed, and this catching up and shrinking of the gap of per capita income is precisely the driving force of growth.

Secondly, we must continue to improve the quality of the labour force and population. The future economy is the competition of labour quality and ability between countries, whoever has a high level of labour force will get more employment opportunities and a high standard of living. Future society will also comprise competition between machines and people, machines will replace simple labour on a large scale, but for complex labour, such as caring for the elderly and various social services, it is difficult for machines to do this –

these services must be provided by increasingly skilled workers. At present, China's gross enrolment for universities has reached 48.1%, comparatively, senior high school education is in urgent need of popularisation. The future labour force must have a certain humanistic quality, when entering the service industry, they must be able to shoulder the challenge of dealing with the elderly society, but will not be replaced by simple machines, obviously, this is what China needs to improve in the future. At the same time, it also needs to be pointed out that the improvement in labour quality is also an improvement in the effective labour supply, and this can be used to solve the challenges posed by the shrinking demographic dividend.

Thirdly, we must deal with the burden of an ageing population. China's development is characterised by a rapidly ageing population. To effectively deal with ageing, we should launch solutions with Chinese characteristics of combining "social support for the aged" with "family support for the aged". Purely relying on social support for the aged, the social cost will remain high. In the US 18% of GDP was spent on medical expenses in 2017; with social changes, completely relying on family support for the aged is also unrealistic, therefore, we need to explore an elderly care system with Chinese characteristics.

Fourthly, we must strictly prevent the occurrence of systemic and regional financial risks. Looking at it from historical experience, especially the historical experience of the Latin American countries, this risk has the strongest impact on the process of economic development. What a financial crisis brings may be a retrogression in the development of more than a decade or even more, and at present China's financial system undeniably contains factors that may induce systemic risk. For example, China's currency stock accounts for the highest proportion of GDP in the world, the "barrier lake" formed by huge liquidity may turn to huge unstable factors driven by international factors, and this problem needs a systemic solution. At present, China's financial system has entered the adjustment stage, the growth rate of broad money stock is basically the same as that of nominal GDP, and this is a very good development trend. Hard work must continue in the coming years to reduce the growth rate of broad money stock while, at the same time, increasing the proportion of direct financing, including bonds, through the development of the bond market and stock market, so as to reduce the dependence of China's economy on bank loans and the resulting broad money stock.

In short, through hard work, China's economy is expected to realise the beautiful blueprint described in the report of the 19th National Congress of the CPC. China will become the locomotive of world economic development in coming years, and even the role model of economic development for all countries in the world.

Chapter 2

Finance and Real Estate

General Context of China's Financial Development

Since the outbreak of the Asian financial crisis in 1997, the central aquthorities have held a national financial work conference every five years, each time bringing in important changes to the financial pattern. What are the most noteworthy points of the 2017 National Financial Work Conference? Can we see from this the overall context of China's financial development in the next five years?

Preventing and Controlling Financial Risks Is the Top Priority of Financial Work in the Next Five Years

The highlight of the National Financial Work Conference in 2017 was to repeatedly stress the prevention and control of financial risks, elevating them to an unprecedented height. Covering prevention and control risks, the conference put forward that finance must return to its essence, namely not to be self-serving but to serve the real economy.

In order to prevent and control risks, the 2017 National Financial Work Conference also put forward that supervision and control must be strengthened, and specifically the need to set up a national financial stability and development commission, with stability to prevent and control risks, and development to serve the development of the real economy.

I anticipate that the Financial Stability and Development Commission will be an actual executive organisation and that its administrative level and authority will be significantly higher than either the Central Bank, the Banking Regulatory Commission, the Insurance Regulatory Commission or the Security Regulatory Commission; it will not just be a deliberative or coordinating body. Therefore, we can predict that the strength of financial supervision will be raised to an unprecedented height in the next five years.

To serve the real economy, control financial risks and strengthen financial supervision, all of these are inseparable from reform. Therefore, reform will naturally become a key word of this National Financial Work Conference – use reform to promote the financial system, to serve the real economy, to prevent and control financial risks, and to strengthen financial supervision.

Three "Distinct Advantages" in the Development of China's Financial Industry

Why did the 2017 National Financial Work Conference take the prevention and control of financial risks as a top priority? My understanding is that the problems of the present China's financial industry can be summed up as three "distinct advantages".

The first "distinct advantage" in development is that the liquidity in the financial system has exceeded the actual needs of the real economy. Since the outbreak of the 2008 international financial crisis, the liquidity of China's economy has continued to rise. In terms of broad money, it is now about 200% of the real economy, whether for the absolute amount or the relative proportion of GDP, it ranks first in the world. The situation contains huge risks. In fact, I have pointed out many times that this is the biggest "barrier lake" in China's economy.

Some people say that the financial system should either avoid a "black swan" or guard against a "grey rhino", and the biggest "grey rhino" of China's financial system is that the liquidity seriously exceeds the needs of the real economy. In developed economies, the stock of financial assets, especially the stock of fixed-income financial assets is not lower than China, but their structure is different from that of China. In China's economy, the liquid financial assets, namely, bank deposits plus money stock, are far higher than the bonds stock (more than double), but the US and other developed economies are the opposite. Herein lies a hidden danger for China's financial stability.

The second "distinct advantage" in development is that some financial services are ahead of the development of the real economy. This is mainly reflected in the fact that a large number of financial transactions are self circulating, self entertaining. For example, interbank lending is very active, for a large number of financial products among banks the support behind them is actually interbank lending. There is also a large amount of business outside normal channels consisting of peer-to peer lending between non-banking institutions and banking institutions. Insurance funds also flowed into the stock market and other fields some time ago. This kind of self-serving development shows that the added value generated by the financial industry is falsely high, in 2016 it accounted for as much as 9% of GDP, approaching or even exceeding the added value level of financial services in developed economies.

The third "distinct advantage" in development is that the development of the whole financial market is ahead of the binding force of supervision and legal systems. The difference between financial markets and other markets is that transactions in the financial markets are complicated, transcend time zones, transcend regions, the number of people involved is extremely large comprising complex transactions, and emotions among social groups easily fluctuate, therefore, financial transactions must have strong supervision. And strong regulation alone is not enough, the rule of law must also be involved, because for the punishment of serious violations, the regulatory department is far less powerful than the judicial department. Punishment from the regulatory department is limited to fines, and restricting or prohibiting relevant violators from participating in financial trading; it cannot achieve the strength of restricting the personal freedom of relevant personnel as well as having enforcement strength.

Supervision of China's financial market continues the pattern of separate supervision in the past 10 years, and the judiciary does not know enough about the financial industry. Its professional knowledge, expertise and skills are far from keeping up with the complexity of transactions in the financial sector, therefore, financial justice is basically lacking. As a member of the national committee of the CPPCC, in the past ten years I repeatedly put forward suggestions that a higher securities procuratorate and a higher securities court be established in Shanghai or Shenzhen, and I continue to campaign for it.

General Context of China's Financial Development in the Next Five Years

According to the above analysis, it's quite possibile that implementation of the spirit of the 2017 National Financial Work Conference is likely to bring five trends in the development of China's financial industry.

Firstly, there is hope for the growth of money stock to drop below nominal GDP growth. The decline of money stock growth relative to GDP growth is the fundamental requirement for resolving systematic financial crisis, and also the basic spirit of this National Financial Work Conference. Since the first half of 2017, because the management of interbank and interfinancial institution lending has been strengthened, and the speed at which the banking system creates money has slowed down. This has led to a good situation we haven't seen for many years whereby the growth rate of broad money is lower than the nominal GDP. This pattern may continue to develop in the next five years, and the result is that interbank lending activity will continue to decline and the trend toward capital-intensive operation will continue to exist. This is not a bad thing for the development of China's financial industry. It will push all financial institutions to more precisely regulate their capital demand, raise the level of their capital management, and further bring about mergers and reorganisation of a large number of small and medium-sized banks.

Secondly, diversified small financial institutions will flourish. Small and micro enterprises and innovative enterprises can only be connected by innovative small financial institutions. It is entirely possible for these flourishing small financial institutions to be included in the scope of the government's "general supervision". Finance returning to its original intention of serving the real economy requires diversified financial services, hence, in the next five years loan insurance, small loans, consumer finance and even institutions providing financial services based on internet big data transactions will flourish, and relevant regulatory regulations will also gradually follow. This is the most concrete and important measure to strengthen financial services for the real economy.

Thirdly, the pace of opening financial services to the outside world will be accelerated. This means that China's commercial banks, bond companies and insurance companies will further open up to the outside world. When China joined the WTO 15 years ago, the situation we worried about was that foreign banks and bond companies would nibble away at our domestic financial institutions. Not only did this not happen but in recent times China's local financial services have made great progress, showing their own innovative ability. Nowadays, China's financial industry has more confidence and reasons to open up to the outside world. Through opening up to the outside world, we can better learn the best practices of foreign risk control while, at the same time, we can defuse international doubts, especially those of multinational corporations (MNCs), about the reversal of China's economic opening up.

Fourthly, the internationalisation of the Rmb will gradually slow down. Rmb internationalisation, in essence, requires the gradual opening of cross-border capital flows. At present, China's financial market supervision is not in place and liquidity remains relatively abundant, therefore there are huge risks in promoting Rmb internationalisation by simply liberalising cross-border capital flows. In terms of the spirit of the National Financial Work Conference, internationalisation of the Rmb should give way to the requirements of taking finance as the service of the real economy, and also should give way to the need to control overall financial risks. Once the Rmb internationalisation process is too fast, it will trigger some unrealistic views from international investors on China's economy and will directly introduce foreign financial fluctuations into China's financial market. Therefore I think that internationalisation of the Rmb in the next five years will put more emphasis on stability and robustness rather than speed.

Fifthly, the price of financial assets will undergo structural adjustment. Because, on the whole, financial risks will be controlled in the next five years, the prices of low-risk financial products will rise, while the prices of high-risk financial products will decline. For example, treasury yields are likely to decline while the yields of corporate high-risk bonds and local bonds will increase. For another example, the share prices of large blue chips and listed companies with sound performance may rise steadily, while the stocks of those high-risk small and medium-sized enterprises may face moderate downward price adjustment. In essence, China's economy emphasises overall financial stability, so investors will adjust the risk premium. Therefore, generally speaking, China's financial market will undergo structural adjustment in the next five years, it is a bull market for low-risk financial assets but a bear market for high-risk financial assets.

In brief, this National Financial Work Conference contains very important information, the relevant statements must be carefully read. What's more, we should carefully observe the follow-up implementation, from which we can see the general context of China's financial development in the future.

Financial System Modernisation Is the Key to Crossing the High-Income Countries Threshold

The report of the 19th National Congress of the CPC put forward the "two centenary goals", and 2019-2021 is the decisive period for determining victory of the "first centenary goal". If we can further promote financial system reform and the transformation and upgrading of the real economy, there is hope for China's economy to enter the ranks of high-income countries defined by the World Bank around the time when the CPC celebrates the 100th anniversary of its founding. However, since mid 2018, there has been a new round of fluctuations in China's economy, mainly reflected in the lack of confidence of micro subjects (especially privately-owned small and micro enterprises) and a steady slowdown of the real GDP growth rate. Looking forward to economic development in the next three years, we should accurately judge the situation and make adjustments.

What are the reasons for this round of adjustments?

We think that the main reason for this round of adjustments is the rapid financial contraction triggered by downward pressure and investor concerns. From the fourth quarter of 2017 to the end of 2018, the "new regulations on asset management" and other policies have greatly restrained entrusted loans and trust-loan financing, as a result, new social financing fell precipitously. On the one hand, financial tightening has led to a rapid decline in infrastructure investment while, on the other hand, it has led to financing difficulties for small, medium-sized and micro enterprises, thereby negatively impacting the overall macroeconomy. More importantly, when financial tightening, Sino-US trade frictions and other factors are superimposed, this has exposed the deep-rooted problems of China's economy in the financial field. For example, the financing channel of investment is unreasonable and occupies bank credit resources; slow disposal of non-performing financial assets leads to a large number of financial resources flowing to enterprises with low efficiency yet it is hard for them to go bankrupt; it is hard for the short-term interest rate reduced by the Central Bank to lead to a decline in the loan ratio of enterprises, therefore traditional monetary policy does not bring a strong sense of gain to micro enterprises. All these problems are closely related to finance.

Finance is the life blood of the real economy and the body cannot function normally without blood. Severe financial tightening since the end of 2017 has, in fact, restrained steady growth of the economy itself. Unlike previous simple total control, the current round of financial tightening is structural. It takes strict control of entrusted loans, trust loans and other "informal financing" as the main measure to introduce "new regulations on asset management", forcing "shadow banks" to put on the brakes.

Other financing channels such as Rmb loans did not fill the gap left by the "shadow banks", and this led to a rapid decline in new social financing in 2018. Although the meeting of the Politburo of the CPC Central Committee at the end of July released the signal of steady growth, the scale of new social financing in the months during the second half of 2018 was still not higher than the same period in 2017.

True, the "shadow bank" financing contains regulatory arbitrage and evasion of supervision; therefore it is reasonable to restrain and manage it. But, on the one hand, the original intention of "shadow bank" financing is to bypass regulations, so there are institutional obstacles to the return of these assets; on the other hand, the "return" of "shadow bank" assets will reduce the asset adequacy ratio, provision rate and other assessment indicators of banks and other institutions. This will pass on to non-financial enterprises, leading to financing cost increases.

Because of the specific characteristics of China's financial system, SOEs, particularly financing platforms closely related with the government, are still regarded as debt bodies with hidden guarantees so once there is a financial contraction, the impact suffered by privately-owned enterprises is more intense. This is like a swimming pool with deep water and shallow water zones. When it is fully filled, both zones have sufficient water resources but when the water starts to be drained, even if the drain is opened in the deep water area, it results in a lack of water in the shallow water area first. To drain water away from the deep water zone, every effort should be made to fill up the pool floor, namely, reform should be carried out from the deep level of implicit guarantees and infrastructure investment and financing structure, but not be tackled in a simple "water removal" way.

Comprehensively Push Financial System Modernisation as the Breakthrough Point to Promote Transformation and Upgrading of the Real Economy

After 40 years of high-speed growth, China's economy has entered a new development stage, raising a higher requirement for the financial system. In the coming years, China should seize the opportunity to comprehensively push for the modernisation of the financial system and make profound changes to it rather than simply aggregate adjustments. Specifically, the following five aspects need to be solved urgently.

First, promote modernisation of the infrastructure construction investment and financing system. In previous years, China's infrastructure construction developed rapidly, which played an important role in stimulating the economy. However, there are also criticisms that China's infrastructure is saturated and should not be invested in going forward. The suitability level of infrastructure construction is closely related to the degree of a country's economic development, population density, geographic structure and industry structure, making it difficult to accurately estimate or measure a country's reasonable infrastructure level. As a reference, we analysed the total amount of airports, railways, oil and gas pipelines, and highways, in terms of area density and per capita density, and compared them with the US, Germany, Japan and other developed countries. We found that China's infrastructure still has a certain potential.

First, the number of airports in China is still small. The number of China's regional small and medium-sized airports with cement runways, not only after considering population and land area, is much smaller than that of the US, Germany and Japan; even in total, it is also much lower than Germany and the US. Then, after considering the land area, China's railway and highway mileage also falls behind Germany and Japan, and falls far behind the US; and even considering the terrain, this gap is still obvious. Finally, the total amount of oil and gas pipelines in China is nearly 1/20th of that in the US, whereas the pipeline density taking demographic factors into account is much lower than that in Germany, while the pipeline density taking area factors into account is also much lower than that of Japan. Although the simple total amount depends on the population, the area calculation ignores many factors, but it does show that there is still room for China's infrastructure construction. Another factor that must be taken into consideration is that because it involves land planning, spatial agglomeration and other effects, infrastructure construction should be moderately ahead of the development of other economic components. For instance, the construction of underground railways should be moderately ahead of other types of urban construction, otherwise it will be restricted by building foundations, vibration and other conditions.

At the same time, infrastructure construction contains a large number of "public consumption" items. The construction and maintenance of the urban green belt, the improvement and upgrading of snow and ice removal equipment in winter in Northeast China, and the construction of a trans-regional wind and sand prevention forest belt have such attributes. Because they have the characteristics of public goods, it is difficult to provide these services in a market-oriented manner and therefore impossible to determine a market price. However, people's demand for these public services will inevitably increase as their incomes increase. From this point of view, China's economic development has reached the current stage, and an appropriate amount of infrastructure construction is necessary and proper.

To give full play to the potential of infrastructure construction, we need to completely reform China's infrastructure investment and financing system. For this, a national infrastructure investment company can be set up to coordinate management of the planning and analysis of the feasibility of local government infrastructure projects, and to cut infrastructure financing from the credit system of commercial banks.

Second, establish relevant mechanisms for efficient disposal of non-performing financial assets within the financial system, promote the synchronous reorganisation of financial assets and physical assets, promote the transformation and upgrading of the real economy, and improve industrial concentration. According to the calculations of different research teams, among China's industrial enterprises above a designated size, the "zombie enterprises" account for 7% to 10%. These "zombie enterprises" occupy a lot of credit resources, and they should go bankrupt or restructure. However, in China, the road for enterprises to go bankrupt or reorganise is blocked and long. After sorting out the information on the national bankruptcy and reorganisation information network, it is known that by the end of 2018, 297 SOEs filed for bankruptcy and reorganisation. This number only accounts for 14.6% of the 2,041 "zombie enterprises" published by the State-owned Assets Supervision and Administration Commission of the State Council (SASAC) in 2016, among which there were fewer large SOEs. Li Shuguang, the director of the Bankruptcy Law and Enterprise Reorganisation Research Centre, China University of Political Science and Law, said that the number of cases applicable to bankruptcy proceedings in China is less than 0.2% of that in the US and 1.16% of that in Western European countries. More importantly, some industries in China are facing profound adjustments, transformation and upgrading which will certainly require these industries to improve their concentration, which means the withdrawal of a large number of enterprises, either to be merged and reorganised, or to undertake bankruptcy liquidation. This raises the bar for the need to resolve problematic financial assets. China's financial system must get ready, mobilising asset management companies and other professional institutions to digest risks and bad assets. At the same time, decisions must be made to help the "zombie enterprises" go bankrupt or be reorganised, their debts must not be allowed to be extended on an unlimited basis, getting bigger and bigger and thereby unrestrictedly wasting financial resources. Specifically, we should encourage banks to use the present provisions to digest, verify and write off bad loans; we should comprehensively make use of the policies of public finance and social security to solve the re-employment of laid-off workers; we must speed up the trial progress of bankruptcy and reorganisation cases in the courts and strengthen judicial trans-regional implementation.

Third, we must devote major efforts to develop a bond market, making it the most important direct financing channel. Compared to stocks, issuance and pricing of bonds are more transparent and clearer, and bond defaults and their consequences are more easily defined at the legal level. More importantly, due to the existence of clear repayment and interest payment timetables, bond financing requires enterprises to take on more risks and responsibilities. From international experience, the bond volume of the bond market in Germany and other developed economies also exceeds that of the stock market, and this can provide us with a useful reference. At present, for the development of a bond market, efforts can be made in the following four aspects: first, break the division between the interbank market and the exchange market, and build a unified bond market to provide an unblocked channel for individual investors to directly participate in the bond market; second, straighten out product varieties and gradually change the administrative thinking of "one product for one regulatory institution"; third, deal reasonably with default cases, making investors bear the due investment risks, at the same time, speed up the bankruptcy and reorganisation process.

Fourth, promote the legal construction of a stock market, constructing a solid legal foundation. From the experience of successful countries such as the US and Britain in the development of stock markets, the healthy development of stock markets depends on many institutional conditions, it cannot be done overnight, or left to itself. At present, the key for the development of China's stock market is to build a solid legal foundation, consequently professional institutions and talent should be trained to implement the judicial procedures of the capital market. At present, stock market supervision mainly depends on the CSRC but the CSRC lacks investigative and judicial capacity and power, currently, the top grid penalty amount for each case is less than Rmb 1 million, far below the requirements for regulating the development of the stock market. In August 2018, the Shanghai Financial Court was officially inaugurated, taking an important step towards the specialisation of financial justice. However, only having courts is not enough, a securities procuratorate must also be established to cooperate closely with the Economic Investigation Department of the public security organisations, therefore professionally investigating capital market cases. At the same time, law enforcement should be strengthened to increase the level of deterrence and punishment.

Fifth, we must establish financial risk monitoring and a response mechanism to identify and cope with major financial risks on a timely basis. After 40 years' development, the volume of China's financial institutions has greatly increased, as has their complexity, therefore transdepartmental, and transmarket financial risk monitoring and response mechanisms need to be established urgently to carry out unified risk monitoring on credit, loans, capital management, bonds and exchange rates, and they need to be dealt with actively when major incidents take place.

In the coming years, this mechanism should focus on the overall level of financial market liquidity and current account deficit risks. In 2008, through targeted reserve ratio requirement (RRR) cuts, reverse repurchase agreements, repo, medium-term lending facilities (MLF) and other policy tools, the Central Bank maintained the basic stability of the market price of short-term monetary funds. In 2019, on this basis, more attention should be paid to changes in the price of long-term capital markets and to opening up the transmission mechanism of short-term and long-term, risk-free and risky capital markets. In 2018, the Rmb exchange rate experienced fluctuation with the annual average exchange rate being 6.61 to the dollar thereby maintaining basic stability. However, in 2019, the foreign exchange market still faces certain pressures. Following the impact of trade friction on exports, to some extent, it will put pressure on the exchange rate. At the same time, in 2019 the growth rate of the US and other developed economies will slow down. Along with the risk of a financial market valuation adjustment, investors will gradually become more risk averse. Once there is a fluctuation in the international financial market, it will also put pressure on the Rmb exchange rate.

The risk of a current account deficit deserves special attention. In 2018, China's trade in goods was still in surplus, however, due to a large deficit in service trade, in the first three quarters of 2018 there was a deficit of US$5.5 billion in the current account. The deficit risk in 2019 will be significantly magnified. Regression analysis forecasts that the deficit of the service trade in 2019 is about US$310 billion, if the favourable balance of trade for goods narrows at the same rate as 2018 (year-on-year growth rate of 16%), the whole year will have a current account deficit. As the exchange rate and capital flows are strongly affected by expectations, once there is a current account deficit, it is likely to cause a fluctuation in investor sentiment and cause a greater outflow pressure. Therefore, the international balance of payments still need to be managed carefully.

After careful calculation, we think that from now until 2021 is an important stage for China's economy to move towards "high income" from "middle income". If we can further promote financial system reform, promote the transformation and upgrading of the real economy, in the next three years maintain an average annual real economic growth rate of about 6.3% and maintain the basic stability of the exchange rate, at around the centenary of the founding of the CPC, China is expected to enter the ranks of high-income countries as defined by the World Bank (according to the latest standards of the World Bank in 2019, the lowest income limit for high-income countries is US$12,056 per capita gross national income), laying a solid foundation for comprehensively embarking on a journey to build a modern socialist China.

The "Crux" of Stabilising the Economy is Major Financial Structure Adjustment

Starting from mid 2018, there were changes taking place in China's economic situation, showing a trend of changes in stability and a downturn in stability. Then, at present, what are the problems that have led to the economic change? Of which, what are long-term problems that need to be resolved through medium and long-term measures such as a mechanism adjustment? What can be effective in the short term through a series of measures, so as to quickly stabilise the economy? We must identify the problems and prescribe solutions.

The Fifth Phase of Macro Fluctuation after the Financial Crisis

Since the 2008 international financial crisis, China's macroeconomy has experienced four fluctuation periods, and now it has entered a fifth phase. The first phase was from 2008 to mid-2009, being dragged down by the external environment, China's economy fell briefly; the second phase was from mid-2009 to 2011, the economic downturn began to reverse in the second half of 2009, a "V-shaped" rebound occurred; the third phase was from 2012 to 2016, economic growth fell once again; from the second half of 2016 to mid-2018 it reached the fourth phase, namely, the economy was relatively stable and healthy, and in 2016 and 2017 the global economy had achieved a rare overall recovery. However, from mid-2018 China's macroeconomy entered the fifth development phase, that is, it became increasingly unstable.

It is generally agreed that at present the downward pressure on China's economy mainly lies in insufficient power in the "troika" driving the economy. First, it is weak external demand. As Sino-US trade frictions have not been fully alleviated, external demand has been directly affected, especially China's export data in the first half of 2019 will show a significant decline, mostly because exports in 2018 were completed ahead of schedule. Second, there is a downward trend in consumption, retail growth has begun to slow down in the second half of 2018. Third, is the downturn in investment, the general analysis believes that the growth rate of fixed asset investment in 2018 is about 5.8%, of which the growth rate of infrastructure investment is only 3.7%, and all these are far below the GDP growth rate.

At the same time, the lack of enthusiasm of enterprise investment is also an important factor affecting investment, and this reflects some long-term problems that need to be solved urgently in China's economy.

Three deep-seated problems

The long-term problems of China's economy are mainly reflected in the following aspects.

The first problem is that large numbers of industries are facing mergers, transformation and upgrading. At present, a large number of industries in China are in a state of overcapacity, there is nothing strange about this, after 40 years of rapid growth, China's industrial organisation structure is extremely scattered. Take the automobile industry, as an example. At present, China has over 100 automobile factories, the production capacity is significantly in surplus, however, generally, there are no more than five automobile production plants in countries with a mature market economy. This phenomenon is reflected in almost all industries; therefore, China's industries urgently need a process of continuous agglomeration, which means that a certain number of enterprises (especially small and medium-sized enterprises) will face bankruptcy, exit, mergers and reorganisations. Therefore, all the problems of the current private economy are pushed to shallow problems such as the lack of a fair competitive environment, weak property right protection of the private economy, and difficult or expensive financing. The basic problems also include issues such as lack of scale caused by low industrial concentration and low-level excessive competition, therefore many enterprises must be prepared for restructuring and transformation, while private entrepreneurs face the difficult choice of starting a second business or quitting or retiring.

The second deep-seated problem is the lack of incentives for local governments to develop the economy. There are many reasons for this change, the direct reason is that now the assessment of local governments is no longer simply focusing on economic development but is becoming more comprehensive and complex, so compared with the past, government incentives for economic development have decreased significantly. At the same time, the polices enacted in recent years such as "replacing business tax with a value added tax" and the consolidation of local tax and national tax have actually decreased the proportion of tax revenue directly retained by local governments from local economic development, which has also decreased the economic incentive of local governments to help develop local businesses. The problem of local governments being lazy and not caring about enterprise development caused for whatever reason must be resolved from the roots. Local governments are also important participants in economic activities and they also face the issue of incentives, therefore, at present, both political and economic incentives need to be further strengthened.

The third deep-seated problem is that the state-owned economy urgently needs to be repositioned through reform. The current SOEs are completely different from those decades ago. Of the current SOEs, some are more traditional enterprises, such as Gree Electric Appliances, Inc of Zhuhai, Conch Cement and Northeast General Pharmaceutical Factory; some of them are ultralarge enterprises, such as the Baoshan Iron and Steel Group and Wuhan Iron and Steel Plant. Besides, there are also local government financing platforms that have sprung up in recent years. These platform companies do not necessarily operate specific industries, their main function is investment and financing, and the ultimate investment targets are local related infrastructure projects. These enterprises occupy valuable resources to a considerable extent. However, their investment efficiency remains to be seen. The state-owned economy in the new era must be repositioned. We need to answer theoretically why we need a state-owned economy, what is the difference between the orientation of a state-owned economy and a private economy, and based on this to deepen reform.

Facing these medium and long-term problems, we must seek a breakthrough from further deepening reform. Streamlining government and delegating authority, power, tax cuts and SOE reform are undoubtedly very important, and have attracted much attention from all walks of life. What is particularly worth emphasising is that the political and economic incentives for local government to develop the economy needs urgent strengthening. Moreover, our current understanding of this is far from being in place. Without local government incentives, many of the policies of central government are difficult to implement, and for enterprise development, including the private sector, many of the problems we face cannot be resolved efficiently. Economic operations are very complex and many of the problems cannot be solved by simple "streamlining" and "delegating". Many problems that enterprises are facing, from labour and employment to multiple market access, cannot be solved overnight in the short term even if the reform is in place. Even in developed countries the establishment and development of enterprises faces heavy supervision and government permits. At present, what is most needed is that local governments who have a direct relationship with the enterprises should stand up for the perspective of enterprises, actively help them establish and develop, solve and overcome the problems of system and mechanism in their development, and explore practical long-term solutions.

However, deepening reform and solving long-term problems, although the benefits are far-reaching, can never be achieved overnight. Comparatively, what should be promoted most in China's economic field, and what can achieve remarkable results in the short term, is financial reform.

The "Crux[1]" of Stabilising the Economy in the Short Term is to Stabilise Finance

We must realise that the main problem affecting China's current economic operations are neither exports nor consumption nor enterprise enthusiasm to invest; the most direct problem, in the short term, is a financial problem.

At present, exports account for only about 15% of China's GDP, and exports to the US account for only 3.5% of GDP, if the added value of exports to the US really coming from China itself is calculated, it is only about 2%, therefore we can say that the direct impact of Sino-US trade friction is only 2% of China's GDP. In the short term, the decline in consumption is mainly due to the decline in automobile sales, and the main reason for this is that consumers expect tax cuts in 2019 and they choose to wait to buy with cash in hand. Generally speaking, consumption is stable. In respect of the issue of investment, the main bottleneck is limited financing which, in the field of infrastructure, is particularly prominent. Financing in this area mainly comes from bank credit and bond issuance. In 2018, bank credit was tightened, while the issuance of local government special bonds was slow, consequrntly the overall contraction of the financial system directly affected the infrastructure investment of local governments.

In fact, with the rapid growth of China's financial system, the deep integration of industry and finance, and the continuous improvement of asset securitisation, the impact of finance on the economy has increased day by day. At present, the proportion of China's financial assets to GDP has reached 400%, that is to say, the financial assets have reached four times GDP. But six years ago, this proportion was only 300% and 10 years ago less than 200%. It is precisely because the volume of financial assets is very different from before, that financial market fluctuation has become an important reason for economic fluctuations, which was clearly reflected in the market during 2018. Besides, with the increasing integration of China's financial market into world finances, its resonance with overseas markets has increased, thereby exacerbating the frequency of domestic economic fluctuations.

Therefore, to solve the problem of an economic downturn, the most direct and effective focus in the short term is financial structure reform.

The "Crux" of Stabilising Finance is Major Financial Structure Adjustment

Generally, four things must be done well in a financial structure adjustment.

First, we must completely "strip" all the debt financing from all local government infrastructure construction, including both open and hidden debts, from the banking system and transfer them into the bond market. The main reason is that most of the investment projects of local governments are long-term with low returns, which is not in line with the business model of commercial banks and, more importantly, more authoritative institutions of commercial banks are needed to supervise and restrain local governments' investment and financing activities. To achieve this, the best strategy is to establish a national infrastructure investment company to uniformly manage the financing of infrastructure construction projects and to be fully responsible for the feasibility analysis, the specific issuance of bonds, the local government debt scale control and other affairs. According to relevant calculations, at present, the proportion of local debts, including hidden debts, to GDP, has reached 40% or even higher. Such a huge debt is mostly used to support local infrastructure projects and other long-term assets, resulting in the need for a long-term financing channel. According to our calculations, at present, about 15% of bank loans are used to make up the local hidden debts. If we can strip this part of debt from the banking system, it will be a major positive for the whole enterprise sector, especially private enterprises.

Second, financial institutions need to deleverage accurately and actively. It can be stipulated that all financial institutions write off reported bad debts regularly, for example, write off 1/3rd each year, and write off the whole amount over three years, thereby dealing with bad assets promptly, and effectively manage and control risks; to this end, financial institutions can be given relevant fiscal and tax policy support.

Third, it is necessary to focus on developing enterprise bond markets, and securities should become the main tool of direct financing for enterprises. Compared to the stock market, the bond market gives investors a relatively guaranteed return, it also has a stronger binding power on enterprises, and the requirements for corporate governance quality and information transparency are obviously lower. Under the present circumstances, China's legal system is not perfect and the quality of corporate governance quality is unsatisfactory, so bond financing should be the focus for development. Furthermore, the bond market should open up the exchange market, interbank market and OTC (over the counter) market, and while boosting the strength of institutional investors, it will attract ordinary investors from stock investment to bond investment.

Fourth, for the stock market, we urgently need to greatly strengthen the construction of the basic system of the stock market, especially the legal system, thoroughly strengthening the power of investigation, prosecution and judicial sentencing regarding stock market violations. At present, the greatest problem of the stock market is that corporate governance quality lacks an effective guarantee at institutional level, resulting in the emergence of a series of company violations, and the punishment is not effective. The branches of the securities regulatory system have only reached the provincial level, and have yet to reach cities and counties, but the bank and insurance regulatory system has formed a "province/city/county" tripartite framework. Security-related violations are often difficult to prosecute and punish accordingly. In terms of administrative punishment, the top fine of the CSRC is only Rmb600,000, while in terms of penal sentence, the current record is 13 years in prison. This punishment is far lower than that of the US and other developed countries where, for the latter, it is not uncommon to be sentenced to far more than 10 years, in some cases, the punishment can even be life imprisonment. Therefore, we must greatly strengthen the investigation, prosecution, sentencing and execution of stock market violations, strengthen the case handling ability of the Securities Crime Investigation Bureau of the Ministry of Public Security, and add professional securities courts and procuratorates to strengthen the regulatory capability of the securities system.

Taken in a multi-pronged manner, the above measures can solve both the symptoms and the root causes, so that China's economic growth potential can be more effectively mobilised. After two to three years' hard adjustment, China's economy is expected to return to a healthy growth trend.

How to Reform the Financial Supply Side?
The Pain Point is the Point for Reform

With the continuous advancement of the supply-side structural reform of the real economy, at present an increasingly prominent major task on the agenda of China's economic reform is structural reform of the financial supply side. The point of financial supply-side reform, in the final analysis, is to change the way the financial system provides financing for the real economy. Its importance is beyond doubt because the financial supply side directly affects the structural adjustment of the real economy, including the entry of new enterprises and the exit of old enterprises with overcapacity. Then, what is the focus of the financial supply-side structural reform? Of course, we should start with the sore spot of the economic operation. Generally, there are six pain points in the current economy, and they are the points of reform.

Pain Point 1: How Infrastructure Construction is Financed

Currently, infrastructure construction investment has accounted for more than 1/5th of our country's total fixed assets investment, about 8% of total GDP. Infrastructure construction is an important growth point of China's economy in this round, at the same time, it is a breakthrough point to improve China's economy and people's quality of life. Why do I say so? At present, the stock of household appliances such as TV sets and refrigerators has gradually reached periodic saturation, and the growth of automobile consumption has slowed down but, of course, if urbanisation is further accelerated, these needs still have potential. However, at present, many factors restricting the improvement of household quality of life are no longer the stock of ordinary consumer goods or durable consumer goods, but the supply of public goods, including clean water, clean air, convenient public transportation and country parks. Generally speaking, the supply of these public products belongs in the infrastructure investment category, while financing such infrastructure is one of the biggest problems in China's economy.

At present, the main body of our country's infrastructure planning and construction is the local governments, and the pain point is very distinctive. They mainly raise funds through three channels: first, indirectly through banks' supply, namely, through many Public Private Partnership (PPP) projects; second, through issuing infrastructure investment bonds, where the total amount issued is approved by the central government, while each local government applies for an amount, comparatively they are not large in scale; third, through trusts and other non-bank financial institutions. None of the existing investment institutions can act as an effective restraint on local governments which are the main body of planning and investment. Therefore, local governments usually have a tendency toward overinvestment in infrastructure and disorderly financing, causing the problem of high and opaque local government debt. At present, the solution to this problem mainly relies on the higher authorities supervising things through "pulling" and the method of so-called "cutting with one knife" (inflexibility), leading to both overinvestment and underinvestment in infrastructure, including zero real growth in infrastructure investment in 2018, which dragged down GDP growth by at least 0.2%. This is the first big pain point of China's current economy.

The reform to resolve the pain point of infrastructure construction has a very clear direction, namely, to form a relatively unified organisation dedicated to financing local governments infrastructure investment, and this organisation must effectively hedge against local government actions. This financing agency must carry out effective management of local government debt and their infrastructure projects, and the most ideal method is to transform the existing China Development Bank, putting it fully in charge of most local project evaluation, financing and recovery. However, at present, the capital scale and business ability of the China Development Bank is not up to this requirement therefore it is necessary to design a new supply mechanism, for example, to build one or several independent and comparable infrastructure development investment institutions similar to the World Bank, with a clear mission to effectively manage the financing of local government infrastructure investment projects.

Pain Point 2: Bond Financing

Currently, the main financing channel of China's economy is still through commercial banks, however, as a very specialised financial institution, a bank has its limitations. The biggest feature of commercial banks is that the funds come from retail investors, and retail investors have great liquidity. This requires commercial banks to invest very carefully, and this requirement is very reasonable, so the bank investments we see are all implemented very carefully: between enterprises and local governments, they prefer to invest in local governments; between large and small enterprises, they prefer to invest in large ones; between short-term and long-term projects, they prefer to invest in short-term ones... and this is a natural defect in the way commercial banks operate. To solve this problem, the most important thing is to fully expand bond financing channels. In the US, Europe and other modern market economies, bonds are the biggest financing channel. By contrast, China's current bond financing scale still has development potential. At present, the main problem affecting bond financing is that it is concentrated in the interbank market, in 2018 this proportion accounted for about 87%, instead of facing individual investors directly. The bond market should be shifted directly from interbank trading to open trading, or handed over to a bond exchange to trade, or interbank bond trading should be fully opened up for individual investors. It would be fair to say that when the excitement of Chinese investors has shifted from the stock market to the bond market, the basic channels for China's direct financing will also have been opened up, capturing the most difficult fortress of financial supply-side structural reform.

Pain Point 3: The Basic Judicial System of the Stock Market

To do a good job in the stock market, we must build a solid foundation, similar to how Chinese football must lay a foundation in the form of youth football. The rule of law is the basis for the good operation of the stock market. At present, the legal framework of China's stock market is very imperfect, the China Securities Regulatory Commission (CSRC) is mainly responsible for monitoring and handling violations. However, the power of the CSRC is limited and generally the CSRC has no subordinate institutions in prefectural-level cities therefore a large number of rule violations fail to be dealt with. More fundamentally, in essence, the CSRC is a supervisory body rather than a law enforcement agency, which lacks coercive force. Besides, its ability to impose fines is extremely limited to a maximum of only Rmb600,000![2] Under such circumstances, the compliance of China's stock market is worrying, all kinds of counterfeiting, insider trading and illegal operations occur frequently, and the perpetrators cannot be effectively punished. Nowadays, countries with better stock market operation in the world have extremely strict legal fundamentals, for example, in the rule of law storm in the stock market in the 1980s, the US managed to largely eliminate various US stock violations. China now not only needs to set up securities courts in Shanghai or Shenzhen, but also needs the securities procuratorate and even the securities investigation bureau of the public security department to achieve comprehensive transregional supervision of listed companies, and there is an urgent need to seriously grasp several typical cases as a warning to all stock market participants.

Pain Point 4: Angel Investment

China currently has a large number of private equity funds and investors are very enthusiastic about private equity investment. However, venture capital investment and angel investment are quite scarce, accounting for only about 1/10th of total private equity funds, but at the beginning, start-ups in particular lack financing and guidance. Corresponding policies should be introduced in this regard, for example, the amount of losses that can be deducted from the profits so as to reduce the tax burden on venture investors. To use another example, angel investment profits can be spread over several years for tax purposes, allowing this kind of venture capital investment to be issued to society to seek long-term investors thereby promoting the development of innovative Chinese enterprises.

Pain Point 5: Bankruptcy Mechanism

The metabolism of the real economy depends to a great extent on the metabolism of financial assets, and a series of non-performing assets must be resolved. At present, a source of good news in China is the healthy situation regarding China's labour force, unemployment is not a serious problem. Therefore, the main obstacle to exiting from the real economy is financial restructuring, so we should particularly encourage bankruptcy reorganisation led by banks and other financial institutions, breaking the interest barriers of local governments and promoting the metabolism of the real economy in return through the disposal of bad financial debts.

Pain Point 6: Manufacturing Profits are Relatively Low, Financial Support is Insufficient

The manufacturing industry not only has a low rate of return but also finds it difficult to identify risks therefore financial resources are often willing to flow into real estate and infrastructure projects led by local governments rather than manufacturing, and this is a long-standing problem. Financial reform and innovation must be carried out to solve this problem. An entry point is to transform the current trust industry, rather than forcing commercial banks to act recklessly by pushing them to allocate a certain proportion or scale of their lending to the manufacturing sector. Compared with banks, trust companies have a more flexible investment mechanism, including long-term ownership of some manufacturing enterprises. At present, the biggest problem for the trust industry is that it cannot issue long-term bonds in regard of funds, and its capital resources and issuance channels are relatively narrow. In terms of capital, if we can liberalise debt issuance, and at the same time open up equity investment in assets, the real economy will be better served by the trust industry. We should take equipment manufacturing in the manufacturing industry as a breakthrough to carry out a pilot, large-scale reform of the trust industry.

At present, the financial system has many difficult problems which are also very prominent. The financial supply-side structural reform, to which a slight move in one part may affect the whole situation, has become an important task of China's economic reform. Once a breakthrough can be achieved, it will promote the supply-side structural reform of China's real economy.

Local Government Financing Must Be Cut Out of the Banking System

Currently, what are the most important factors that affect the future trend of China's economy?

At present, what everyone talks about little or even ignores are the problems of China's economy itself, the most important one being the problem of financing China's financial system and local public finance. To me, this may be the most critical factor affecting the future trend of China's economy.

The Crux of the Financial Problem Lies in Local Governments Occupying Financial Resources

What is wrong with China's financial system? From the current circumstances, poor monetary transmission means there is obviously a hidden danger that liquidity cannot be smoothly injected into the real economy.

In 2018, one distinctive manifestation was that large numbers of listed companies did not get loans, so shareholders needed to pledge their equity for financing. The data of the China Securities Depository and Clearing Company (CSDC) showed that until 30 November 2018, the number of pledged shares in the A-share market was 641.437 billion, accounting for about 10% of the total share capital, the total market value of pledged shares was Rmb4.53 trillion. Compared with earlier months, the number of pledged equities has increased recently but the market value has decreased, the reason being that the stock price continues to fall. When the stock market falls, the value of the pledge decreases and the financing channels such as bank/securities companies require major shareholders of listed companies to replenish their deposit or collateral. If the stock price falls below the warning line, they are even forced to close their positions. Although this tests the cash flow of the shareholders, it obviously puts pressure on the stability and market value of listed companies, and leads to further volatility of stock prices, which may form a negative cycle.

If this is the case for listed companies with convenient financing, it is not surprising that the longstanding problem of difficult and expensive loans of a large number of private, particularly small and medium-sized, enterprises has been further aggravated.

Why is it difficult for enterprises to acquire finance? In 2018, what was denounced most by the capital market and even the whole of society was that the regulatory authorities deleveraged in a rigidly uniform way. This simple and crude deleveraging policy is like starving cancer cells to lose weight, the consequence is that the body's own immune system decreases significantly while the growth of cancer cells is ultimately irresistible, and the end result is the deterioration of the overall health level. This is definitely not a good way to treat cancer, a precise and targeted treatment is the foundation of cancer treatment. The fundamental problem of China's economic and financial system today is that a large number of low-quality financial assets must be removed, similar to cancer cells, reducing loans and controlling the total amount of social financing is by no means a permanent solution. Targeted therapy is needed to solve the root of the problem.

If a large number of enterprises lack financing, what is the crux of this problem?

To get to the root of the matter, we must understand that the fundamental problem is the institutional problem of China's finance and public finance. At present, China's financial system is, in fact, dominated by bank credit. However, banks are willing to invest in projects with low risk, guaranteed returns, high interest rates and large single loan amounts, and these are precisely the type of loans related to government. A lot of bank loans are local government related SOE loans and the end users of these loans are local governments. Under China's political system, local governments have no ability to finance independently – in essence, they are wholly-owned subsidiaries of the central government. The bank system knows very clearly that although the loans are granted to local SOEs, they are actually used by the local governments who have an obligation to repay, and local governments will not go bankrupt (once a problem occurs, the central government has to compensate), therefore there is no default risk. Besides, local governments often seek loans regardless of cost and these are often short term because the local officials' time in office is usually no more than five years. Under such circumstances, the main target of local officials is to ensure local economic growth and financial stability in the short term, therefore they do not hesitate to rely on short-term, high-cost debt to expand investments or borrow more money to repay old debts.

How much debt do local governments have? According to Finance Ministry published data, by the end of 2018, direct local government debt was about Rmb18.4 trillion. As well as this debt, they have a large amount of hidden debt, mostly accumulated by local governments bypassing higher-level government supervision, and through various borrowing channels. Regarding the scale of hidden local government debt, estimates from research institutions differ between Rmb9 trillion to Rmb47 trillion with the consensus beingf around Rmb30 trillion. This Rmb30 trillion debt ultimately stems from the banking system. The bank loans are mainly medium and short-term loans. By our calculation, a 5-year loan of Rmb30trillion has to be recycled every five years, comprising about Rmb6 trillion of bank loans annually. However, the annual scale of new loans in the banking system is about Rmb13.5 trillion to Rmb14 trillion which, together with the recovery of the transfer refinancing, adds up to about Rmb25 trillion, or a total of Rmb40 trillion. This means that the maintenance of local government implicit debt accounts for 15% percent of bank loan resources every year. For banks, lending to local government affiliated institutions and enterprises is a very simple way of lending with a low transaction cost. However, this has also led to a squeeze on resources, therefore enterprises, especially small and medium-sized enterprises, have the problem of difficult and expensive financing.

"Major Surgery" Resolves Financing Difficulties and Improves Leverage Transparency

Then, how should we solve this problem? I think China's financial and public finance system needs major surgery. There are two goals for this surgery. First, cut the implicit debt of local governments out of the banking system. We must not allow financing of local governments to squeeze out and occupy valuable bank loan resources. Second, we must fundamentally and effectively, working with both administrative and market means, manage the lending behaviour of local governments.

The key for this "major surgery" is to set up a national infrastructure investment company, which can consult the operation of the World Bank and other international development institutions. On the one hand, under the guarantee of the central government, make large-scale, low-cost financing from the capital market. At present, the annualised rate of 10-year debt is about 3.5%, much lower than the interest rate that local governments raise from the market. On the other hand, and more importantly, this company can comprehensively, professionally and uniformly manage all infrastructure project financing of local governments, in other words, local government financing of infrastructure projects must be made via this company. This infrastructure investment company can transfer functional personnel from the National Development and

Reform Commission (NDRC), the Ministry of Finance, the National Audit Administration and other related departments to carry out its operation, thereby professionally, comprehensively and effectively auditing the financial situation of local governments, estimate the actual scale of fixed assets, assess their repayment ability and, on this basis, form an overall and long-term judgment. At present, the China Development Bank has partially played this role, however, the scale of the CDB has ranked first among the world's development finance institutions. It is undertaking the important task of various channels of development finance, including financing of Belt and Road Initiative (BRI) projects, so it is difficult for it to focus on the supervision and management of domestic local government financing.

In this way, local government financing costs can be greatly reduced. Calculated according to the scale of an implicit debt of Rmb30 trillion at a market interest rate of 7% separately financed by local governments, and assuming that the overall financing cost of the infrastructure investment company is 3.5%, it can save the government Rmb1 trillion of financing costs every year. More importantly, suc a scenario enables local government infrastructure investment to be uniformly managed and restricted, thereby achieving long-term, stable and efficient growth.

If this surgery is successful, the bank's loan resources will be fully released, and the financing situation of the whole industry will experience large-scale improvement while the financing pressure of listed companies will be greatly eased. The problem of difficult and expensive financing for small and medium-sized enterprises will also be solved, hereafter enabling China's capital market to embark on a relatively healthy and sustainable development road.

Besides, through this operation, the leverage of China's economy will be more transparent. The leverage of China's economy is not a simple "high or low" problem but a problem of quality and transparency. In fact, the leverage of China's economy itself is not high, in 2018 the debt rate of non-financial departments was about 2.6 times GDP, close to the US, but lower than Japan's 3.6 times, yet China's national savings rate is more than double that of the US and 1.5 times that of Japan.

In short, the current most important factor affecting the future trend of the economy is China's economic system itself, especially the institutional problem in the financial field, which needs structural adjustment, and the key to it is a "major surgery" for China's finance.

Need for Targeted Therapy with Loose Mobility on Structural Deleveraging

In the first half of 2018, many considered that China's economy was weak on the demand side and that therefore we needed certain policies to stimulate steady growth.

I disagree with this judgement. My viewpoint is that China's macroeconomy is still recovering, the driving force of spontaneous economic growth is continuing to recover, and that the core indicators show that the investment growth rate of the private economy rebounded to about 8% in the first half of 2018 from 4% in the same period in 2017. At the same time, the profits of the whole real economy rebounded steadily and economic resilience and sustainability are increasing.

Some macroeconomic fantasies are mainly brought about by the rigidly uniform policy of deleveraging, consequently all economic activities that rely heavily on external financing have dropped significantly, banks' off-balance-sheet business and other activities, including the business scale of the so called "shadow banks", decreased Rmb2.1 trillion compared to the same period in 2017, and this directly led to a decline in the growth rate of infrastructure investment to 9% in the first half of 2018 from 19% in the same period of 2017.

More importantly, the rigidly uniform deleveraging measures led to a series of chain reactions in the capital market, including many shareholders of listed companies often obtaining financing by means of stock pledges, however, the continuous decline of share prices triggered a liquidity crisis; besides, at present, bond issuance is difficult in many cases and even if they are issued, they fall below the issue price. In mid 2018, the overall financial market was tense and investor sentiment was unstable.

It should be said that the main factor affecting the economic trend in the first half of 2018 was not the decline in the vitality of China's economy itself but on the policy side, implementation of structural deleveraging policy has not been effective and accurate.

Need To Revisit Understanding of the Essence of Structural Deleveraging

At present, the rigid and uniform deleveraging method is unreasonable. In the financial field, without external intervention, non-performing assets are often more likely to be granted loans than normal assets because creditors are often reluctant to expose problems but like to repay old debts with new debts and repay old loans with new loans. Therefore, in the absence of accurate, targeted therapy, what this rigidly uniform method, relying on reducing loans and deleveraging, brings about is an overall financial tightness, rather than a real decline in leverage.

In order to deleverage structurally, we must revisit our understanding of two problems.

Firstly, the leverage of China's economy is not high on the whole but the problem is that the structure is unreasonable. It is generally believed that China's economic debt is equivalent to about 260% of GDP. This overall leverage is basically consistent with that of the US and many other developed economies and, compared with the overall leverage of 350% in Japan, it is obviously very low.

The reasonable leverage for an economy is decided by two factors. One is the economy's own national savings rate. If the rate is very high, such as in China or Japan, where their savings rate is as high as 35%, then naturally there will be a lot of savings to find the investment direction, therefore the leverage will naturally be higher.

Second, it depends on the financing structure of the economy. If the equity financing market foundation in the economy is not solid, as is the case with the current Chinese economy, or the legal basis including the equity market is not perfect, for example, there is no special securities procuratorate or securities court, under such circumstances, savers' funds either bypass intermediaries from informal channels to invest in enterprises or families, or are directly converted into investment in the form of bonds or bank loans because, compared to equity financing, bonds and bank loans have stronger constraints on the risk of default and bankruptcy while it is difficult for equity financing to have such explicit provisions, and the fund users of equity financing may not pay dividends to shareholders indefinitely. In China, on the premise that it is difficult to vigorously develop the stock market, given the same scale of national savings, the leverage will certainly be higher.

Therefore, it should be said that the leverage of China's economy in 2018 was not high at about 260%. The problem is that the leverage structure of China's economy is unreasonable. On the one hand, local debt is too high in relation to central debt while local debt lacks an overall restraint mechanism. It is difficult for investors to grasp the quality of local debt. This implies financial risks. On the other hand, the debt of enterprises is relatively highand needs adjustment. The main problem of high corporate debt is reflected in a large amount of low-quality debt not having been adjusted on a timely basis.

According to my analysis, "zombie" enterprises account t for 7% to 10% of China's industrial enterprises above a designated size. Even if that calculation is 5%, that means there are nearly Rmb6 trillion of non-performing assets that need to be restructured. However, the speed at which the financial system disposes of non-performing assets is not satisfactory. According to the financial statement data of 16 listed banks, although at present the disposal of non-performing loans has accelerated, the accumulation rate of new non-performing loans is accelerating. By offsetting the two, the balance of non-performing loans increased by nearly Rmb50 billion in 2017. In the first quarter of 2018, the non-performing loan ratio of banks rose by 0.01% - 1.75%. At the current rate of restructuring, it will take at least five years to clear up the Rmb6 trillion of non-performing assets.

The second understanding is that the crux of structural deleveraging is accurately eliminating non-performing assets. According to the above analysis, leverage itself is not a problem, the problem is to eliminate bad debts through precise deleveraging.

Three Essentials of Accurately Implementing Structural Deleveraging

Based on the above analysis, we can draw three policy predictions.

First, relatively loose liquidity must be maintained in the process of structural deleveraging. Structural deleveraging itself can easily cause panic in the overall financial market because this means that some non-performing assets will be disposed of, which often causes a chain reaction, leading to good enterprises also being suspected of becoming problem enterprises; at the same time, the disposal process of non-performing assets also leads to the shrinkage of assets invested in problem enterprises by relevant good enterprises.

Second, accurately eliminate a batch of non-performing assets. At present, the provision for non-performing assets of China's major financial institutions, especially the five state-owned banks, is sufficient, generally more than 150%, however, these provisions are not used to resolve non-performing assets. The approach for some time to come can be that the regulatory authorities require these major financial institutions to dispose of considerable non-performing assets within a certain period of time. For example, each large state-owned bank could dispose of 500 non performing loans with a total scale of more than Rmb50 billion within half a year. These disposals do not turn non-performing loans back into normal loans in the form of new loans, but actual reorganisation or bankruptcy. The China Bank and Insurance Regulatory Commission (CBIRC) can directly assess the amount of non-performing loans handled by the banks, flexibly handling the loan assessment history of relevant bank staff so as to help reduce the burden of history, then carry on light and speedy asset restructuring. At the same time, it is suggested that the vicious circle of mutual insurance between enterprises should be broken, in principle, to eliminate the mutual insurance treaty on non-performing loans in the history of commercial banks, so as to get rid of the stumbling block of asset restructuring. Through this large-scale removal of dead wood in China's economy, the quality of leverage will be greatly improved.

Third, merge some local debts into central debts. Local governments generally do not borrow directly because the terms of office of local officials are generally about three years so their natural mentality is to borrow without concern for the repayment term. Under China's current political system, a better way is for the Ministry of Finance to establish a unified infrastructure investment fund, its role being similar to that of the World Bank. This fund can cooperate with local government to invest in local infrastructure projects with all funds needed for local infrastructure construction being uniformly borrowed by this fund. In this way, we can monitor local government activity and make all local debts more transparent while credit ratings can also be unified.

At present, central government debt only accounts for 15% of GDP, however, local debt, including local government-related debt, accounts for more than 30% of GDP; this is a very unreasonable structure. Once the local debt system is unified, all kinds of local government investments in infrastructure projects can mainly be completed by debt uniformly issued by the central government, and the credit level of related bonds will increase significantly while the interest rate will fall.

We have reason to believe that once the above three adjustments are in place, the task of China's structural deleveraging will be advanced in an orderly manner, domestic and foreign investors' expectations of China's macroeconomy can be stabilise relatively quickly, and the capital market can also rebound. In the future, the direction and precision of China's structural deleveraging will also be significantly improved, and China's macroeconomic problems and the relative downturn in the capital market are expected to be alleviated.

Probing the Causes of China's Real Estate Bubble

A Case Study from the 'Cosmic Centre'

With the rise in house prices, the saying "Tsinghua education is far less valuable than Tsinghua school district housing" has become a hot topic of discussion for netizens. Some families have struggled for a long time and finally sent their children to Tsinghua University only to experience that after graduation their children cannot afford a school district home near Tsinghua.

This problem is not difficult to explain. I will analyse it at the end of this paper but first let me analyse why house prices near Tsinghua University are so high – this is a more interesting example of the real estate bubble in China that has yet to be unearthed in detail.

Wudaokou 'Cosmic Centre'

Outside the east gate of Tsinghua University, when I first studied there in the early 1980s, it was still a piece of farmland, with only a small path leading to the university. Outside the path was Shuangqing Road, which could only accommodate two cars passing side by side but it connected to Qinghe Woollen Mill, a typical example of the SOE reform at the time.

The east gate of Tsinghua University was very desolate at that time. After four o'clock every afternoon (especially in winter), like many of my classmates, I would start from the east gate and run to the railway line at Wudaokou, then turn back, passing the abandoned thermal power plant near the north gate and return to Tsinghua, the whole journey being about five kilometres. At that time, Tsinghua students studied hard and they also paid special attention to sports. Everyone vied with each other in doing physical exercise, hoping to get good results in the standard test of a 1,500-metre run.

Things change with the passage of time. Now the land has completely changed, being broadly known as Wudaokou, as well as "Cosmic Centre".

50,000 vs 100,000: Supported by the High-Quality School District, House Prices Have Double

The high house prices in this area are indeed related to it being a school district. Close to Tsinghua University, one stop west on the underground train takes you to the east gate of Peking University where there are high-quality schools like the Tsinghua University Affiliated Primary School, the Peking University Affiliated Primary School, the Zhongguancun No.1 Primary School, the Zhongguancun Middle School, as well as the No. 101 Middle School and the Tsinghua University Affiliated Middle School which are a little farther.

To what extent can a school district explain high house prices? Here is a very good comparison.

Because the houses in this area belong to school district housing, in 2017 property prices were generally close to or even more than Rmb100,000 per sqm. For example, in Wudaokou and south of Chengfu Road, there is the Shuiqing Muhua community housing estate, of which the current building age is about 15 years where house prices have been close to Rmb100,000 per sqm.

However, one road away, the price for another apartment located closer to Tsinghua University (also with 70-year property rights) has only recently risen to Rmb50,000 per sqm, the reason being that until now that none of the apartment owners were allowed to "settle down for household registration", that is to say, they cannot enjoy school district treatment. The reason for this apartment not being eligible for household registration is that it has not been able to join the residents' committee, so the Zhongguancun police station would not agree to undertake the household registrations for them. The reason for them being unable to join the Residents' Committee is that the Owners' Committee could not be established because the owners come from all over the world and are too scattered, moreover, nearby are five-star hotels and many of their facilities are connected to this apartment building, so the circumstances are rather complicated. I often said to young colleagues of mine that they should consider buying property there before the household registration issue is settled and the house price is still low, because the issue will be resolved eventually, and the house price will certainly rise to a level equivalent to that of the surrounding communities.

Prioritising GDP Gives Rise To Conflicts Between Residential Housing and Commercial Real Estate

Wudaokou has been jokingly nicknamed the "Cosmic Centre" by Tsinghua students because the area is very busy with a lot of people coming and going, and the same is true on weekends and holidays. Many young entrepreneurs, young students and professionals are gathered here. However, on this five-square-kilometre plot of land, in the first 20 years of the 21st century most of the new buildings built here were mainly office buildings, while residential buildings were extremely rare.

The office buildings include the Tsinghua Science and Technology Park of about 500,000 square metres. It consists of seven or eight high-rise buildings with about 25 floors, including the one that the government specially granted land to Google to build, and the Weisheng Building, which was specially granted to Taiwan Weisheng Electronics to build themselves. In addition, there are a large number of new office buildings built by the Academy of Sciences.

In sharp contrast to commercial real estate, there are only three or four new residential buildings, including the Shuiqing Muhua community housing estate I mentioned just now with a floor area of less than 100,000 square metres. Another larger building is Huaqing Jiayuan built 15 years ago with a floor area of about 150,000 square metres. Ren Zhiqiang, the CEO of Huayuan Property should be thanked for this. Speaking frankly, looking at it from today's perspective, the construction standard, quality and design level of Huaqing Jiayuan were very rough. Besides, there is Tangning ONE built by Longhu Real Estate in 2011, which is a high-grade apartment building where the average price is about Rmb150,000 per sqm. The above-mentioned apartment is one that cannot be settled for household registration, its total floor area is about 50,000 square metres and its name originates from the fact that it is part of the supporting facilities for the Tsinghua Science and Technology Park. Compared with the millions of square metres of commercial real estate, the supply of residential property can be counted on the fingers of one hand.

The direct consequence of this is that the supply of residential real estate is in seriously short supply and its price is rising rapidly. Taking Huaqing Jiayuan, which Ren Zhiqiang was proud of, as an example, its opening unit price was about Rmb3,000, while in 2017 it had exceeded Rmb120,000. The teachers, who were a little bolder and had some spare money and bought a house at the time, have now become multimillionaires. Most of these teachers have moved out of Huaqing Jiayuan because the place has become popular for rentals to foreign students, particularly South Korean students. In addition to young students, with a lot of people coming and going, it is very noisy and therefore not suitable for families. Ren Zhiqiang often said that as a property developer he had created huge wealth for house buyers while he himself did not get much. His words are reliable at least in respect of the "Cosmic Centre" in Wudaokou.

However, the more important question is why the Beijing municipality, or even the Haidian district government, knows that the house prices in Wudaokou are so high but are not willing to grant more residential land there? The reason lies in GDP. Because in Wudaokou providing office buildings, science and technology parks, building high-rise buildings for Google and for Taiwan Weisheng Electronics can directly boost GDP. Therefore, large numbers of company headquarters are concentrated in Wudaokou today, including companies such as Sohu, Netease and Google, let alone the National Examination Centre, as well as the China Education Network, provider of the earliest internet information services for colleges and universities. This has indeed led to the continuous growth of GDP in Wudaokou which is also known as a high-tech centre but the direct consequence is that local house prices remain high and many high-tech personnel working in Wudaokou and teachers from Tsinghua University and Beijing University must buy houses outside the district.

The Cases of Harvard and Stanford

At this point, we might as well make a detour, leave Wudaokou temporarily but take a look at the real estate near Harvard University and Stanford University.

In the past hundred years, America's Harvard University has become a model of higher education that drives the continuous development of the surrounding economy. However, the land around Harvard University is mainly owned by residents. Except for the tiny Harvard Yard, Harvard University has no main gate. The university and the city are completely integrated. Then, how does Harvard University meet its rising housing demand?

The university has already set up its own real estate company, continuously purchasing the land and houses of surrounding residents in the market. But this is not enough because without the planning permission of Cambridge Town where the university is situated, these residential houses cannot be converted to office use. Therefore, Harvard University needs to take a stand against the planning commission, which is trying to transform some residential houses into office buildings, which often strains the relationship between Harvard University and the Cambridge Town planning commission.

In addition, the reconstruction of the university's existing buildings will also experience intervention by the Cambridge Town planning commission, which is elected by the residents. The planning commission often considers the interests of existing residents rather than the overall development of the city, thereby leading to many absurd stories. For instance, in 2010, when the university was renovating an office building, the architect designed two completely symmetrical buildings on either side of Cambridge Road – now they have become the Asia Centre and Fairbank Centre for Chinese Studies, and the Department of Government of Harvard University – and an underground passage was also designed to connect the two buildings without damaging the street view. However, the planning commission disagreed with the building of the underground passage, despite the fact that it would not affect the view at all. It is said that one planning commission member, whose child was rejected by Harvard University and therefore felt very annoyed, objected to the idea. Although Harvard University has become increasingly famous in the era of globalisation, it is difficult to expand nearby. It is also difficult for Cambridge Town's GDP to grow, not least because of Harvard University.

It was because of the long-term uncertainty of its relationship with Cambridge Town, before the outbreak of the global financial crisis, that Larry Summers, the president of Harvard University, decided to bypass Cambridge Town and to develop in the small town of Austin across the Charles River because Austin had a lot of vacant land and, at the time, the Harvard sports ground as well as the Harvard Business School were located there. But due to the outbreak of the financial crisis, this development planning was delayed for ten years.

Stanford is much luckier than Harvard in this regard. Stanford has indeed promoted the development of high-tech industry in Silicon Valley, resulting in a huge rise in the value of the surrounding land. Fortunately, the Stanford campus used to be a huge rural area. The university is not worried about land. In response to high house prices, the university took part of its own land and developed it into housing with large property rights, while small property rights were transferred to professors. According to regulations, these houses can only be sold to teachers at Stanford University. This partly solves the development problems experienced by Stanford University brought about by high house prices in Silicon Valley.

Tsinghua University and Peking University are partly imitating this model. Tsinghua bought some land in the nearby Qinghe area and built houses with restricted leases and sold them to its staff. Like Stanford, they can only be transferred to people on campus. This also partly hedged the rising house prices in Wudaokou.

The Institutional Dilemma and Rural Dilemma of Residential Land Supply

It is not that there is no land near Wudaokou, but it is difficult to get planning permission for development.

The A-class land here is owned by Dongsheng Township. It is somewhat unexpected that in the middle of Wudaokou with such high house prices, the land has been reserved for a township, but not been incorporated into urban planning. Until now the Dongsheng Township has kept its own health centre and offices. There the buildings are all low-rise with about five floors, which should have been developed and utilised by increasing the plot ratio through land replacement. However, if the land of a township is to be changed into urban land, the township government itself cannot directly derive much benefit, so this kind of transaction is difficult to carry out.

In addition, there are many institutions near Wudaokou, including Tsinghua University and the Chinese Academy of Sciences, who have a lot of land of their own. However, this is government land which is impossible to develop for residential purposes. For example, the buildings of the Chinese Academy of Sciences have been continuously renovated in recent years, changing from five-storey to 15-storey buildings but, one after another, they have been designated as office buildings which cannot be re-zoned as residential land. The Tsinghua campus occupies nearly 400 hectares of land, being one of the largest universities in China without having another campus. The Tsinghua campus has large numbers of low four to five-storey residential buildings and dormitories. These buildings are also difficult to transform into higher buildings, such as houses with seven or eight floors, because it is difficult for the existing residents to relocate and, more importantly, Tsinghua University has absolutewly no right to dispose of its own land.

This creates a dilemma, namely, that although house prices are high, it is difficult for land to be allocated for residential construction and it is difficult to provide solutions on the supply side. This is probably a common problem in major cities in China, especially in Beijing.

Why is it Difficult for Tsinghua Graduates to Afford Tsinghua School District Housing?

Finally, I will analyse why house prices in Wudaokou school district are so high, far far out of reach financially of a talented Tsinghua University graduate.

First, one of the goals for parents sending their children to study at Tsinghua University is to feel a sense of achievement in life, and this sense of achievement often comes from non-economic factors, including personal happiness and social recognition. Therefore, even if the salary of graduates is not high, parents still expect their children to go to famous universities.

Second, in terms of the economy, the income of a university graduate is rising, so it is difficult to measure economic income in the short term. In the long run, the human capital premium conferred by a Tsinghua degree should be quite high.

More importantly, the high house prices near Wudaokou are an investment phenomenon, and are not as daunting as ordinary expensive consumer goods. As long as investors expect house prices to continue to rise in the future, someone will continue to enter the market. This should explain the problem that high house prices and higher education are difficult to correlate to the relatively high income of talented students.

Chapter 3

The Internet and the New Economy

Cnsumption Integrated With Production: China's Internet Economic Model is Just Getting Started

The War at the West Gate of Tsinghua University: Is Online "Eliminating" Offline?

At the end of August in Beijing, several autumn rain showers would make people feel chilly. At this time of the year, I would go to the bicycle street at the west gate of Tsinghua University and stroll around, getting my bicycle repaired to get ready for the new school term.

In recent years, the bustling street only has a few bicycle shops left. I made an enquiry to a shop owner, who said that the bicycle shops are fewer and fewer, one of the reasons being that many of the customers buy their bikes online and, more importantly, in recent years, the rise of bike sharing has greatly reduced the demand for self-owned bicycles. Not only are there fewer bicycle shops but the variety of options is also shrinking. A shop owner told me that the wholesalers can't see the demand and dare not purchase goods.

In sharp contrast to the decline of physical stores, online bicycle sales are abundant. I got some high-tech accessories, such as a stepless internal variable speed hub, and front and rear-linkage brakes from the internet. Carefully I fitted the parts to my very ordinary bike, which looked inferior but was wonderful to ride. Of course, finally, I had to rely on Xiao Li from Anhui, who was working at the west gate of Tsinghua University to help install and debug.

The decline of the bicycle shops at the west gate of Tsinghua University is one of the typical scenarios in which the internet economy is destroying offline stores and services but the question is: is China's internet economy just eliminating traditional retail and services? Let's look at the following three examples.

Three Cases Showing the Scope of Internet Platform Integration

First, ecommerce sells wine. All wine buyers know that they'd rather spend more money than buy fake wines to make themselves suffer. In order to prevent counterfeiting, each major winery has its own unique tricks. At present, one of the main advertising themes for three Chinese *baijiu* industry brands - Maotai, Wuliangye and Yanghe - is "combating counterfeiting", and the goal is to attract customers who are worried about counterfeit goods threatening their own brands. Customers know very well that the difference in taste between these *baijiu* liquor brands and the cheap genuine liquors produced by some other wineries is far less exaggerated than the price difference. However, in order to prevent counterfeiting, they all buy well-known brands to protect against counterfeiting.

An entrepreneur from Shandong purchased a batch of wineries around the Wuliangye Winery in Sichuan. He invited me to have a taste of his wine. Even after years of wine tasting, it was hard for me to tell the difference between his wine and Wuliangye. The production cost of his wineries is very low, only 1/20th of the retail price of Wuliangye, but how to get consumers to believe that his wine is good wine? A possible strategy is to find a retail ecommerce site with a good reputation for OEM sales. At present, some ecommerce companies have convinced buyers that self-operated stores do not sell counterfeit goods and that, moreover, the logistics and after-sales service are of an extremely high standard, therefore once the wine he produced is put on these ecommerce sites, consumers do not worry about the quality of the wine he produces. This is the secret of self-owned brands.

It can be inferred from this example that further down the line, ecommerce with a good reputation and logistics services will be involved in production, so as to supervise the production process of these wines and become the actual production controller of these wines and even the owner of the brands. In short, ecommerce integrated with manufacturing!

Second, supermarkets. The most traditional supermarket comes from the morning market in the free market, fresh and convenient, but its disadvantage is that supermarkets are labour-intensive for consumers, and it is also extremely hard for suppliers to supply to them. It requires suppliers to supply early in the morning, often causing problems due to insufficient or excessive supply. Now, Jingdong, Taobao and other ecommerce companies have established online supermarket brands, and their direct advantage is that consumers can buy fresh vegetables and food without leaving home.

The greater potential advantage of this business model is that the ecommerce companies can accurately grasp and analyse various data, such as consumer consumption characteristics, consumption habits and other data of a certain region. This big data is fed back to the production side, enabling manufacturers to accurately provide a variety of products and matching demand and consumption to the greatest possible extent. It can be imagined that this process will finally cause ecommerce to evolve into several super distribution platforms for vegetables and food. These distribution platforms will, in return, integrate many farms and plant growers, using big data to accurately guide their production. Ecommerce platforms not only provide various types of data, more importantly, they control the production process, because their own reputation and product quality are decided by accurate control of the production process. It can be imagined that the future of ecommerce will be direct or indirect ownership of a production base for a large number of commodities.

Third, take small commodities, for example. One of my hobbies is to refit motorcycles and bicycles by myself, such as to add indicators, a mobile phone bracket, power sockets and other accessories. My experience is that compared to offline purchases, buying these items online is generally more convenient. But the problem is that finding the items you really want on the Jingdong or Taobao platform is often a painful process. For example, when I search for a wire connector for a brake light, hundreds of search results appear. Although such search results can be further filtered, it is still very time-consuming and laborious. More importantly, the industries manufacturing these small commodities are often in a state of overcapacity, so the market is flooded with cheap and shoddy products . Because I can't see the quality of these accessories and worry about buying counterfeit or shoddy products, I'm in the habit of look from for higher-priced products first then working my way down to lower-priced products. As a consumer, this makes the process very laborious for me and I ternd to spend more money than necessary to guard against counterfeit products. I believe that in the next step, ecommerce will integrate thousands of producers, which will be organised into several highly reputable manufacturers with reliable quality and good service, while the data in the hands of ecommerce can, in turn, guide these enterprises with excess capacity to produce more accurately, therefore avoiding cheap competition.

The Future of Bicycle Stores at the West Gate of Tsinghua University

From analysis of the above three cases, we can generally deduce the future of the bicycle stores at the west gate of Tsinghua University. My prediction is that these physical stores will still exist and even expand in scale, and perhaps the craftsman Xiao Li's business will be more prosperous. However, unlike today, Xiao Li and his guys will probably be integrated into a shared bicycle platform. Although bike sharing is now in a period of "Warring States", a "First Emperor of Qin" who will certainly use bicycle users' data to customise the services we need, is coming. For example, to provide a personalised long-term bicycle rental service for teachers and students at Tsinghua University, which is easier than the commonly used system of renting by the hour, and if you have a problem, you can go to the west gate to repair or replace the bike for free or pay some money to upgrade various parts. Going further up the line, the bicycle platform will certainly integrate some bicycle manufacturers and accurately provide products.

This integration will not only happen at the west gate of Tsinghua University and in the bicycle industry but in more manufacturing and service fields, becoming the new model for China's internet economic development.

Consumption Integrated With Production: China's Internet Economy Model

With the development of e-commerce, the sharing economy and other digital platforms, the basic trend of China's internet economy has emerged: starting by exerting energy in consumption, gradually advancing from downstream to upstream. No matter if it is sharing bicycles, or an ecommerce platform, they all start from the consumption end, through grasping consumption information (including consumers' quality requirements), thereby integrating upstream manufacturers, making the quality, quantity and variety of their products better match the demand of downstream consumers, which will finally resolve the basic market economy problem of either overcapacity or "insufficient supply".

This important prospect for China's internet economic development is different from that of other countries. In the US and Germany, the internet development, or even the digital technology revolution in a broad sense, often begins from the production side. German industry 4.0 is largely a revolution in the field of production. However, China's digital technology development starts from the consumer side. Therefore, China's internet development model is very distinctive and is walking along a unique path. There is no doubt that China needs to learn from the advantages of German industry 4.0, for example, industrial production automation and the wide application of new materials and new energy. But it is also undeniable that there are also aspects of the China model that are difficult for Europe and the US to learn from because of the high population density of China's cities and its young consumer groups, as well as a large number of young engineers and innovative, well-educated young workers and entrepreneurs. This causes the development of China's internet not only to lead the new economic era, but also makes it highly innovative on a global scale.

To this end, China's traditional industries must make sufficient mental preparation. In the short term, we can directly observe that because it is extremely convenient for internet enterprises to secure financing because they are sought after by investors, they can use a lot of the cash they have in hand to merge and integrate the traditional real economy. And this is the logic of capital, behind it is the logic of efficiency, that is, that through this integration, the problem of overcapacity has been solved to a great extent, making demand and supply more matched, and making the production and distribution of the whole society more coordinated. This is a new trend for China's economy to lead the world economy in the future, so observers and policy makers of China's economy should pay a lot of attention to it. In fact, because China has a strong manufacturing base, once the consumer and production ends are fully connected in the internet era, China's economy will radiate new growth energy.

The Biggest Starting Point of "Internet+" Should Be to Promote Reform

In London's streets, foreign visitors often find a very strange phenomenon, namely, that there are many electric scooters with a special sign hanging on them. On the front of these scooters there is a glass panel attached with a London map. Riders of these scooters wear a special yellow jacket. After they ride for a while, they stop and begin to write something on the map.

What are they doing?

In fact, this is the local taxi driver applicants becoming familiar with the London map, addresses and road conditions. It is said that the tests for taxi drivers in London are the strictest in the world and applicants generally must pass multiple rounds of tests, therefore, they must be familiar with the condition of every street and even every shop, and be able to quickly answer the best route from point A to point B when asked.

It is so difficult, but why do so many people still want to take the tests for a taxi driver license in London?

This is because, once you have become a taxi driver in London, your life's work can be done. Although taking a taxi in London is very expensive, most people don't use taxis, but because the barriers to becoming a taxi driver in London are very high, taxi drivers have formed trade unions, so the income of taxi drivers is still very good.

What is this? This is the most intuitive illustration of a monopoly.

However, from the perspective of consumers, you will find that although the taxi drivers in London are very professional, they are not the most hospitable, in my experience, they sometimes have a bad temper, and it is not always easy to talk to them. More importantly,

London's taxi provides excessive service, because most passengers today do not need to take a taxi as large as the ones in London, neither do the taxi drivers need to know the details of every street. With the popularity of satnav today, this is not necessary, what passengers want is nothing more than a safe and comfortable basic service from point A to point B. Obviously, taxi drivers in London charge too much.

This situation has been known for many years. However, once a monopoly is formed, it is difficult to break it.

The situation of the taxi industry in Beijing and other parts of China is the same as in London in nature, the difference is that it is the government, not the taxi guild, that monopolises taxi supply. For the present taxi companies, many are owned by individual bosses or indirectly owned by local governments, and they control the licensing of these taxis.

The number of taxis in Beijing has hardly increased in the past few years, resulting in a serious shortage of taxi supply and a decline in service quality. Unlike London, taxi drivers in most parts of China are workers. They do not own the cars, and each month they must pay very high contract fees, therefore, they can only be forced to accept a rather low real income. This has resulted in a shortage of taxis, so the drivers work overtime, and the service attitude is poor. In the long term, today's taxi drivers are working at the cost of their health, those who have become ill from overwork may suffer from all kinds of chronic diseases in the near future, and society will eventually pay for these chronic diseases. In other words, the excess profits of local taxi companies are based on low-quality and insufficient service as well as the long-term health cost of taxi drivers paid for by society. This is obviously unreasonable.

The internet is changing all this. In London, Uber has emerged; in China, there emerged Didi taxi and Kuaidi taxis, Uber and other companies have all entered this market. This business model, in which individuals bring their own cars, the taxi software companies provide the basic service platform and drivers provide personal service, is having a huge impact on the taxi industry. The reform of the taxi industry that has been discussed by all parties over the years, is finally breaking the problem.

What does this case tell us?

It tells us that developing an internet platform, which is affordable and accessible to a broad group of people, provides a strong formula for success. It has a top-down power to promote social progress and it can achieve the effect that top-down reform or discussion among social elites failed to achieve for a long time in the past.

At present, "internet+" has been regarded as a sharp weapon of China's economic transformation. However, what I want to emphasise more is that "internet+" should become a sharp weapon for promoting reform. "Internet+" is a people's war, it will break down the interest groups opposed to reform one by one, and finally form the driving force of comprehensive reform. In the end, in concert with top-down reform, it will play a role which should not be underestimated in this round of reform.

It is Not "Autonomous Driving" But "Smart Driving" That Will Disrupt the Automobile Industry

On 7 March 2016, BMW held its *Next 100 Years* celebration; followed by the symbol of artificial intelligence (AI) AlphaGo successively beating a Korean Go superstar, and with giants such as Google and Apple showcasing their autonomous driving R&D. All these developments pose one big question: has the era of autonomous driving arrived? Is a new revolution brewing in the automotive industry which has a history of more than 100 years? I've been paying attention to auto products and the auto industry for a long time. I'd like to share some of my thoughts about the issue with you.

Autonomy is Still a Long Way Off

Why do I say so? First, we must understand that, in essence, autonomous driving is completely different from using AI to create a chess grandmaster. The essence of autonomous driving is a game between AI and people on the road, although the goal of the game is not "victory" but to avoid traffic accidents. The rules of chess are much simpler compared to traffic regulations, although traffic rulebooks only have dozens of pages, people don't rigidly follow the rules when driving vehicles; in reality the traffic rules are very complex.

For example, we often see cars not following the traffic rules but forcing their way into a line of cars. Theoretically, the aggrieved party can hit the car without any legal responsibility, however, because of the high cost of dealing with an accident, few people do so, therefore, when someone cuts in, the vast majority of drivers often just reluctantly give way.

On top of this, road conditions are constantly changing. For example, in an alleyway where two cars are at an impasse, who should give way? Under such circumstances, a normal driver will often make a quick and basically correct judgement, and good and bad drivers don't differ much in this basic judgement. However, it is not easy for machines to flexibly and naturally respond to this type of situation.

I can imagine, many years later there may be autonomous cars on the road but many people will consider self-driving car to be silly and a bit of a gimmick, and the majority will continue to drive human-operated cars. There are also legal issues. Owners of autonomous cars must be very careful to avoid possible traffic accidents, especially in China's road environment. A manned car will try its best, fighting with wits and courage, ultimately forcing the pilotless car to be overcautious so that it can only crawl along carefully all the way which will make its owner very annoyed.

The Era of Smart Driving Has Come

Smart driving and autonomous driving are different concepts, smart driving is broader. It means that machines help people to drive, as well as being a technology capable of completely replacing the driver under special circumstances.

The era of smart driving and autonomy has come. For example, now many cars have automatic brakes, and the technical principles are very simple, namely, install radar and infrared sensors in the front of the car. When foreign objects or pedestrians are detected, they automatically help the driver to brake. Another technique is very similar, that is, to realise adaptive cruise control on the motorway during stable road conditions, that is, keep a certain distance from the car in front, when the car in front accelerates, the car also accelerates, and when the front car decelerates, the car also decelerates. This kind of smart driving can greatly reduce traffic accidents, so as to reduce the losses of insurance companies.

I believe that smart driving technology will be popularised soon, and one mechanism is that insurance company premiums will decline with the arrival of smart driving, incentivising car manufacturers and car purchasers to manufacture and purchase vehicles with smart driving technology. It is said that in the US, intelligent brake technology will become the basic configuration of future vehicles mandated by the government.

Smart driving can not only assist, but more importantly, help parking. Both Audi and BMW have introduced models that park the car automatically. BMW's new 7-series can fully realise automatic parking after the separation of people and vehicle, which not only reduces the requirements for driver parking technology but the car can also park in a small parking space because it doesn't need to consider leaving space to open the door after parking. Audi has also demonstrated the concept whereby, after arriving at a shopping mall, a hotel or home, the car finds its own parking space like a dog. When the owner comes out, it drive to the owner itself, greatly reduces the time to find parking spaces.

Another factor worth considering regarding the pace of popularisation of smart driving technology is that smart driving does not provide the flexibility and fun that many people get from driving a car. In many cases, drivers still enjoy driving, at the same time, they can also take the initiative to tackle the most complex situations according to their own judgement instead of relying on machines or AI. I firmly believe that most of the new models launched in the next five years will be equipped with smart driving functions.

As Smart Driving Disrupts the Automotive Industry, Who Will Dominate the Two Software and Hardware Camps?

Since the smart driving era has come, will there be disruptive changes in the automotive industry? I think there will be.

First, the era of smart driving has further promoted general technological R&D.

What is general technology? For example, all drivers have this experience, the built-in navigation provided by the original manufacturer, no matter how expensive or good, is not as easy to use as the mobile navigation apps such as Baidu Maps or Gaode Maps. The reason is very simple, that is, because Baidu and Gaode can upgrade the maps at any time, they are very easy to search, and provide the best driving route at any time as road conditions change. While for built-in navigation systems, often the maps are old, and the user interface (UI) is complex and inconvenient, and it is difficult for the road conditions to be dynamically updated.

Why does this happen? The users of Baidu and Gaode navigation systems are calculated in tens or hundreds of millions. In order to keep these users, Baidu and Gaode must continuously invest in R&D, they have so many consumers that their R&D costs are comparatively insignificant. On the contrary, even for large car makers like Toyota and Volkswagen, their cumulative navigation users would not exceed 10 million which does not justify such a large R&D investment, also it is very difficult for them to update maps and UIs.

This example tells us that there will be two camps in the future automobile industry, one camp being companies specialising in smart driving and human vehicle interaction interfaces. Such companies are most likely to emerge from internet companies such as Apple and Google with focus on designing general software for smart driving and standard procedures and systems for human vehicle interactions and vehicle-to-vehicle communication. The most interesting thing is that these companies are likely to eventually integrate into one or two. They will have their own platform, like today's Apple and Android. These platforms allow cars to communicate with each other, with mobile phones and cars as well as people, and cars will be able to communicate with each other. Whoever controls these platforms to a great extent controls the users and the car makers.

Another camp is the traditional car makers that produce motor vehicles in contact with the ground and in physical contact with consumers. Their advantage is in developing engines, batteries, power train systems, control systems and other car-related physical comfort systems. The number of such car makers is most likely to decline gradually in the future because there are many common technologies between them, resulting in increased competition. In fact, now a large number of automatic braking and cruise control system components are produced by Bosch. Car makers producing hardware must be more focused and professional in the future. In order to be more focused and professional, the scale of car factories should be larger, and the technical universality should be strengthened.

In the future, these two camps will exist and the key lies in who dominates who: will software producers Google and Apple lead hardware producers BMW and Mercedes, or will BMW and Mercedes lead Google and Apple? Or are the two relatively evenly matched?

I am inclined to the view that in the future, either Google and Apple will lead BMW and Mercedes, or they will have a relatively equal relationship. Because Google and Apple are large in scale and have abundant financial resources, they can afford a protracted war and are able to put in a lot of financial resources. If BMW, Mercedes and some Chinese car manufacturers cannot quickly integrate, they will be crushed by these software companies. The benefits of the segmentation of the future automobile market will flow more towards the software companies, a bit like how Bosch today dominates the world's hardware market. But for now, the answer is not clear, in another five years we may see things more clearly. The key lies in the extent to which the car makers that produce hardware can accelerate integration.

The last question that must be asked is for the Chinese car makers, where is the future of the smart driving era? My viewpoint is that the Chinese car makers must accelerate the elimination of backward production capacity and accelerate integration. Only in this way can they occupy a place in the fiercer, more platform-based and larger-scale competition in the future.

At the same time, I also particularly appeal to China's Baidu, Tencent and other internet companies to join the R&D ofinto smart vehicle platforms and to develop various software for smart driving according to China's road conditions and Chinese people's driving habits. Otherwise, in the huge industry of smart vehicle software, China will lag behind the developed countries – just like the smartphone market where the dominant platforms globally are developed by two American companies, Apple and Android. China should not repeat this mistake.

Traditional System Should Embrace Internet Finance

Since 2013, there has been an upsurge in internet finance in China. The internet monetary fund represented by Yu'e-Bao quickly collected hundreds of billions of Rmb, a considerable part of which was transferred from bank deposits being, which has aroused the concern of the whole society about the traditional banking industry. The core problem is – will internet finance have a substantial impact on traditional financial services?

My answer is that after reasonable supervision, the impact of internet finance on the traditional financial system is limited. The impact of internet finance simply using internet channels of traditional financial institutions does exist, but it is limited; while the internet finance based on internet transactions will not have an impact on traditional financial institutions, it will bring beneficial supplements, the premise is reasonable supervision, especially to strictly prevent the malicious misappropriation of funds in the name of internet finance through public fundraising.

Two Types of Internet Finance

First, it is necessary to clarify the two types of current internet financial services.

The first category is something we might as well call non-primary internet financial services. This refers to financial services that take the internet as a tool and essentially serve as an offline economic activity and belongs to traditional financial services. Yu'e Bao belongs to this category. This kind of financial business has not broken through the scope of traditional financial businesses, it just uses the internet as a more efficient means of information exchange to broaden the spread and sales channels of traditional financial businesses.

Taking Yu'e Bao as an example, its essence is nothing more than taking the internet as a marketing channel, gathering the funds of internet users and depositing them back to commercial banks in the form of a deposit agreement. This process speeds up the transfer of depositors' funds from banks to monetary funds, but the basic business is bank deposits, and the final investment destination is to invest in the real economy through bank loans.

The second category can be called primary internet finance, that is, real provision of financial services for economic activities on the internet. For example, there are a lot of economic activities due to transactions between Taobao's online stores and buyers – such as ordering, shipping, receiving, payment and evaluation. This series of trading activities leaves an extremely rich data trail on the internet, and this data can reflect the behavioural characteristics of internet transaction participants very effectively, such as credit, consumption habits and consumption preferences. Such data can be fully utilised to provide financial services for various participants in online transactions, such as providing loans to sellers, and providing facilities for buyers to pay in instalments. Such transactions are in line with the basic principle that finance serves the real economy, which is also an expansion of traditional financial business.

Limited Impact of Non-Primary Internet Finance

The first type of non-primary internet financial business has a certain impact on traditional finance but it is relatively limited.

First, this kind of business uses the internet as a distribution tool, which can enhance the relative position and bargaining power of individual depositors to banks – because it can quickly pool the funds of depositors scattered everywhere, bargaining with relevant banks through internet funds, so as to obtain a relatively high deposit interest rate and lower the normal interest spread of banks. In essence, this process is not brought about by the internet but is caused by breaking the monopoly of traditional commercial banks.

A monopoly enables traditional commercial banks to enjoy high interest margins and obtain excess profits. Even without the emergence of this kind of internet financial business, with the emergence of a series of new financial institutions in China's financial reform and the further promotion of interest rate marketisation, the interest rate spread of existing commercial banks will also gradually decline.

Therefore, the impact of a non-primary internet financial model on traditional banks is not essentially caused by the internet, but should be regarded as a new financial institution. It is brought about by breaking the monopoly, and Yu'e Bao is equivalent to a new third-party financial institution.

But we must see that this impact is limited. Because the potential risks of Yu'e Bao and other products are huge, reasonable supervision will lower their market competition. On the internet, Yu'e Bao and other products have a very strong ability to accumulate wealth, and it is precisely this strong ability to gather wealth that also brings a very strong ability to generate money because once depositors' confidence in Yu'e Bao decreases, there would be a quick run on the bank, therefore internet-based monetary funds, such as Yu'e Bao, must be reasonably supervised.

A goal of reasonable supervision is to reduce the probability of these funds being run, the basic method being to limit the liquidity of such funds and the difficulty of withdrawal, at the same time, such monetary funds should also set aside higher deposit reserves for banks. From this point of view, the interest rate that Yu'e Bao and other products can give investors will continue to decline. As Yu'-e Bao is incorporated into the normal regulatory system, so its safety will be improved, while interest rates will also fall, and the impact on traditional banks will gradually decline.

Primary Internet Finance and Traditional Finance Are Complementary

Primary internet financial business is based on online activity deployment, and these transactions are an extension of the real economy to a certain degree, therefore, this type of business can be regarded as an extension, rather than a replacement, of traditional finance. More importantly, online trading has its uniqueness, as large quantities of transaction information can be easily gathered and analysed by big data arms of internet financial institutions, so as to increase the accuracy and efficiency of financial business.

Primary internet financial activities are not covered and cannot be reached by traditional financial institutions, conversely, this type of internet financial activity cannot replace, in essence, traditional financial activities, and it does not affect traditional financial transactions. Specifically speaking, what traditional financial transactions are generally concerned with is to provide loans to large customers including enterprises but these kinds of transactions must be carried out face to face offline, while direct data analysis of key customers cannot replace face-to-face demand communication as well as an actual survey.

Speaking more theoretically, primary internet financial business uses hard data with a variety of information about both parties to a transaction that can be converted into computer code; however, what traditional financial business needs more is soft information, including the subjective impression of financiers after meeting with all parties to the transaction; soft information is the soul of the traditional transaction.

As for part of the offline transactions of the real economy turning to online transactions, some traditional financial businesses will also turn to primary internet finance, but this should be a gradual change instead of a rapid change in attracting a large amount of funds from banks in the short term like Yu'e Bao. Traditional financial institutions have plenty of time to learn and transform so as to expand their business space in the internet era.

Traditional Financial Institutions Should Embrace Internet Finance

The emerging internet finance is becoming a new wave affecting the development of the financial industry, we must calmly analyse its business essence and type. In the short term, although represented by Yu'e Bao, financial activities carried out by using the distribution capacity of the internet have a certain but controllable impact on the traditional financial industry, but what we should expect more is the primary internet financial activities based on actual online economic activities. This kind of financial activity will greatly expand the coverage of the traditional financial industry, which means an expansion of the entire financial industry in response to the changing times rather than a simple division of the traditional financial business field. Internet finance is worth looking forward to, it will certainly become an important entry point for China's economic transformation and financial development.

In particular, it should be noted that internet finance needs special supervision and institutional guarantees. On the one hand, the internet spreads information very quickly and if bad expectations about internet finance are formed, it is easy for them to spread on the internet, causing excessive shock and panic divestment by investors, bringing greater risks; on the other hand, we should also do a good job in investor protection. China has a large number of savers, and many small savers have a weak sense of self protection, therefore the regulatory authorities must strictly prevent criminals from committing financial fraud in the name of the internet; investor protection in the internet age is particularly important.

Three Questions About Facebook's Libra Currency:

Angels or Demons in the Era of Globalisation?

In June 2019 Facebook published a white paper, announcing that it would create a new type of cryptocurrency – Libra - and also establish an association to manage this currency - the Libra Association.

As a social media giant, Facebook has more than 2 billion users. What impact would the birth of the Libra currency bring to the current monetary system by quickly triggering a heated discussion in the global financial community and even among central banks? How should we view and respond to this ambitious plan? We might as well start by understanding this new concept.

Different Libra Currency

From the information in the public domain, the Libra currency is very different from existing digital currency, specifically, it has three basic characteristics.

First, its currency value is linked to a basket of currencies, which eliminates the concerns of many investors and traders who are reluctant to use it for fear that its currency value might fluctuate too much, therefore not triggering speculation. At this point, the Libra currency is different from other digital currencies which are produced in some form (such as computer mining) and have a limited circulation, which in fact leads them to become a financial speculation product rather than a liquid currency.

Second, the Libra currency makes cross-border transactions safe and convenient through a set of technical solutions. One of the main goals of Libra is to solve the difficulties of cross-border transactions because current cross-border transactions are very complicated, the time and economic costs are very high for the currency conversion, and inter-bank payment and clearing system involved, and they are more affected by geopolitical factors. Russia, Iran and even Huawei's troubles with the US government are related to this issue, which has constantly aroused controversy in the international community.

Third, the Libra currency has a governing association which is open. To become a member of the board of directors, you must make an initial investment (purchase Libra tokens) of at least US$10 million, getting one vote for every US$10 million.

Three Questions about Libra Currency

Regarding the Libra currency, we must ask three questions.

First, what is the essence of the Libra currency?

In essence, it is the same as Alipay and WeChat Pay, but Alipay and WeChat Pay are directly linked to the Rmb, one yuan of Rmb corresponding to one yuan in WeChat Pay and Alipay, while the value of the Libra currency is linked to a basket of currencies. This is also the motive for Facebook wanting to create the Libra currency – because until now Facebook hasn't been involved in the payment field, but seeing that Alipay and WeChat Pay have a robust business, it certainly has the same idea.

The great difference between Libra and Alipay and WeChat is that Libra has the identity of an independent currency, it does not correspond one on one to any sovereign currency, but is linked to a basket of sovereign currencies, while Alipay and WeChat are directly linked to the Rmb. In addition, the Libra Association established by Facebook looks very open and transparent, in fact, its high-threshold design is also suspected of making money by hook or by crook.

Second, is the Libra currency an angel?

Because Facebook repeatedly claims it "passively generates money" or that "the value of the currency is based on the value of the world's major currencies", so far, its move has not aroused hostility from central banks.

In the future, the Libra currency is most likely to succeed in two areas. One is in some economically fragile countries where people do not believe in their own currency and may prefer to price and save in the Libra currency which can be expected to become the currency used by local people for daily transactions. Under normal circumstances, this is conducive to the economic development of the relevant countries.

On the contrary, in economically developed countries, for example, in the EU and the US, the Libra currency is unlikely to completely replace their own currencies for the simple reason that in their own countries, people's shopping, dining and rent are priced in local currency, and this is the basic regulation of the local central bank. If transactions are conducted in a currency whose value does not correspond directly to that of the local currency, it will cause a lot of problems for consumers and manufacturers, as they must always be concerned about the exchange rate between their local currency and the Libra currency.

Another field in which the Libra currency may succeed is cross-border transactions. Current cross-border transactions are extremely complex. Libra provides a breakthrough for this problem due to technical reasons and the convenience of the internet. This is the reason for many financial companies wanting to be first to join the Libra Association. The Libra currency is expected to become a sharp weapon to promote economic and financial globalisation.

Third, will the Libra currency turn into a demon?

In an emergency, the management of the Libra currency is likely to become an extremely complicated geopolitical issue. In some special cases, some powerful countries are likely to force Facebook to intervene in individual country transactions, with some Libra accounts in the country even being frozen and confiscated. If Facebook has only managed to control public opinion so far, then with the Libra currency, Facebook will be able to paralyse the economy or even collapse the regime of any country that uses a lot of Libra currency.

Regarding the Libra currency, another issue that we need to pay attention to is when more and more financial companies begin trading in Libra currency, then many financial assets will be denominated in Libra. It is conceivable that when major fluctuations occur in the world economic and financial system in the future, the governments of major countries in the world will ask the Libra Association to adjust the specific rules of the Libra currency flows and transactions, so as to expand or shrink its currency issuance. By then, the Libra Association will in fact become a super central bank, and the Libra currency will truly become an independent currency, having its own independent monetary policy, and this is completely different from the case of Hong Kong dollars, for example; central banks must be well aware of this prospect.

If the Libra Association actually becomes a super central bank and the Libra currency becomes a truly independent currency, then who will dominate its monetary policy? What is the purpose of its monetary policy? Based on the economic situation of which country or region? Which country or region's economic interests will be damaged? These are devilishly complex international political issues.

How Does China Treat Supra Sovereign Currency?

According to the above analysis, then, what attitude should China and other emerging market economies take towards the Libra currency?

First, China and other major developing countries must adhere to the principle that the Libra currency cannot be used in domestic transactions. Even in countries with large numbers of Facebook users, it is also necessary for their governments to require that all transactions and pricing in the country must be based on local currency, so as to limit the scope of the Libra currency used by domestic residents and to control the popularity range and depth of the Libra currency.

Second, it should be necessary for these sovereign states to declare in advance that in case of emergency, cross-border transactions of the Libra currency can be restricted to prevent large amounts of capital flight and an economic crisis.

Third, for a large country like China, we must consider letting our major companies join the Libra Association. After all, the Libra currency may evolve into a major international currency in the future. Rather than refuse to deal with it, we'd better join it and participate in the formulation of its rules. In a sense, Libra may evolve into a new currency such as the special drawing right (SDR) that the IMF has long wanted to operate. Since China has actively participated in the operation of the IMF and its SDRs, why not join the Libra Association on Facebook? Its essence is the same.

Fourth, countries like China with super social and ecommerce platforms should encourage the platforms to be more internationalised, promoting their own internet payment tools, so as to increase the influence of their own currency internationally. Only when the local currency becomes stronger will it be more able to participate in the issuance of international currencies in the future.

For a large country like China, we must clearly recognise that no matter how high the degree of internationalisation of the Rmb, it is a sovereign currency. However, in the future, the world will certainly produce a supra-sovereign reserve currency, which is not necessarily produced by Chinese local enterprises – in fact, due to the restrictions of internet transactions and cross border transactions, China's local financial institutions and enterprises are unlikely to create such a supra-sovereign reserve currency. China and other major countries should also actively participate in the operation and management of this supra-sovereign reserve currency during the process of promoting the internationalisation of their local currencies. This would be a positive and pragmatic approach.

Chapter 4

Reform Practice and Chinese Economic Thought

Economic Summary of 40 Years of Reform and Opening Up

China's 40 years of reform and opening up has created the largest economic growth in human history. Over the past 40 years, China's economy has developed rapidly, and its proportion of world GDP (calculated according to PPP) rose from 4.9% to 18.2%. By contrast, in the 40 years after the Industrial Revolution, Great Britain's share of world GDP rose from 3.8% to 5.9%; in the 40 years following the American Civil War, the US share of world GDP rose from 7.9% to 17.3%; in the 40 years after the Meiji Restoration, Japan's share of world GDP rose from 2.3% to 2.6%, and from 3.3% to 8.9% after the second world war; in the 40 years of rapid growth experienced by the "Four Asian Dragons" (South Korea, Singapore, Chinese Hong Kong and Chinese Taiwan), the their combined share of world GDP rose from 0.7% to 3.5%. In terms of volume, in the past 40 years, China experienced the largest economic growth in human history.

From China's own perspective, the past 40 years is of great significance. According to our research,[1] China's share of world GDP peaked (at 34.6%) in 1600, then it began to decline. After 1820, with other countries starting the process of industrialisation, China's share of world GDP began to decline rapidly. Until the beginning of reform and opening up (1978), China's share of world GDP was only 4.9%, however, 40 years later, it rebounded to 18.2%. From an economic perspective, the past 40 years has indeed witnessed the first rejuvenation of China in more than 400 years.

Why Should We Summarise the 40 Years of Reform and Opening Up at the Economic Level?

Despite the remarkable development achievements, 40 years is short in the long river of human history. Why is it necessary to make an economic summary based on the practice of China's reform and opening up? The first reason is for China's own further development. Since the reform and opening up, China has done many things right and achieved the largest economic growth ever seen, however, the goal of reform has not been fully realised, and there are still many aspects that need further reform. Therefore, for Chinese economists, it is very important to study and summarise the reform and opening up from the perspective of economics. In addition, foreign economists should also pay attention to the Chinese economy, because China has become the world's second largest economy, contributing to the largest economic growth in history, therefore economic theory needs to explain this important economic phenomenon.

The second reason is, compared to other 40-year periods in history, the economic growth since China's reform and opening up is very unique, therefore we need to distill the economic summary from it. One of the most noteworthy is that the starting point of the reform is an economy under highly unified government management.

Starting from the planned economy of highly unified management, China tries to adjust the relationship between the government and the economy. The uniqueness of this process is self-evident. Looking back on the process of human exploration of the world, it is not difficult for us to find that many theoretical breakthroughs originate from some "accidental exceptions". Although these exceptions revealed many universal principles, they were not conventional or common phenomena in the context of the times. For example, it is those experiments from accidents that have helped humans discover radioactivity, invented penicillin for curing diseases and saving people, and vulcanised rubber for making automobile tyres. Starting from the important "economic experiment" of the 40 years of China's reform and opening up, economists are most likely to elicit valuable and enlightening conclusions in the field of the relationship between government and the economy. At the same time, these conclusions will also have universal significance and will be closely related to the development of other economies.

At the economic level, the third reason to summarise the 40 years of reform and opening up is that many emerging economies are deeply interested in China's experience of rapid development. Leaders and people from many countries in the world are trying to learn and summarise universal, replicable policy and institutional arrangements from China's experience. It is true that China has many distinctive political and economic systems, and that these features may be difficult to simply replicate in other countries, however, China's practice will certainly sum up universal experience that can be learned and applied by other countries.

How to Summarise the 40 Years of Reform and Opening Up from the Economic Level?

Many explanations have been put forward for the high-speed economic growth since China's reform and opening up. From the most macro level, Comrade Deng Xiaoping's exposition of "emancipate the mind and seek truth from facts" is undoubtedly commendable. In other words, the systems and polices that are most conducive to development need to be achieved through trial, practice and exploration, but not made based on subjective assumptions based on a doctrine of book worship. There is no doubt that this is one of the most important experiences of China's economic reform.

The second angle to understand China's economic take off is to analyse it from the principles of classical economics. Beyond all doubt, these common-sense knowledge points of economics have indeed played a great role. For example, China's success is inseparable from its emphasis on education, even before the reform and opening up, China had promoted equal access to elementary education for girls and boys; China pays attention to the protection of property rights and promotes the ownership reform of many SOEs and collective enterprises; China has played a comparative advantage through international trade. These analyses are reasonable and China's achievements in these fields have attracted worldwide attention.

The third angle to understand China's economic take-off is to analyse China's special institutional factors. For example, some theories show us why progressive reform can succeed in China.[21]Many studies believe that China's reform is based on the "province", this relatively independent unit carries out decentralised work, therefore, local governments can carry out differentiated experiments under appropriate incentives. Taking these experiments initiated by local governments as materials, the central government can identify the most effective measures and promote them. However, in the former Soviet Union, each region produced only a small part professionally and was vertically managed by the central government, therefore it was difficult to promote the reform experiment of decentralisation. Other studies, starting from China's political system, believe that the Communist Party is not controlled by any interest group, therefore the ruling party's decision-making is neutral, and this "neutral government" contributes to the sustained growth of China's economy.³

These analyses provide us with powerful analytical tools for understanding China's special institutional system.

Compared with these existing studies, our research adopts a different perspective. We try to answer the following questions: from China's reform and opening up, can we summarise some economic principles that can be written into textbooks that are universal and previously ignored? From China's rapid economic growth, can we refine the economic principles of universal significance and the development of these principles in other economies, for instance, the role they played in economic growth after the British industrial revolution and the American Civil War, as well as the Japanese economic take-off, but that were ignored by us? Can these economic principles provide policy suggestions that can be learned and copied by other countries?

To this end, I led the establishment of a special research team, and a systematic study was carried out for nine months. The team went deep into the grassroots level and went to the frontline to obtain first-hand and informative information, for example, we went to Jiangsu and Liaoning Provinces to do field research. Jiangsu Province has the highest per capita GDP and the second highest total GDP in China. We investigated two cities in the province, Jingjiang City to the north of the Yangtse river and Jiangyin City (Southern Jiangsu is one of the regions with the most economic vitality and the most active enterprises in history) to the south of the Yangtse river respectively. We also investigated Shenyang, the capital city of Liaoning Province. Shenyang can be called "China's 'Detroit'". In the process of opening up to the outside world, it has suffered the "pain of transformation". Shenyang was once China's industrial centre and undertook most of the industrial assistance from the Soviet Union in the 1950s. During this prosperous period, there were more than 1,400 municipal SOEs but there are only 26 left. In addition to field research, we also had a discussion with former and current leaders of more than 10 ministries and commissions such as the NDRC, Ministry of Finance, Central Bank, Ministry of Natural Resources, Ministry of Housing and Urban Rural Development, CSRC, former CBRC (the China Banking Regulatory Commission) and former Ministry of Coal. As the witnesses of reform and opening up, they provided us with useful information and profound insight into the specific decision-making process of reform and opening up. We also consulted large numbers of academic papers and government documents, as well as the relevant expositions of the state leaders, such as the *Collected Works of Deng Xiaoping*, *Collected Works of Chen Yun*, *Collected Works of Jiang Zemin*, *Zhu Rongji on the Record*, and a series of important speeches by General Secretary Xi Jinping.

Here are two points that need to be explained in particular. First, we do not believe that China's reform and opening up is perfect and has been successful in all aspects. In fact, China's economic system needs further reform in many aspects. In the process of reform and opening up, some policies are unreasonable. One of the purposes of our study was to discuss the success of China's reform and opening up and the need for further improvement. Second, we hope, based on the theory of economics and specific practices in the economic field, to discuss the universal economic principles behind China's reform and opening up.

Economic Summary of 40 Years of Reform and Opening Up

Reviewing the 40 years of China's reform and opening up, we believe that the following five experiences can be summarised at the economic level.

First, economic growth requires the creation and development of new enterprises, and this requires a complete market and good business environment. However, in reality, the market is not perfect, so this requires local governments to help enterprises solve the problems in their growth with appropriate incentives. The Chinese governments at all levels, especially local governments, have played a significant role in helping enterprises solve practical problems in land, employment and coordination of transportation, and in guiding coordinated development of both upstream and downstream enterprises, as well as for the development and growth of new enterprises, especially private ones. Even in the US, new enterprises also encounter problems which need government help to solve. For example, some enterprises may need to import a highly-skilled labour force and this requires local government to relax immigration policies; for another example, the high house prices in Silicon Valley have raised the labour costs of enterprises, and this also needs local government help to solve. The experience of China's reform and opening up tells us that the incentive of local governments to help enterprises is very important for the entry and development of enterprises, and this incentive comes from two aspects. Of course, sometimes there exist some irrational decisions in local governments' process of helping enterprises establish and develop, consequently there is also a need for corresponding restraint systems to regulate the behaviour of local governments. Looking forward to the future, the government should focus on further lowering the market threshold and continuously improving the business environment, continuously promoting the establishment and development of new enterprises.

The second experience is that rapid land conversion is the key to economic growth but this is ignored by contemporary economics as a whole. The land needed for a certain economic activity may have been occupied for other purposes, therefore how to transfer the land use, or re-zone land, from one economic subject to another is very important. And this process is usually very expensive because the transaction cost of resolving conflicts over pricing of property values via Coase Theorem negotiation itself is high. In China, local governments have the incentive as well as the jurisdiction to fast-track this land conversion process. The process sees most of the land used for economic development transformed from agricultural land into non-agricultural land and this transformation is negotiated by the local government. Both industrial parks and real estate developers obtain land use rights directly from the local government: either they acquire land through auction to develop residential projects, or the government directly subsidises land for industrial enterprises at a low price. Rapid land conversion is also crucial for accelerating the entry of enterprises.

The third experience is that financial deepening and financial stability play a key role in economic growth. Here financial deepening means that residents actively hold more and more financial assets, and that the growth rate of financial assets exceeds that of the economy. Financial deepening is crucial to real economic growth because it promotes the transformation of residents' savings into investment in the real economy. Otherwise, residents with additional money need to start their own businesses or find suitable investment projects alone, in which case capital turnover is slow and efficiency is low. An indicator of financial deepening is the ratio of total financial assets to GDP. According to our calculations, in 2018 China's total financial assets were close to four times that of GDP, while in 1978 it was only about 0.6 times as much. The premise of financial deepening is financial stability, otherwise residents reduce their holdings of financial assets and even cause a run on banks and other financial institutions. In order to make financial deepening serve the domestic economy, it is also necessary for financial deepening to be based on domestic currency. Financial deepening based on local currency, on one hand, makes domestic enterprises rely on "domestic debt" rather than "foreign debt", thereby avoiding an external debt crisis; on the other hand, it can also avoid capital flight. In order to maintain financial stability, the central government needs to actively defuse financial risks, especially risks related to the banking system.

The fourth experience is that the most fundamental role of openness is learning instead of simply giving full play to comparative advantages or using foreign capital and technology. Opening up forces the main part of a country's economy to learn the most advanced knowledge, systems and concepts in the world, and to put it into practice in combination with the actual situation of the country. This is the key to cultivating endogenous economic growth capacity and to gradually realising transformation and upgrading. In order to achieve sustainable economic development, all sectors of the economy including entrepreneurs, workers and government officials, must learn, even if opening up to the outside world is the most effective way to learn. Admittedly, opening up is indeed conducive to giving full play to comparative advantages, but only giving full play to comparative advantages is not enough. As far as China is concerned, there are numerous examples of opening up to developed economies and giving domestic economic sectors learning opportunities. Through these opportunities, they learn new business models, management skills and how to expand new markets, thereby gradually developing and expanding themselves. However, opening up is also accompanied by shocks and risks, with many economic sectors also paying a high price and making arduous efforts to deal with external shocks. At this time, the government should play a role to help workers, entrepreneurs and other micro sectors deal with the negative impact of opening up. Chinese entrepreneurs, workers and government officials have worked together to resolve these shocks. In this process, China's central government and local governments have made great efforts: on one hand, they provided basic social security for laid-off workers in affected industries and promoted their re-employment; on the other hand, they actively attracted investment and boosted the local economy by securing large enterprises and projects. From this perspective, the open process also needs careful management.

The fifth experience is that the central government should actively regulate and control the macroeconomy. Economic growth, especially rapid economic growth, is inevitably accompanied by macroeconomic shocks, leading to cooling and heating of the economy. As far as China is concerned, when the macroeconomy is in an upward cycle, there is fierce competition and jockeying among enterprises. Most enterprises are eager to expand their production scale and gain the initiative, as they believe that as long as they can expand their market share and take the lead, they can succeed. On the contrary, if enterprises cannot achieve a market leadership position, they suffer heavy losses. Due to the high expected income, it is reasonable for micro enterprise entities to expand production through "gaining the initiative". However, this simultaneous expansion of production scale leads to over investment, consequently leading to overcapacity. In addition, when the macroeconomy is too cool, existing enterprises are reluctant to quit without a fight. They believe that if other enterprises are forced out of the market they themselves can persist and survive, and can gain considerable profits from the price rebound. What the "consumption war game" in microeconomic theory describes is this phenomenon. The result of this rational game of micro actors is that the market clearing process is very slow.

From the micro level, the decisions made by enterprises in the "gaining the initiative game" and "consumption war game" are rational. However, from the whole macro level, the long process of the market clearing has brought about low socioeconomic efficiency. China's central government actively regulates and controls the macroeconomy in order to speed up the market clearing process which improves social efficiency from the macro level. When the economy is too cool, the government forces loss-making enterprises with excess capacity to withdraw and helps solve the problem of unemployment through financial subsidies; when the economy is too hot, the government suspends the approval of new projects and orders commercial banks to reduce loans to enterprises. China's central government comprehensively applies market-oriented means, including fiscal and monetary policy, administrative fiat, reforms and other measures, to deal with cyclical macroeconomic fluctuations.

Overall, the most basic economic summary of the 40 years of reform and opening up is that a successful economy must carefully adjust the relationship between the government and the economy, especially the relationship between the government and the market. As participants in economic activities, governments at all levels must adjust their incentives and behaviour in place, only in this way can the government work in the same direction as the market economy, and can the economy develop healthily for a long time. In economics hypotheses, economists often ignore the role of government, or think rigidly that the government is either benevolent or evil. However, the reality is much more complex, and the government's behaviour of participating in economic activities and the incentives behind it are very important issues in economic practice and worthy of careful study. In terms of the practice of China's reform and opening up, in many cases, the government is the power to boost the development of the market.

Based on the economic analysis of the practice of China's reform and opening up in the past 40 years, we believe that China's economy should continue to make efforts in the following directions and further deepen reform. In terms of entry and development of new enterprises, we should deepen the reform of the fiscal and taxation system, give local governments reasonable financial power and fully mobilise local government enthusiasm for economic development; we should appropriately increase the share of tax retained by local governments and encourage them to continuously improve their business environment, create a fair and open market, and promote local economic development; we should liberalise the industry access threshold and strengthen corresponding regulatory constraints; we should promote implementation of the policy of reducing taxes and reducing burdens. In terms of land and the real estate market, we should challenge local governments' singular pursuit of GDP and encourage them to pay more attention to people's livelihood and sustainable development, and shift to operating long-term assets. Drawing on the experience of Germany, Singapore and other countries, land supply can be helpful for people's livelihoods as it increases the supply of residential land. In terms of finance, the bond market should be regarded as the breakthrough point for deepening China's financial reform, detaching local government infrastructure financing from the banking system and redirecting it toward the bond market; we should vigorously build and improve the institutional foundation needed for the development of stock markets, strengthen the force in investigation, prosecution and judicial in the bond field, severely crack down on violations of laws and regulations; we should promote the orderly opening up of financial services and carefully manage capital flows. In terms of opening up to the outside world, we should continue to speed up learning with an open, mature and confident attitude to absorb all the advanced knowledge, technology and ideas in the world, expand opening up and promote personnel exchanges to promote learning in science and technology, social governance, financial rule of law, foreign investment and international economic governance. In terms of macro control, we should strengthen the marketisation and legalisation of macro control means and avoid unfair treatment of private enterprises caused by macro control; we should establish an efficient policy feedback mechanism, improve the foresight, timeliness, pertinence and flexibility of macro control, avoid over regulation and lagging behind in control; and we should pay more attention to the counter-cyclical regulation of fiscal policy to prevent pro-cyclical fiscal policies from amplifying macroeconomic fluctuations.

The Song Dynasty Led the World, the Qing Dynasty Fell Behind Western Europe

What Does the Study of Ancient Chinese Economic Development Tell Us?

Today, no one can tell clearly the big picture of China's economic history. Although many of our predecessors and colleagues have done outstanding research, most of their findings are about individual regions or topics, such as in cases where they have a special understanding of the fluctuation in the price of rice in Jiangnan, the repair and dredging of the Jiangnan canal, and so forth. Only with a complete understanding of the past can a nation better understand the present. The basic work of understanding the past is to understand the overall situation of the nation's economic development and to undertake international comparisons.

Our research draws the following basic conclusions.

First, the level of economic development in ancient China was very backward by today's standards. For example, we found that, measured against the value of the US dollar in 1990, the per capita GDP of the Ming Dynasty (1368-1644) was about US$920 and that of the Qing Dynasty (1644-1911) was US$760, lower than the level after reform and opening up (1978). Notice that the absolute value of the above dollar valuation depends on the value of ancient and modern currencies. In an article we published previously, calculated by multiplying the physical output by today's world prices, the above income level was lower. As a deduction, we can better understand that the economic value of ancient people's lives was far lower than that of modern people. The economic cost of life lost in war was much lower than today.

Second, from the Northern Song Dynasty (960-1127) to the Ming Dynasty, China's per capita GDP fluctuated at a high level whereas in the Qing Dynasty it showed a downward trend. Our analysis shows that the reason for the decline was mainly that the population growth rate exceeded the accumulation rate of capital and land. In nearly 900 years, the per capita cultivated land area continued to decline, and this decline could not be made up for by the increase in grain yield per hectare. In other words, the amount of land occupied per capita and the number of labour tools including livestock decreased, leading to a continuous decline in labour productivity.

Third, through international comparison, we find that the standard of living in Song Dynasty China was among the best in the world but lagged behind that of the Eastern Roman Empire before 1300 (the fourth year of Dade in the Yuan Dynasty) and was overtaken by the Kingdom of England around 1400 (the second year of Jianwen in the Ming Dynasty); prior to 1750 (the 15th year of Qianlong in the Qing Dynasty), although the standard of living in some parts of China was not far from that in the richest parts of Europe, China as a whole lagged behind Western Europe, therefore the great division between East and West began before the industrial revolution. This finding is closely related to the above finding that per capita GDP was gradually declining, that is to say that the continuous decline of China's per capita labour productivity was a negative factor for economic development and national progress.

An Objective Evaluation of Ancient Economic Development Is to Understand the Present and Look Forward to the Future

The above findings are the result of our research team's long term efforts over the course of the previous decade. Recently, our research has also been supported by major projects of the National Social Science Foundation of China, and papers have been gradually published in academic journals at home and abroad. These findings have attracted some attention in Chinese economics circles, but their importance has not been fully realised. In 2017, the British journal *Economists* and the Japanese journal *Japan Economic News* reported on our findings, which was fed back to the domestic media and inevitably triggered some discussions. To this end, it is necessary to make some explanations.

First, this was a long-term, systematic and arduous research project. We used the production method to measure the total, per capita and structure of GDP in ancient China, and the measurement was based on various official and folk records of relevant dynasties. For example, for the Ming Dynasty, we used the *Ming Veritable Records*, *Wanli Accounting Record*, local chronicles and other historical materials to calculate. These historical materials have detailed records of population, grain and the handicraft industry (including ceramics, paper, pig iron and copper). The Song Dynasty data came from the *Draft Institutional History of the Song Dynasty*, *Records of Food and Goods from the History of the Song Dynasty*, *A Continuation of the Comprehensive Mirror to Aid in Government*, *Comprehensive Investigations Based on Literary and Documentary Sources*, and other documents. In fact, China's historical data record in this regard far exceeds that of other countries in the same period. Thanks to the completeness of China's historical data, compared with international peers, our research is far ahead in methodology and data rigour.

Accordingly, we disagree with the point of view of Chinese economic history from the California School, which believes that China's economic development level in the Qing Dynasty was world leading. Our data is more comprehensive than that of the California School. Similarly, we also overturned some conclusions of the British economist Angus Maddison on the study of Chinese economic history.

Maddison's research has received extensive attention. He believes that China's per capita GDP rose from US$450 to US$600 in the Song Dynasty (note that his ancient and modern price conversion rates are different from ours) and that since then, it has been maintained at this level, which is different from our research conclusion. Maddison had originally planned to attend the second annual conference on Asian historical economics organised by us in May 2010. Sadly, he didn't get the chance to attend the conference due to his unfortunate death at the beginning of that year. Before he died, we had corresponded with him many times and had repeatedly asked him what the basis for his calculation of China's economic aggregate was. In the end, via email, he told us he had assumed the per capita GDP level of China's past dynasties entirely through his own estimation and then multiplied it by the number of people to arrive at the economic aggregate. By contrast, we used specific data for rigorous calculations and tests. Although there are still many areas that need to be improved, it should be said that it is a bigger step forward than Maddison had estimated.

Second, how to interpret our study findings? Some people say that our findings prove that China was not so powerful in history; some people even say that the dream of rejuvenation of the Chinese nation is actually an illusory dream and that China's history was not so brilliant. All these sayings have misinterpreted our findings.

Our finding is that China's per capita GDP was at the highest level in the world around 1000AD, beginning to lag behind Italy from about 1300, and beginning to lag behind the Kingdom of England in 1400, and which means that China historically did not do so badly. On the contrary, this shows that the economic development of ancient China was much earlier than previously thought, that the ancient society reached the peak of per capita development level earlier than we previously realised, and that the period when China's economy began to lag behind the West was also earlier than imagined globally.

Then, how to interpret the finding that the economic development of ancient China was much earlier than we previously thought and that the period where we were lagging behind the West was earlier than we had thought? Academic circles must have different views on this, and this is obviously beyond the scope of our academic research project. I am personally inclined to make the following interpretation: China's social and political system had entered a high level super-steady state very early. China is one of the few countries in the world to have reached ideological reunification very early and this unification had been achieved in the Western Han Dynasty (206BC – 25AD). What followed is that the political system of ancient China also matured relatively early. Because China is at the easternmost end of Eurasia, it has not been invaded or attacked by too many outsiders, therefore it has developed a relatively unified system, a political and economic structure that is politically relatively stable, and a relatively unified ideology with Confucius and Mencius at the core.

This structure enabled China's economy to fufil its potential level of growth and enter a steady state. Because Chinese society is relatively stable, and the way of Confucius and Mencius, which is in the mainstream ideology, advocates more children and more happiness, while traditional Chinese medicine (TCM) also was more highly developed, resulting in precocious healthcare and reproductive technology, the population grew very fast. In this way, China formed a large but not strong, stable but relatively fragile empire. This does not mean that Chinese civilisation lagged behind the world but means that Chinese civilisation is a unique branch within world civilisation.

The corollary to that is that if China does not engage in direct exchanges and conflicts with the outside world, it cannot have a British-style industrial revolution. China's per capita GDP has declined, but there is no shortage of labour, and there is insufficient demand for labour-saving technological innovation. Although in some parts of China, such as Jiangnan, the per capita GDP is relatively high, it is inconceivable that under a unified system, the capitalist system would appear in some areas but that the whole country is still in a feudal state.

Frankly speaking, these viewpoints are different from those of leaders and predecessors in economic history, such as Mr Wu Chengming and Li Bozhong. We believe that different conclusions are drawn by doing basic research carefully and this is with the greatest respect for our predecessors.

Turning to today, why has China been able to develop rapidly? Because the traditional culture that China has adhered to for a long time has strong stability and vitality, and this self-sufficient and stable civilisation system has generated the power of self-innovation and self-transformation under the impact of Western powers, promoting China's self-improvement and gradual opening up since modern times, and eventually bringing about great achievements in China's reform and opening up over the past 40 years.

Studying history tells us about the past, the purpose being to look forward to the future. Studying the past makes us understand our own development process, it also makes us understand the importance of reform and opening up. This is the driving force that inspires us to move forward and to persevere with reform and opening up.

Establish a People-Centred Official Assessment System

China's Economic Development Has Shifted from High Speed to High Quality

Reform and opening up have solved the problem of food and clothing for the people and since 2017, China has entered the decisive period of comprehensively building a moderately prosperous society. The report of the 19th National Congress of the CPC clearly points out: "From 2035 to the middle of the 21st century, we will, building on having basically achieved modernisation, work for another 15 years and develop China into a great socialist country that is prosperous, strong, democratic, culturally advanced, harmonious and beautiful."[4]

In terms of guiding ideology for economic development, the report of the 19th National Congress of the CPC also pushed forward a new development ideology. China's rapid economic growth in the past 40 years has been extremely rare in world economic history; looking to the future, the greater challenge before us is to maintain 33 years of steady and rapid development from 2018 to 2050, that is, China's goal is to maintain solid and steady economic development for 73 consecutive years, which will create a true miracle in human economic history.

In fact, to achieve this goal, China's economy in the next 33 years does not need to develop very fast. According to the calculations of the Centre for China in the World Economy of Tsinghua University, if calculated from 2017, China's GDP maintains a growth rate of 5.5% for the next eight years, 4% for the next 15 years and 3% for the last ten years, then China's economy will reach the median level of the world's most developed economies by 2050, equivalent to the economic development level of today's developed countries such as Japan and Britain, and this calculation takes into account that developed countries are still moving forward according to their average economic growth rate of the past 20 years.

Therefore the fundamental task of China's economy in the next 33 years is to maintain a steady but not rapid development. This is one of the reasons why the Central Economic Work Conference at the end of 2017 proposed that economic work be shifted from high speed to high quality. The core requirement for high quality is sustainable, steady development.

Establish New Assessment Indicators to Press Local Officials to Improve the Quality of Development

The biggest feature of China's economy is that both government and market forces act in the same direction and are organically integrated. Compared with other countries, China's local economic officials play an outstanding role in promoting development, they are the promoters and planners of economic development. Therefore, local government behaviour directly affects the speed and quality of China's economic development.

In China's past period of rapid growth, what concerned local officials was their assessment indicators. Among various assessment indicators, the most important one was the local GDP growth rate, fixed asset investment, the rate of tax rises, as well as the ranking of these indicators in relevant regions. Officials went all out and worked overtime around these indicators, and this is the biggest, as well as the most distinctive, driving force for China's economic development.

If China's economy wants to shift from high speed to high quality, the assessment indicators of local officials must also be changed accordingly. According to the report of the 19th National Congress of the CPC, the most important task is to establish people-centred assessment indicators. I think that for some time to come, the people-centred assessment indicators should include the following three aspects.

First, the whole country approaches every situation holistically, and each region shifts from total economic development to per capita economic development. Economic development is still an important topic of concern to local governments because a series of major social contradictions must be solved in the process of economic development. However, it must be noted that as China has entered the era of a great-power economy, the flow of population and funds between different regions will greatly accelerate. Therefore, in some regions which have received outflows of population and funds from other regions, GDP will grow a little faster while in other areas, the growth rate will be slower because of the loss of population and capital. This is a natural characteristic and inevitable requirement of the economic development of major powers and also demonstrates the superiority of the economic growth of a major power. For example, individual coastal areas will also develop rapidly while the economic growth of some central and western regions that need to protect the ecological environment will be slower, and this is the development need of the ecological civilisation construction in the five-pronged integrated plan to promote and coordinate economic, political, cultural, social and ecological advancement, and is the requirement to implement the concept that "Clear water and lush mountains are invaluable assets".[5] In this situation, local leaders should not only focus on a region's absolute economic growth rate. What should they do? The concept and goal of growth should be placed on a per capita development level. When formulating economic indicators in the future, it should be emphasised that the per capita development level of a region should be continuously improved, even if the local total economic level is likely to decline. This is a fair and reasonable mechanism.

Second, various indicators of people's livelihood and development should be taken into account. The livelihood development indicators should include the growth rate of per capita disposable income, educational level (especially in senior high school), increased university gross enrolment among local people, local surveys on the unemployment rate, and the life expectancy and health level of residents in this area. In particular, it should be pointed out that the assessment of some indicators affecting social stability, such as the proportion of middle-income families in the region, the natural growth rate of the region's population and the fertility rate of women of child-bearing age in this region should also be considered. These are important indicators affecting China's economy and its ability to cope with an ageing population and to realise the healthy and balanced development of its economy and population.

Third, it is particularly important to consider not only some objective indicators but also subjective indicators of people's satisfaction in various regions. An important requirement for building a moderately prosperous society in all respects should be that people's subjective perception of happiness has been continuously improved. This subjective perception of happiness is , to a considerable extent, directly related to the ruling performance of the local government. For example, in this region, if the society and people's lives are relatively stable and there are few malignant events, then the recognition of the people will increase, and this is the public-opinion basis for governance. We suggest that this series of subjective indicators be investigated by the organisation and statistics departments independently of the administrative agencies in the region, only in this way can we obtain data objectively and fairly.

If these subjective indicators are properly measured and can be comprehensively considered with reference to the corresponding objective indicators, popular public opinion can be better integrated with government governance. To a large extent, this will incorporate some of the advantages of the so-called Western democratic states into the socialist national governance system with Chinese characteristics. The disadvantage of democracy is that public opinion is easily manipulated by politicians, and the method of "one person, one vote" tends to go to extremes, resulting in social division. Trump's rise to power actually exacerbated the division within American society. However, if an objective public opinion survey is used as an auxiliary index for assessing officials, it should be conducive to better reflecting the social situation and public opinion while , simultaneously improving the current tendency of local leaders of paying more attention to their superiors.

In short, the new era and new development ideology needs a new set of official assessment systems. This new assessment system should promote sustainable economic development in the future, as well as guide local government officials to shift their energy toward listening to public opinion and improving people's livelihood, only by doing so can we ensure the successful realisation of the grand goals set by the 19th National Congress of the CPC.

Institutional Innovation Key To Xiong'an New Area Development

Since the establishment of Xiong'an New Area on 1 April 2017, the news has triggered discussion and analysis from all walks of life. Some people believe that the Xiong'an New Area will become the highlight of China's economic growth in the 21st century, and its position will be similar to that of the Shenzhen and Shanghai Pudong new areas. This simple comparison, I'm afraid, is not in accordance with reality because the natural geological condition of Xiong'an New Area is different from that of the Shenzhen and Shanghai Pudong new areas. It is neither close to a river nor the sea, nor does it have access to the sea, and there is also a lack of economic centres with a thriving market economy in the surrounding areas. Therefore, I'm afraid, the idea of hoping to turn Xiong'an New Area into a new type of city with a GDP of more than a trillion and an economic scale comparable to large cities is unrealistic.

Then, in what aspects can the establishment of Xiong'an New Area bring long-term and overall influence? I think the Xiong'an New Area should become an important milestone in the exploration of China's modernisation system in the 21st century. Specifically speaking, it has set the benchmark and provides innovative significance in the institutional exploration of economic development, social governance and ecological civilisation construction.

Economic System

After many years of development, China's market economic system has begun to take shape, therefore there are some innovative points worthy of review and summary on a global scale. However, it is undeniable that many existing systems of China's economy must be continuously reformed and innovated.

First, in terms of land management, the existing system relies too much on the market-oriented land transfer mechanism, which makes local governments at all levels rely too much on the income from land transfers. The direct consequence of land finance is the short-term behaviour of local governments, the phenomenon of living beyond their means is very serious.

At the same time, land finance has pushed up the real estate price dominated by the market mechanism, which has brought a series of social consequences. For this, Xiong'an New Area should explore a land management method closely combined with government management and market mechanism, for example, a three-tier real estate management model can be explored. First, government can hold a considerable number of real estate businesses for a long time for rental to residents living and working in the Xiong'an New Area. Second, the government can also build a batch of "small property rights" houses and, according to the principle of market pricing, sell them to people who work long term in the Xiong'an New Area, similar to the houses built by Stanford University for its professors. Such housing can be limited only for internal circulation of local staff. Third, another part of the property in the Xiong'an New Area can also be fully open to the market on the premise of also providing personnel with long-term residence permits in the new area. Through these three methods, land use can support long-term local economic development and avoid real estate becoming a tool for investment and speculation while also providing long-term financial resources for local finance.

In terms of public finance, Xiong'an New Area should carefully study the model of Chinese Hong Kong and Singapore, namely, where the main fiscal revenue should still come from taxes paid by enterprises while personal income tax is kept at a low rate but is spread over a wide base. In this way, the local finances of Xiong'an

New Area can be closely linked with the local economic level, letting local government more actively support the development of local enterprises and also ensuring that the middle class, whose main income is wage-based, does not bear a heavy personal tax burden while, at the same time, making personal income tax simpler and more manageable, and avoiding the model of individual personal income tax in Western developed countries. The facts have proved that, in developed countries, this local financial model based on personal income tax and real estate tax is not successful because this makes the relationship between local governments and enterprises relatively loose, and personal income tax has become extremely complex, allowing the personal income tax system to become the object of bargaining and lobbying for all political forces, and this is the tragedy of American public finance.

In terms of economic development, Xiong'an New Area should also actively explore areas, for example, where the government holds long-term non-controlling shares in some local enterprises but does not directly control these enterprises. This is equivalent to the model of Temasek State-Owned Enterprise Management in Singapore whereby the government controls the equity of some enterprises so as to strengthen the relationship between the government and enterprises, and also provides a solid financial foundation for the development of local government but with no government interference enterprise operations.

Social Governance

Social governance is especially noteworthy in terms of potential for innovation in the Xiong'an New Area. In terms of traffic management, public transportation should become the main component of transportation in the Xiong'an New Area. In particular, it should be emphasised that fast, convenient and seamless connections are needed between different public transport modes, for example, linking high-speed rail and underground rail to buses and shared bicycle facilities beside bus stops to form a one-stop public transport service. In the management of private cars, congestion charges should be collected to guide residents to own cars but to use fewer cars so that residents who really need cars can afford to buy them and use them when they really need to. Xiong'an New Area should become a new transportation area with special charging and guidance methods for smart transportation. Xiong'an New Area should say no to car purchase restrictions and car traffic restrictions.

In terms of governance, we should especially explore the establishment of channels for direct communication between grassroots government (for example, neighbourhoods) and residents, public policy seminars and hearings for local residents should be held regularly, many major public affairs should be left to residents to vote on, and some grassroots official posts can try differential elections; grassroots taxes, such as property taxes and even personal income tax may be administered and used by grassroots government. Educational funds of Xiong'an New Area should be uniformly arranged by the new area, and educational resources among school districts in the area should be relatively balanced to avoid the quality of education in school districts being uneven.

Ecological Civilisation System

In terms of ecological civilisation construction, Xiong'an New Area should also become a national benchmark. The natural conditions of Xiong'an New Area are not ideal, the diffusion capacity of air pollution is not strong and water resources are relatively scarce, and this will promote the establishment of a strict system for natural resource management in the new area. For this, the government should design and guide the establishment of a set of mechanisms to reasonably allocate scarce natural resources. For example, water resources and emission rights are priced by the market but the government should play its role in safeguarding the market and severely crack down on illegal acts of secretly discharging sewage and extracting groundwater. Natural resources are priced according to the market, the water price for the new area is likely to be higher than in the surrounding areas, which only fully reflects the objective situation of water shortage in the new area, it should not cause any particular controversy.

In short, if the new area can carry out some advanced and popularised institutional innovation exploration in economic development, social governance and ecological civilisation system, it will become the benchmark of a new round of national modernisation system innovation so as to substantially accelerate the process of national overall modernisation.

Learn from the World Bank's Experience To Reform the Infrastructure Investment System

In recent years, the growth rate of China's economy has slowed down significantly compared with before. Is there any potential for China's economy to maintain a relatively fast growth rate? If so, where are the new growth points? How to promote the formation of new points of China's economy through reform and innovation? These are three questions that must be answered in analysing the current macroeconomic situation.

China's Economy Still Has Rapid Growth Potential

To answer the question about China's economic growth potential, we must examine the current stage of China's economic development against a broad historical background.

After years of rapid economic growth, China has become the second largest economy in the world, and the size of the economy is nearly double that of Japan, which ranks third. Nevertheless, we must see that China's current per capita GDP development level is still only 20% of that of the US in terms of purchasing power parity (PPP) exchange rates.

Throughout the development history of the modern market economy, we find that the main determination of an economy's growth potential is the gap between the per capita GDP of the economy and the benchmark set by the world's developed countries. In recent decades, among the world's large countries with a total population of more than 10 million, the US has always maintained the highest level of per capita GDP development and is the benchmark for global economic development. The per capita GDP development level of European countries, including Germany, calculated according to PPP, is basically 80% to 90% of that of the US, Japan is currently 70% (it once reached 85%) of that of the US, and South Korea and Chinese Taiwan are also close to 70% of that of the US.

The historical experience of East Asian economies catching up with the US tells us that when the gap between their per capita GDP and the US is large, the speed of catch-up is relatively fast; as they approach the US, the pace slows down. The basic reason for this is that the economies with a large gap can learn advanced technology and business MOs (modus operandi) from the US and other developed economies, and can also export to the developed countries so as to improve the income level of their nationals.

Japan's per capita GDP reached 20% of that of the US after the second world war, the per capita GDP of Chinese Taiwan and South Korea reached 20% of that of the US in the 1970s and 1980s respectively, and in the five to ten years afterwards, the growth rate of these economies was above 8% (see Table 1). Therefore, we can confidently predict that China's economy still has a growth potential of 8% or more in the next five to ten years. Of course, this potential needs to be released by improving the socioeconomic system.

In the long run, China's economy has three major development advantages. First, as a large economy, China has a huge hinterland and does not have to rely too much on the international market. Second, China's economy is a catching-up and surpassing economy, and it can continuously learn new business models and technology from the developed countries. Third, and also most importantly, China's economy is different from that of Japan in the late 1980s, it still has the original driving force for system innovation.

If China can continuously improve the government's comprehensive social governance capacity, improve judicial efficiency and improve the efficiency of the financial system, its long-term growth prospects are considerable. According to our calculations, between now and 2049, that is, when the PRC celebrates the centenary of its founding, the development level of China's per capita GDP (calculated according to PPP) is likely to reach 70% to 75% of that of the US, and the overall economic scale will be close to about three times that of the US. According to this analysis, we should appreciate that some of the difficulties in China's economy today are temporary, and that China should have the confidence to take appropriate measures today to deal with the slowdown in economic growth. This is because China can make up for some of the current social costs of maintaining economic growth through the rapid economic growth rate in the future and the simultaneous rise in national financial resources.

Reasons for China's Current Economic Slowdown

In essence, the main reasons for the current slowdown in China's economic growth are that the traditional growth points are fading while new growth points have not yet fully erupted.

There are two traditional economic growth points in China: real estate and exports. In the first decade of the 21st century, real estate development and its related industries were the driving force for China's economic growth. Investment in real estate development has long accounted for about 20% of China's total fixed asset investment and 10% of GDP. At the same time, a particular characteristic of the real estate industry is that not only does it drive the growth of many related industries but it also produces a huge wealth effect, making families who have bought a house gain a great sense of wealth appreciation along with the rise in house prices, thereby leveraging the consumption of a considerable number of people. After China's accession to the WTO, exports maintained double-digit growth for a long time, even as high as 20%; in 2007 exports accounted for more than 30% of GDP and the foreign trade surplus accounted for 8% of GDP.

But these two major economic growth points are gradually fading. The growth of real estate has encountered difficulties for two reasons: first, the housing needs of urban residents have been basically met, more than 97% of families own their own real estate, and the per capita housing area has also reached 33 square metres, the residence of a family of three is close to 100 square metres, and it is rising every year. Second, due to the acceleration of financial reform, many families can easily make gains of more than 5%, that is, low risk and highly liquid financial investment returns that exceed the inflation level by more than 2.5%. This has changed the longstanding pattern of residents adopting investment in housing purchases as a means of wealth appreciation and preservation.

At the same time, as the driving force of China's economic growth, exports have lost their aura. The most important reason is that the size of China's economy has increased from US$5.1 trillion before 2009 to US$13.6 trillion in 2018, and global import demand can no longer keep pace with China's economic growth, not to mention that China's rising labour costs and interest rates have also brought various obstacles to exports.

Where Is the New Growth Point of China's Economy?

Since China's economy still has great long-term growth potential, where is the future growth point? My analysis is that there are three growth points for China's economy in the future. Here are some examples in the order of possible breakthroughs.

The first growth point is people's livelihood and public consumption infrastructure investment. Public consumption infrastructure investment refers to investing directly into future people's consumption, with a certain nature of public goods, including high-speed rail, underground rail, urban infrastructure construction, disaster prevention and resilience, waste and water treatment in rural areas, and improvement of air quality, and construction of public affordable housing. These public consumption investments are different from general fixed asset investments because they do not form new production capacity and do not bring about overcapacity. More importantly, this kind of public consumption investment is not done solely to provide public goods. For example, many people benefit from the installation of high-speed rail and underground rail networks. The nature of this type of product is different from cars, refrigerators and televisions because public consumption must be carried out by large numbers of people together, for example, thousands of people benefit from high-speed rail but it would be impractical to run a train for one person . But a mobile phone is used by one person. Public consumption goods require a lot of upfront investment. From the perspective of social welfare, commercial returns from investment in public consumption may be low, once the service capacity is formed, the social welfare return can be gradually formed.

Why is this kind of public consumption infrastructure investment the first growth point of China's economy at present and in the future? The most fundamental reason is that this type of investment is what the Chinese people need most at present and can directly improve people's future happiness. The gap between the quality of life of Chinese nationals, especially urban residents, and that of developed countries is no longer the possession of refrigerators, the popularity and quality of mobile phones, or even the quantity and quality of cars, but the quality of air and the degree of traffic congestion, the popularity and quality of public transport, as well as the ability to respond to natural disasters. These essentially belong to the category of the public consumption level. Raising the level of public consumption requires a very long investment cycle while business returns are very low and require long-term government subsidies. However, this kind of investment can greatly stimulate economic growth. At present, about 25% of China's fixed asset investment is used for such investment, and this proportion still has room for improvement in the future. It is worth mentioning that such investment does not aggravate the problem of overcapacity, on the contrary, it helps resolve this problem.

The second growth point of China's economy is green growth and the upgrading of existing production capacity. In terms of production capacity and output, China's manufacturing industry ranks among the best in the world, however, all kinds of production equipment are often highly polluting and energy consuming. Upgrading such capacity to modern and effective capacity requires investment, and this investment process will drive China's economic growth for a long time. According to my incomplete calculations, just for five energy-consuming industries – nonferrous metals, iron and steel, electric power, chemical industry, and building materials - it will take 10 years to update highly-polluting production capacity with high energy consumption, and drive GDP growth by 1% a year. Moreover, the resulting low pollution and low energy consumption will benefit the Chinese people for a long time.

The third growth point of China's economy is consumer spending. Since 2007, the proportion of Chinese residents' consumption in GDP has been rising every year and at present has risen to about 54%.

To sum up, the biggest growth point that China is most likely to expand in the short term and can rely on for a long time is public consumption investment.

How to Promote Public Consumption Investment, the Largest Growth Point of China's Economy?

In order to release growth points for China's economy, the most important thing is to find a stable, sustainable and highly effective financing channel. At present, the main funding resources for local government investment are bank loans and similar trust products, the proportion of public bond issuance is very low.

There are many disadvantages to relying on bank loans for long term-investment. The first disadvantage is maturity mismatch, supporting fixed asset investment for more than 10 years with bank loans of three years or less often means local governments need to seek refinancing from banks, and each round of refinancing has risks for both banks and the government.

The second disadvantage is that, faced with the pressure of short-term debt repayment, local governments consequently rely too much on land development. This is like a negative spiral, constantly forcing local governments to auction land while, at the same time, worrying about declining land prices, resulting in many local governments being unable to carry out long-term land development plans.

The third disadvantage is that because large numbers of fixed asset investments rely on bank loans, these investments are largely made by government, and have priority in funding sources which, to a considerable extent, has squeezed bank loans to small and medium-sized enterprises which often must raise money at high interest rates, thereby raising the loan interest rate of the whole private economy.

What should we do? We must innovate the mechanism, opening financing channels for long-term fixed asset investment through innovation. Firstly, macro leverage should be allowed to increase. At present, China's leverage, that is, the debt balance of government, the non-financial sector and residents accounts for about 250% of GDP. Internationally, many people think this ratio is too high but it must be noted that China's national savings rate is 47%, so there is no problem using these savings to support the debt accounting for about 250% of GDP. The leverage ratio of the US economy is also 250%, but the US national savings rate is only about 17%. Moreover, the US is still an economy dominated by direct financing markets such as equity.

According to this analysis, we believe the key to reducing leverage in China's economy is to adjust the debt structure, intrinsically, we need to convert some public consumption infrastructure investment from bank loans to low-interest government loans, or to loans guaranteed by the government, thereby releasing the banks' loan potential to better serve enterprises.

Specifically speaking, first, the issuance of treasury bonds should be increased year by year, making the ratio of national debt to GDP increase from 16.6% to 50%. We can use the net additional treasury-bond income to establish a special national livelihood construction investment and development company, similar to the China Development Bank, but its function should be purer, that is, particularly to evaluate the use of long-term fixed asset investment funds of local government. A rolling (refunding the old with the new) investment fund should also be set up specifically to be used for investment and construction of projects that support people's livelihoods.

Second, the debts issued and borrowed by local governments shouldon a timely basis be converted into local government public debt (guaranteed by the central government) but local governments would also need to disclose their financial information and balance sheets at the same time. This can form a social supervision mechanism for local government finance, and this is also a mechanism innovation.

Third, we should gradually reduce bank loans' share of GDP through asset securitisation. If it can be reduced from the current 155% to 100%, it will help resolve the financial risks of banks and can also solve the longstanding problem of economic growth relying on currency issuance.

In other words, through the above operations, some functions of money can be gradually adjusted to be provided by quasi-monetary financial instruments such as treasury bonds so as to greatly reduce risk in the financial market. At the same time, it must be noted, the current infrastructure loans issued by banks have certain risks, therefore we should allow banks and credit companies to restructure, allow partial projects and products to default, only in this way can we disinfect the financial system and gradually resolve systematic financial risk.

In short, China's economy still has good prospects for development in the future, while the biggest new growth point that can be seen at present is long-term, sustainable investment in people's livelihoods and public consumption infrastructure. In order to release this growth potential, we must innovate financing channels from now on to establish large numbers of quasi-monetary financial instruments such as treasury bonds in China, by using long-term bonds with relatively low interest rates to support a large number of investments, so as to open up the financing channels for enterprises and reduce the financing cost, thereby laying a solid foundation for the transformation and updating of the whole Chinese economy.

China's SOE Reform Viewed from German Car Maker VW's "Diesel Emissions Scandal"

In 2015, a major scandal broke regarding Volkswagen: it deceived the US environmental protection agency (EPA) and configured illegal software in diesel-engine vehicles sold in North America, reducing the pollutants in the detection process of automobile exhausts, while pollutants emitted during normal driving exceeded the standard. This scandal inflicted serious reputational damage and economic losses on Volkswagen while the American judicial system is bound to prevail and the incident is likely to end with huge compensation from Volkswagen.

It is difficult to imagine this incident occurring in China where diesel engines are not widely used in passenger cars, mainly due to the poor quality of diesel fuel. Diesel engines from Volkswagen and other European car makers entering China are often not acclimatised to local conditions which soon leads to mechanical damage. However, for China, and particularly for the reform of China's SOEs, the Volkswagen's scandal is of profound and enlightening significance.

Volkswagen Scandal: Deep-Seated Systemic and Operational Reasons Merit Reflection

I have paid close attention to the automobile industry, particlarly the automobile industry in Germany, and I also have some contacts with senior executives of the main engine manufacturers. Speaking realistically, Volkswagen's achievements are commendable. It is not only a strong player among the forest of global enterprises but its performance is obvious; taking the lead in gaining insight into the importance and growth potential of the Chinese market, it became the first major car maker to jointly invest with Chinese enterprises which has played a role in the development of China's auto industry. At the same time, Volkswagen has been actively involved in public welfare affairs, including donations to support China's education. We cannot deny its contribution completely just because of one incident.

From the people I have met, staff at all levels of the Volkswagen Group are also very active, competent and dedicated. This "diesel fraud" incident, in my opinion, has its long-term institutional reasons but the fundamental problem lies in the system.

In Germany, the Volkswagen Group, similar to China's FAW Group Corporation, SAICMOTOR, and Dongfeng Motor Corporation, is a quasi-SOE with a strong "enterprising spirit". It has long pursued the crown of being the number one passenger car company in the world and tried to catch up with Toyota, and finally in the first half of 2005 its sales exceeded those of Toyota.

Supporting Volkswagen to catch up with Toyota and win the crown was its continuous expansion. Some famous sub-brands within the Volkswagen Group, such as MAN in trucks, Bentley in luxury cars, Bugatti Veyron and Lamborghini in supercars, Ducati in motorcycles, all of them were acquired through a series of dazzling mergers and acquisitions. Volkswagen executives have often proudly said to me that Volkswagen covers all automobile categories and has become the world's largest automobile group. Undoubtedly, Volkswagen has adopted a very positive strategy in the process of expansion, having a very strong "enterprising spirit". And such an "enterprising spirit" reflects the determination of the top leaders to shape the auto industry empire.

In contrast, as a large enterprise group, Volkswagen's internal hierarchy is relatively strong. Compared with other auto enterprises, its internal management operation is similar to that of government departments, the superior is strict with the subordinates and in order to complete the tasks assigned by the superior, the subordinates must work conscientiously. This is in sharp contrast to companies such as BMW. The HR department of BMW once showed me their outline of corporate culture construction, among them, employees must have ten attributes, the first being to have the courage to express different opinions.

Volkswagen's "enterprising spirit" can be seen from the active and bold introduction of DCT into passenger cars in recent years. Many people in the auto industry told me that this decision was extremely risky because the DCT technology was not very reliable. As expected, in recent years, there were accidents where the protection system was started due to overheating, resulting in cars breaking down.

The context of the "diesel emission fraud" incident is still under investigation; however, I believe the fundamental factor is nothing more than that the upper level put forward a sales target, the subordinates did everything to complete the task, and finally took the risk to fake it. The senior level of Volkswagen urgently wanted to promote diesel technology to North America because the North American market is Volkswagen's weak point, the constraining factor for Volkswagen struggling to surpass Toyota in sales for many years. The upper level demanded the promotion of diesel technology in the US and kept pushing it, the subordinates could only complete the task by resorting to any means. I think this is the most reasonable inference of how and why this "diesel emission fraud" incident occurred.

Volkswagen Does Not Represent the German Model, BMW Is the Model

Many people think that Volkswagen is representative of German manufacturing and that since the Volkswagen Group is the largest company in Germany, therefore it represents German manufacturing and the German entrepreneurial spirit. I don't agree.

In 2015, I wrote *The German Model for the Chinese Economy*

together with Roland Berger, the famous economist and founder of Roland Berger Company, to discuss the market economic system of Germany, and one chapter is devoted to German enterprises. We found that the mainstream group of German enterprises is modern enterprises with long-term family control, management by professional managers and the participation of all levels of the enterprise. According to this analysis, Volkswagen is actually an alien.

Volkswagen is a quasi-SOE. Lower Saxony, where it is headquartered, owns about 20% of Volkswagen, moreover, according to its extremely complex system of voting rights, it has the right to vote against resolutions of the general meeting of shareholders. Moreover, from the perspective of ownership structure, Volkswagen has had no family influence for a long time. From the history of the Volkswagen Group, it is a quasi-SOE producing cost-effective products for the people in Germany.

In recent decades, Volkswagen has also received constant attention from the German government and senior officials. Former German Chancellor Schroeder is the most important supporter of Volkswagen, he changed his Mercedes Benz to a Phaeton to support Volkswagen. He also tried his best on the joint venture between Volkswagen and China but this does not change the fact that Volkswagen is not the mainstream of German enterprises.

The typical representatives of German enterprises should be family-controlled enterprises such as BMW, Henkel and Bosch. Most of them have been controlled and carefully managed by the family for a long time but at the management level, family members do not appear in person, but ask professional managers to take care of the business, and trade unions and employees participate in management through the board of supervisors. This system ensures that the company has long-term goals rather than pursuing short-term sales, there is no desire for quick success and instant benefit such as seizing first place in the world. In research and development, this kind of company is more forward-looking and attaches importance to fundamental and long-term innovation.

Among Germany's three major car manufacturers, Volkswagen is the quasi-SOE, Mercedes Benz is an American-style public company with extremely dispersed equity, only BMW Group is controlled by the Quant family. The three companies have completely different personalities. Volkswagen is energetic and proactive, its internal management is strict, thereby leading to today's mistakes. Mercedes Benz is a listed company with large-scale shareholding of retail investors, so at the end of the 20th century, Mercedes Benz merged with Chrysler, wanting to take a path of complementary strength, the result was a great failure. This M&A case is often commented on by the German business community, some people sarcastically say that the reason why Mercedes Benz does this is because the top management wants to learn from the US, through the merger with American companies, to get super-high wages and bonuses. Indeed, among the three major German automobile manufacturers, the salary of the boss of Mercedes Benz is much higher than that of the other companies.

By comparison, among the three car factories, BMW can better represent the mainstream of German enterprises. Over the past few years, BMW has surpassed Mercedes Benz to become the leader in luxury car sales. This typical German family business has been carefully managed by the Quant family since the second world war. They recruit professionals to engage in frontline management but the family does not stand idly by. On major issues, the family always carefully studies and judges issues from the perspective of the company's long-term development. More importantly, BMW encourages internal employees to innovate boldly, to put forward opinions different from, or even contrary to, those of their superiors but that are conducive to the long-term development of the company, and to constantly surpass themselves.

In the field of technological innovation, BMW's performance in recent years has been impressive. For example, in the past, BMW took rear wheel drive as its foundation but it has recently announced the start of production of front-wheel drive vehicles; the superb operation and accurate positioning of BMW's acquisition of Mini and

Rolls Royce are also amazing; moreover, BMW used to stick to naturally aspirated engines, however, seeing that energy conservation and emissions reduction are the general trend, they quickly turned to turbocharging, and from turbocharging to carbon fibre to build electric vehicles, and then launched electric scooters. This series of operations made people highly admire its innovation and foresight.

BMW is different from Volkswagen. It does not blindly pursue market share and blindly expand market share. Instead, it seriously grasps its own market positioning. When I communicated with BMW executives, they repeatedly asked me a question: will the rapid growth of BMW's sales in China hurt the gold content of the BMW brand? No matter what the answer is, it is very difficult to have such a long-term consideration, and this is inseparable from the long-term prudent control of the family.

Bosch, another German enterprise that is very well run, has more control than the BMW family. This enterprise has long been controlled by the Bosch family. It adheres to a policy of not being publicly listed, pays attention to sustainable development, puts innovation first, and has a large number of R&D and technical reserves. Although the competition among car manufacturers around the world is very lively and fierce, however, in terms of core technology and components, Bosch is far ahead of its competitors. This transcendent status is inseparable from its long-term vision, adhering to R&D and not being influenced by short-term profit fluctuations.

Similar German enterprises include Henkel and many family enterprises that are not well known to Chinese people, and they are the essence of German manufacturing.

World Capitalism Enters Version 3.0

At the end of July 2015, I went to the US to conduct rather systematic research. I participated in many seminars and was left with the deep impression that the global capitalist model is changing.

If the family-owned enterprise in Adam Smith's time was the

first-generation enterprise model in the development of the capitalist market economy, then by the early 20th century, large-scale listed companies rapidly gathered social resources and formed considerable production capacity, and this can be regarded as the second-generation form in the development of capitalist enterprises. Through research at this time, I clearly feel that the third stage of the capitalist development model has arrived, that is, for the financial capital represented by Wall Street, rather to hold industrial enterprises long term not short term.

The typical modus operandi of Wall Street funds after the 1980s was via private equity fund M&A activity, and buying and selling enterprises, pushing up the shares of enterprises in the short term and obtaining huge profits. Now this era is passing and being superceded by the capitalist version 3.0, namely, whereby a lot of financial capital is repeatedly and carefully looking for listed or unlisted companies with potential growth value and, through long term holding, controlling these industrial enterprises and helping them improve their value, while the business is managed by professionals. This model coincides with Germany's model of long-term family control combined with professional management.

In my opinion, this is a new trend of market economic development. An investor in Wall Street said to me, in his hand he controls many enterprises with long-term investment value, many people want to buy his shares at a 100% or 200% premium, but he is unwilling to sell because his goal is the long-term profitability of these enterprises.

Enlightenment About China's SOE Reform

Where will the reform of China's SOEs go? I think in the future China should support a number of enterprises whose families focus on long-term strategic management and control, and are directly run by professional managers. The state can take shares in such enterprises at the capital level but not directly participate in strategic planning and daily operation. Through this model, China should be able to produce world-class enterprises just like BMW.

Japan has a negative experience in this regard. Japan's decline is largely due to difficulties with the continuity of its family businesses. For example, for businesses such as Panasonic, Toyota, Nissan and other companies, family control is very weak, or has even lapsed. This is related to Japan's blind adoption of the inheritance law enforced by the Americans after the second world war. In Japan, inheritance tax is so high that family heirs can't inherit any wealth at all. Although Germany has inheritance tax, we found in our study that Germany's estate tax is absolutely open to family businesses, as long as the family continues to run a business for more than ten years, the operating assets passing from the previous generation to the next generation do not pay any estate tax.

There are large numbers of family-controlled enterprises in China today, such as New Hope. The key to the long-term development of these enterprises is that the next generation should inherit the entrepreneurial spirit of the previous generation and have a long-term focus on the business. In order to encourage the long-term operation of these enterprises, estate tax must be lenient and inheritance tax must be reduced. A long-term family-run business is the greatest contribution to society, otherwise, if family businesses are sold, turning them into financial capital or even consumer capital, such as big houses and luxury cars, this is a great loss to society.

Mr Liu Chuanzhi has repeatedly mentioned on different occasions that his dream is to build Lenovo into a family business without a family. I personally think that this saying is overly modest. Objectively speaking, Lenovo's long-term future development requires a family to control it strategically for a long time while, at the same time, uniting large numbers of professional managers to jointly build the company, and with partial equity participation of employees, Lenovo Group may not be surnamed Liu but it should let some family members come in to maintain the company's long-term development. Such family members should be conscientious, diligent and decent, focussing on their own businesses rather than on politics or society, and they should be pillars of national economic development. State-owned capital should participate in such enterprises to build the foundation of national public finance.

This is the enlightenment we gain from Volkswagen's "diesel emissions scandal".

Tackle Urbanisation Today on Behalf of Future Generations

Urbanisation has been regarded as the biggest driving force for China's future economic development, and urbanisation places various expectations on China's socioeconomic development – the driving force of economic growth, the improvement of people's livelihood and consumption structure, and so on. It can be said that nowadays, China's economic growth structure and efficiency improvement are all focused on urbanisation. However, on this important subject that has attracted much attention, there are many silent stakeholders who cannot participate in the discussion, and they are our descendants.

Urbanisation has played a major role in changing China's economic outlook, a major role in changing China's economic geography and territorial outlook, and is an irreversible event. What kind of urbanisation path we walk along today will irreversibly change the future of China's economy and society. Therefore, on the bright side, urbanisation is a once in a lifetime opportunity for China's socioeconomic development. If urbanisation can be planned well and promoted in place, it will make China's economic structure relatively rational and even ahead of the current developed countries; on the contrary, if urbanisation is not carried out well, it will put a heavy burden on China's economy and society.

Urbanisation Decision-Making Must Focus on the Interests of Future Generations

Even countries today that have achieved modernisation do not necessarily walking along the best path on the issue of urbanisation.

In the US, the large city of San Francisco and the metropolis of

Los Angeles on the west coast are not the best form of urbanisation in the eyes of Americans themselves. They cover a large area, have a large population, consume a lot of water and have high transportation costs, and for quite a long time in the past, they also suffered from air pollution. All this shows that the development model of many big cities in the US is not optimal.

In Europe, over the past 500 years, the urban development pattern has basically not changed, most of the small towns 500 years ago are still towns today. In terms of the natural endowment with relatively high population density in Europe, this pattern is not necessarily optimal. This leads to a relatively scattered population, while the space outside the city for citizens to hike, explore and discover nature is relatively limited, the intensity of land development is relatively high.

For China, although the overall land area is large, much of the land is uninhabitable and not even suitable for economic activities such as agriculture, forestry and animal husbandry.

Under many complex conditions, today's urbanisation as well as population policy may be the major strategic decision with the most long-term impact in the whole process of China's modernisation. On the issue of urbanisation and population, we must consider the issue from the standpoint of future generations hundreds of years to come, the vision must be long term but not limited only to today's society.

The Scale of Cities and Towns Should be Relatively Concentrated, and the Layout Should Focus on the Coast and South China

Then, from the standpoint of future generations of the Chinese nation hundreds of years hereafter, what are the major issues that deserve our main attention when we look at today's urbanisation process?

The first major issue is the relative concentration of urbanisation.

For Chinese people living today, they usually want to live more spaciously which will also lead to an increase in the land area of a city. But in the longer term, the impact of human socioeconomic activities on the environment should be as small as possible, only in this way can the support and harmony of the whole environment to humanity be improved. Therefore, if we consider the problem from the most long-term perspective, the size of a city should be concentrated, and the population density inside the city should also be relatively increased, thereby reducing the impact of human activities on nature. At the same time, with the continuous improvement of labour productivity in the future, urban residents will have more and more leisure time which they can use this to get out of the city more and go to the suburbs, or even the remote wilderness, to get closer to nature.

According to this principle, Chinese Hong Kong's overall urbanisation development model can be used for reference. In Chinese Hong Kong, only 15% to 20% of land is developed, the remaining 80% of the land is undeveloped and basically in a natural state. Compared with this model, the continental European model may not be the best urbanisation choice conducive with long-term human development.

The US has a huge territory and very low population, the overall natural conditions are excellent. Therefore, urban development is divergent, and the area expands without limitation. Although it often brings inconvenience to the life of urban residents, overall it has not greatly affected its long-term environment quality. Its model may not be applicable to China with a small amount of usable land and a large population.

The second major issue is the layout of urbanisation.

According to the principle that human activities should have little impact on the environment and that the urban density is relatively large, the layout of urbanisation should focus on areas more suitable for human socioeconomic activities.

Over the past 200 years, in the period of industrialisation, especially in the post- industrial era, the pattern of human social life has changed significantly. Before the industrial revolution, due to the limitations of science and technology, as well as the lack of living environment and temperature regulation ability, the world's major cities were concentrated in temperate and cold zones. This was because there were relatively few infectious diseases in these areas in summer and, having already mastered various technologies to keep people warm, human beings could also survive well in winter.

In the post-industrial era, humankind had mastered the medical knowledge and technology to control most infectious diseases and also fully mastered air-conditioning technology, therefore the basic trend of modern society was for populations to be concentrated in subtropical and even tropical areas where life expectancy is also relatively high. This is because cold winters often have a negative impact on human emotions, which can be very detrimental to people's rehabilitation and recovery from modern diseases such as hypertension and diabetes. As a result, living in colder areas led to a reduction in life expectancy.

Specific to China's grand urbanisation planning, more consideration should be given to developing large cities along the coast and in the south. Compared with the northwest and northeast, the coast and the south are more suitable for human habitation, therefore appropriately increasing the scale and intensity of urbanisation in these areas can reduce the pressure of economic development on the environment in other regions. In terms of the overall layout of the country, it is in line with the basic laws of the economy and the environment. The traditional idea was that the population distribution of a whole country should be evenly spread but this view does not conform with the concept of modern social development. Under the condition of modern warfare, national defence relies on sophisticated technology, and the relationship with population distribution is becoming increasingly alienated.

On the Basis of Long-Term Planning, Flexibly Promote Urbanisation

If the above analysis of urbanisation is agreed, how should China's urbanisation process be promoted?

First, we should plan as a whole and establish a national urbanisation development strategy committee, similar to the central leading group for comprehensively deepening reform, it should have a high degree of authority transcending departments and regions, to ensure planning is carried out to the end and remains unchanged for decades.

Second, flexible market-oriented methods should be adopted as far as possible but avoiding simple and crude administrative intervention to affect the process of urbanisation. Today, Chinese society has shown a pattern of diversified interests, and people increasingly advocate economic freedom, freedom of movement and freedom of speech, therefore it is also impossible to prevent population migration and urban development via traditional coercive methods, instead market mechanisms should be adopted as guidance. For example, prices for water, electricity and energy in different regions can be different; for another example, where the ecological environment is not suitable for long-term development and is already too congested, higher house prices should be tolerated. Higher house prices in these areas are actually a mechanism to limit the continued excessive influx of population.

Third, we should use industrial development planning to guide population development. The mechanism of economic research tells us that there are two factors affecting the development of urbanisation. In addition to climate factors and living conditions, another factor is employment. And employment is closely related to industry. In areas where resources and the environment do not support sustainable development, the industry scale should be controlled via market methods, such as electricity and water prices, thereby limiting the size of cities and towns.

In short, on the issue of urbanisation today, we should plan from the standpoint of future generations of the Chinese nation, plan at the highest level and try to adopt a market-oriented approach to flexibly promote the implementation of the overall plan. If China can walk along a road of urbanisation that can stand the test of history, it will be China's major contribution to global modernisation.

Notes

9. China's new role

1. *Xi Jinping: The Governance of China*, Vol. II, Foreign Languages Press, 2017, page 480.

10. Understanding that capital in the 21st century cannot do without China

1. National income, rather than gross domestic product (GDP) was repeatedly used by Piketty in his book. The former is a country's gross earnings excluding depreciation, not the total output generated in the economic activity in a country, it is more closely related to the welfare of a country's residents.

1. Macro Control

1. *Xi Jinping: Secure a Decisive Victory in Building a Moderately Prosperous Society in All Respects and Strive for the Great Success of Socialism with Chinese Characteristics for a New Era – A Report*
2. This data is based on statistics from the National Bureau of Statistics. According to UNESCO statistics, China's illiteracy rate in 1982 was 34.49%.
3. From the *Selected Compilation of Important Documents Since the 18th National Congress of the CPC*, the Central Party Literature Press, 2016, page 774.
4. *Xi Jinping on Building a Moderately Prosperous Society in All Respects*, Central Party Literature Press, 2016, page 154.
5. *Xi Jinping: Secure a Decisive Victory in Building a Moderately Prosperous Society in All Respects and Strive for the Great Success of Socialism with Chinese Characteristics for a New Era – A report at the 19th National Congress of the CPC*, People's Publishing House, 2017, pages 28-29.

2. Finance and Real Estate

1. "Ox nose" means the crux of a matter, or the key to resolving a problem.
2. . Proceeding from the problems, China's relevant laws and regulations are constantly improving. On 27 July 2019, the speaker of the CRSC expressed in his answer to journalists: "The problems reflected by the market and investors, such as the punishment stipulated by the law being too light, lack of diligence and responsibility by intermediary agencies, and failure to carry out investigations, even

though they are objectively in existence. We are working with relevant parties to promote the amendment and improvement of relevant provisions of the *Security Law of the PRC* and the *Criminal Law of the PRC*, regarding illegal securities acts such as false information disclosure of the issuer, the listed company and its controlling shareholders, and the securities violations committed by accounting firms, sponsors and other intermediaries without due diligence and responsibility. It is proposed to significantly increase the maximum term of imprisonment and the amount of fines to strengthen civil liability for damages and implement joint punishment for dishonesty, therefore effectively increasing the cost of violations of laws and regulations in the capital markets." See *The Top Grid Fine of Rmb600,000 Will Become History! The CSRC Is Taking Action*, the *China Fund*, 27 July 2019.

4. Reform Practice and Chinese Economic Thought

1. Broadberry, S., Guan, H. & Li, D., "China, Europe, and the Great Divergence: A Study in Historical National Accounting, 980-1850", *The Journal of Economic History*, Vol. 78, No. 4 (2018), pp. 955-1000.)
2. Maskin, E. & Xu, C., "Soft Budget Constraint Theories: From Centralisation to the Market", *Economics of Transition*, Vol. 9, No. 1 (2001), pp. 1–27.

    Lau, L. J., Qian, Y. & Roland, G., "Reform without Losers: An Interpretation of China's Dual-Track Approach to Transition, *Journal of Political Economy*, Vol. 108, No.1 (2000), pp. 120–143.

    Bai, C. E., Li, D. D., Tao, Z. & Wang, Y., "A Multi-Task Theory of the State Enterprise Reform", *Journal of Comparative Economics*, Vol. 28, No.4 (December 2000), pp. 716–738.

    Li, D. D., "Changing Incentives of the Chinese Bureaucracy", *The American Economic Review*, Vol. 88, No. 2 (1998), pp. 393–397.

    Qian, Y. & Xu, C., "Why China's Economic Reforms Differ: The M-form Hierarchy and Entry/Expansion of the Non-State Sector", *Economics of Transition*, Vol. 1, No. 2 (1993), pp. 135–170.

    Berglöf, E. & Roland, G., "Soft Budget Constraints and Credit Crunches in Financial Transition", *European Economic Review*, Vol. 41, No. (3–5) (1997), pp. 807–817.
3. Yao, Y., "Neutral Government: An Explanation of the Success of China's Transitional Economy", *Economic Review*, Vol. 3 (2009), pp. 5-13.
4. *Xi Jinping: Secure a Decisive Victory in Building a Moderately Prosperous Society in All Respects and Strive for the Great Success of Socialism with Chinese Characteristics for a New Era – A Report at the 19th National Congress of the CPC*, People's Publishing House, 2017, page 29.
5. *Xi Jinping: The Governance of China*, Vol. II, Foreign Languages Press, 2017, page 209

ABOUT ACA

We hope you enjoyed these insights into the Chinese economy.

ALAIN CHARLES ASIA publishes an exciting range of China-focused non-fiction. From the soaring highs and grim lows of China's tumultuous history to the vivid life stories of its major and minor players, ACA has books for anyone eager to learn more about this vast, diverse nation.

To let us know what you thought of this book, or to learn more about the eclectic selection of titles we offer, find us online. If you're as passionate about books as we are, then we'd love to hear your thoughts!

alaincharlesasia.com
@aca_pub